GREEK
MYTHS

Robert Graves

GREEK
MYTHS

Illustrated Edition

BOOK CLUB ASSOCIATES LONDON

This edition published 1985 by
Book Club Associates
by arrangement with Cassell Ltd.

FIFTH REPRINT 1989

Originally published in two volumes
by Penguin Books in 1955
Hardback edition first published
by Cassel & Co Ltd in 1958
Condensed and illustrated edition
first published 1981

This condensation of *Greek Myths* is the work of John Buchanan-Brown

Printed in Belgium

frontispiece: *Statue of Zeus (Vatican Museum)*
opposite: *Battle of the Centaurs and Lapiths (Vatican Museum)*

CONTENTS

ACKNOWLEDGEMENTS

The publishers are grateful to the undermentioned for permission to reproduce the illustrations appearing on the following pages:

Sonia Halliday: 27, 34 top, 67, 135 top, 141

Michael Holford: 18 top, 19, 30, 34 bottom, 48, 62 top, 63, 90, 94, 122, 123, 147, 162 bottom, 171, 175, 184, 206, 207, 217

The Mansell Collection: 5, 13, 31 bottom, 55, 66, 73, 91 top, 120, 129, 131 bottom, 155, 185, 192 top, 222, 224, 228

Photoresources: 59 top, 71, 87, 102, 103 top, 117, 131 top, 151, 187, 231 bottom, 238

Scala: 2, 58, 62 bottom, 170, 230, 239

Rev. Professor Raymond V. Schoder: 18 bottom, 23, 49, 59 bottom, 84, 103 bottom, 109, 114, 115, 136 bottom, 157, 165, 174, 192 bottom, 197, 198, 199, 202, 203, 210, 211, 231 top

Ronald Sheridan: 11, 26, 31 top, 35, 39, 77, 91 bottom, 111, 126, 130, 145, 146, 162 top, 177, 219, 246

Weidenfeld & Nicolson: 16, 17

1

IN THE BEGINNING

The Pelasgian Creation Myth

IN THE BEGINNING, EURYNOME, the Goddess of All Things, rose naked from Chaos, but found nothing substantial for her feet to rest upon, and therefore divided the seas from the sky, dancing lonely upon its waves. She danced towards the south, and the wind set in motion behind her seemed something new and apart with which to begin a work of creation. Wheeling about, she caught hold of this north wind, rubbed it between her hands, and behold! the great serpent Ophion. Eurynome danced to warm herself, wildly and more wildly, until Ophion, grown lustful, coiled about those divine limbs and was moved to couple with her. So Eurynome was got with child.

Next, she assumed the form of a dove, brooding on the waves and, in due process of time, laid the Universal Egg. At her bidding, Ophion coiled seven times about this egg, until it hatched and split in two. Out tumbled all things that exist, her children: sun, moon, planets, stars, the earth with its mountains and rivers, its trees, herbs, and living creatures.

Next, the goddess created the seven planetary powers, setting a Titaness and a Titan over each. But the first man was Pelasgus, ancestor of the Pelasgians; he sprang from the soil of Arcadia, followed by certain others, whom he taught to make huts and feed upon acorns, and sew pig-skin tunics such as poor folk once wore in Euboea and Phocis.

The Homeric and Orphic Creation Myths

Some say that all gods and all living creatures originated in the stream of Oceanus which girdles the world, and that Tethys was the mother of all his children.

But the Orphics say that black-winged Night, a goddess of whom even Zeus stands in awe, was courted by the Wind and laid a silver egg in the womb of Darkness; and that Eros was hatched from the egg and set the Universe in motion. Eros was double-sexed and golden-winged and, having four heads, sometimes roared like a bull or a lion, sometimes hissed like a serpent or bleated like a ram. Night lived in a cave with him, displaying herself in triad: Night, Order, and Justice. Before this cave sat the inescapable mother Rhea, playing on a brazen drum, and compelling man's attention to the oracles of the goddess. Eros created earth, sky, and moon, but the triple-goddess ruled the universe, until her sceptre passed to Uranus.

The Olympian Creation Myth

At the beginning of all things Mother Earth emerged from Chaos and bore her son Uranus as she slept. Gazing down fondly at her from the mountains, he showered fertile rain upon her secret clefts, and she bore grass, flowers, and trees, with the beasts and birds proper to each. This same rain made the rivers flow, so that lakes and seas came into being.

Her first children of semi-human form were the hundred-handed giants Briareus, Gyges, and Cottus. Next appeared the three wild, one-eyed Cyclopes, builders of gigantic walls and master-smiths, whose sons Odysseus encountered in Sicily. Their names were Brontes, Steropes, and Arges, and their ghosts have dwelt in the volcano Aetna since Apollo killed them in revenge for the death of Asclepius.

Marble statue of the Cycladic Mother Goddess (National Archaeological Museum, Athens)

The Five Ages of Man
Some say that Earth bore men spontaneously, as the best of her fruits. These were the so-called golden race, subjects of Cronus, who lived without cares or labour, eating only acorns, wild fruit, and honey that dripped from the trees, drinking milk of sheep and goats, never growing old, dancing, and laughing much; death, to them, was no more terrible than sleep. They are all gone now, but their spirits survive as genii of happy rustic retreats, givers of good fortune, and upholders of justice.

Next came a silver race, eaters of bread, likewise divinely created. The men were utterly subject to their mothers and dared not disobey them, although they might live to be a hundred years old. They were quarrelsome and ignorant, and never sacrificed to the gods but, at least, did not make war on one another. Zeus destroyed them all.

Next came a brazen race, who fell like fruits from the ash-trees, and were armed with brazen weapons. They ate flesh as well as bread, and delighted in war, being insolent and pitiless men. Black Death has seized them all.

The fourth race of men was brazen too, but nobler and more generous, being begotten by the gods on mortal mothers. They fought gloriously in the siege of Thebes, the expedition of the Argonauts, and the Trojan War. These became heroes, and dwell in the Elysian Fields.

The fifth race is the present race of iron, unworthy descendants of the fourth. They are degenerate, cruel, unjust, malicious, libidinous, unfilial, treacherous

The Castration of Uranus
Uranus fathered the Titans upon Mother Earth, after he had thrown his rebellious sons, the Cyclopes, into Tartarus, a gloomy place in the Underworld which lies as far distant from the earth as the earth does from the sky; it would take a falling anvil nine days to reach its bottom. In revenge, Mother Earth persuaded the Titans to attack their father; and they did so, led by Cronus, the youngest of the seven, whom she armed with a flint sickle. They surprised Uranus as he slept, and it was with the flint sickle that the merciless Cronus castrated him, grasping his genitals with the left hand (which has ever since been the hand of ill-omen) and afterwards throwing them, and the sickle too, into the sea by Cape Drepanuum. But drops of blood flowing from the wound fell upon Mother Earth, and she bore the Three Erinnyes, furies who avenge crimes of parricide and perjury — by name Alecto, Tisiphone, and Megaera.

*Curetes clanging armour to drown the cries of the infant
Zeus. A terracotta relief (British Museum)*

The Titans then released the Cyclopes from Tartarus, and awarded
the sovereignty of the earth to Cronus.

However, no sooner did Cronus find himself in supreme command
than he confined the Cyclopes to Tartarus again together with the
Hundred-handed Ones and, taking his sister Rhea to wife, ruled in
Elis.

The Dethronement of Cronus
Cronus married his sister Rhea, to whom the oak is sacred. But it was
prophesied by Mother Earth, and by his dying father Uranus, that one
of his own sons would dethrone him. Every year, therefore, he
swallowed the children whom Rhea bore him: first Hestia, then
Demeter and Hera, then Hades, then Poseidon.

Rhea was enraged. She bore Zeus, her third son, at dead of night on
Mount Lycaeum in Arcadia, where no creature casts a shadow and,
having bathed him in the River Neda, gave him to Mother Earth; by
whom he was carried to Lyctos in Crete, and hidden in the cave of
Dicte on the Aegean Hill. Mother Earth left him there to be nursed by
the Ash-nymph Adrasteia and her sister Io, both daughters of
Melisseus, and by the Goat-nymph Amaltheia. His food was honey,
and he drank Amaltheia's milk, with Goat-Pan, his foster-brother.

Around the infant Zeus's golden cradle, which was hung upon a
tree (so that Cronus might find him neither in heaven, nor on earth,
nor in the sea) stood the armed Curetes, Rhea's sons. They clashed

their spears against their shields, and shouted to drown the noise of his wailing, lest Cronus might hear it from far off. For Rhea had wrapped a stone in swaddling clothes, which she gave to Cronus on Mount Thaumasium in Arcadia; he swallowed it, believing that he was swallowing the infant Zeus.

Zeus grew to manhood among the shepherds of Ida, occupying another cave; then sought out Metis the Titaness, who lived beside the Ocean stream. On her advice he visited his mother Rhea, and asked to be made Cronus's cup-bearer. Rhea readily assisted him in his task of vengeance; she provided the emetic potion, which Metis had told him to mix with Cronus's honeyed drink. Cronus, having drunk deep, vomited up first the stone, and then Zeus's elder brothers and sisters. They sprang out unhurt and, in gratitude, asked him to lead them in a war against the Titans, who chose the gigantic Atlas as their leader; for Cronus was now past his prime.

The war lasted ten years but, at last, Mother Earth prophesied victory to her grandson Zeus, if he took as allies those whom Cronus had confined in Tartarus; so he came secretly to Campe, the old gaoleress of Tartarus, killed her, took her keys and, having released the Cyclopes and the Hundred-handed Ones, strengthened them with divine food and drink. The Cyclopes thereupon gave Zeus the thunderbolt as a weapon of offence; and Hades, a helmet of darkness; and Poseidon, a trident. After the three brothers had held a council of war, Hades entered unseen into Cronus's presence, to steal his weapons; and while Poseidon threatened him with the trident and thus diverted his attention, Zeus struck down with the thunderbolt. The three Hundred-handed Ones now took up rocks and pelted the remaining Titans, and a sudden shout from Goat-Pan put them to flight. The gods rushed in pursuit. Cronus, and all the defeated Titans, except Atlas, were confined in Tartarus and guarded there by the Hundred-handed Ones. Atlas, as their war-leader, was awarded an exemplary punishment, being ordered to carry the sky on his shoulders.

The Birth of Athene

Athene's own priests tell the following story of her birth. Zeus lusted after Metis the Titaness, who turned into many shapes to escape him until she was caught at last and got with child. An oracle of Mother Earth then declared that this would be a girl-child and that, if Metis conceived again, she would bear a son who was fated to depose Zeus, just as Zeus had deposed Cronus, and Cronus had deposed Uranus.

Therefore, having coaxed Metis to a couch with honeyed words, Zeus suddenly opened his mouth and swallowed her, and that was the end of Metis, though he claimed afterwards that she gave him counsel from inside his belly. In due process of time, he was seized by a raging headache as he walked by the shores of Lake Triton, so that his skull seemed about to burst, and he howled for rage until the whole firmament echoed. Up ran Hermes, who at once divined the cause of Zeus's discomfort. He persuaded Hephaestus to fetch his wedge and beetle and make a breach in Zeus's skull, from which Athene sprang, fully armed, with a mighty shout.

The Fates
There are three conjoined Fates, robed in white, whom Erebus begot on Night: by name Clotho, Lachesis, and Atropos. Of these, Atropos is the smallest in stature, but the most terrible.

Zeus, who weighs the lives of men and informs the Fates of his decisions can, it is said, change his mind and intervene to save whom he pleases, when the thread of life, spun on Clotho's spindle, and measured by the rod of Lachesis, is about to be snipped by Atropos's shears.

Others hold, on the contrary, that Zeus himself is subject to the Fates, as the Pythian priestess once confessed in an oracle; because they are not his children, but parthenogenous daughters of the Great Goddess Necessity, against whom not even the gods contend, and who is called 'The Strong Fate'.

The Birth of Aphrodite
Aphrodite, Goddess of Desire, rose naked from the foam of the sea and, riding on a scallop shell, stepped ashore first on the island of Cythera; but finding this only a small island, passed on to the Peloponnese, and eventually took up residence at Paphos, in Cyprus, still the principal seat of her worship. Grass and flowers sprang from the soil wherever she trod. At Paphos, the Seasons, daughters of Themis, hastened to clothe and adorn her. She takes the air accompanied by doves and sparrows.

Hera and Her Children
Hera, daughter of Cronus and Rhea, having been born on the island of Samos or, some say, at Argos, was brought up in Arcadia by Temenus, son of Pelasgus. The Seasons were her nurses. After banishing their father Cronus, Hera's twin-brother Zeus sought her

out at Cnossus in Crete or, some say, on Mount Thornax in Argolis, where he courted her, at first unsuccessfully. She took pity on him only when he adopted the disguise of a bedraggled cuckoo, and tenderly warmed him in her bosom. There he resumed his true shape and ravished her, so that she was shamed into marrying him.

All the gods brought gifts to the wedding; notably Mother Earth gave Hera a tree with golden apples, which was later guarded by the Hesperides in Hera's orchard on Mount Atlas. She and Zeus spent their wedding night on Samos, and it lasted three hundred years.

To Hera and Zeus were born the deities Ares, Hephaestus, and Hebe, though some say that Hephaestus was her parthenogenous child — a wonder which Zeus would not believe until he had imprisoned her in a mechanical chair with arms that folded about the sitter, thus forcing her to swear by the River Styx that she did not lie.

Zeus and Hera
Only Zeus, the Father of Heaven, might wield the thunderbolt; and it was with the threat of its fatal flash that he controlled his quarrelsome and rebellious family of Mount Olympus. He also ordered the heavenly bodies, made laws, enforced oaths, and pronounced

Birth of Aphrodite
(Museo delle Terme,
Rome)

16

*Dionysus springing
from the thigh of Zeus
(Vatican Museum)*

oracles. When his mother Rhea, foreseeing what trouble his lust would cause, forbade him to marry, he angrily threatened to violate her. Though she at once turned into a menacing serpent, this did not daunt Zeus, who became a male serpent and twining about her in an indissoluble knot, made good his threat. It was then that he began his long series of adventures in love. He fathered the Seasons and the Three Fates on Themis; the Charities on Eurynome; the Three Muses on Mnemosyne, with whom he lay for nine nights; and, some say, Persephone, the Queen of the Underworld, whom his brother Hades forcibly married, on the nymph Styx. Thus he lacked no power either above or below earth; and his wife Hera was equal to him in one thing alone: that she could still bestow the gift of prophecy on any man or beast she pleased.

A time came when Zeus's pride and petulance became so intolerable that Hera, Poseidon, Apollo, and all the other Olympians, except Hestia, surrounded him suddenly as he lay asleep on his couch and bound him with rawhide thongs, knotted into a hundred knots, so that he could not move. He threatened them with instant death, but they had placed his thunderbolt out of reach and laughed insultingly at him. While they were celebrating their victory, and jealously discussing who was to be his successor, Thetis the Nereid, foreseeing a civil war on Olympus, hurried in search of the hundred-handed Briareus, who swiftly untied the thongs, using every hand at once, and released his master. Because it was Hera who had led the conspiracy against him, Zeus hung her up from the sky with a golden bracelet about either wrist and an anvil fastened to either ankle. The other deities were vexed beyond words, but dared attempt no rescue for all her piteous cries. In th end Zeus undertook to free her if they swore never more to rebel against him; and this each in turn

above: *The birth of Athene. Detail of a vase (British Museum)*

opposite: *Eros (British Museum)*

above: *Zeus and Hera (Archaeological Museum, Palermo, Sicily)*

grudgingly did. Zeus punished Poseidon and Apollo by sending them as bond-servants to King Laomedon, for whom they built the city of Troy; but he pardoned the others as having acted under duress.

Births of Hermes, Apollo and Dionysus

Amorous Zeus lay with numerous nymphs descended from the Titans or the gods and, after the creation of man, with mortal women too; no less than four great Olympian deities were born to him out of wedlock. First, he begat Hermes on Maia, daughter of Atlas, who bore him in a cave on Mount Cyllene in Arcadia. Next, he begat Apollo and Artemis on Leto, daughter of the Titans Coeus and Phoebe, transforming himself and her into quails when they coupled; but jealous Hera sent the serpent Python to pursue Leto all over the world, and decreed that she should not be delivered in any place where the sun shone. Carried on the wings of the South Wind, Leto at last came to Ortygia, close to Delos, where she bore Artemis, who was no sooner born than she helped her mother across the narrow straits, and there, between an olive-tree and a date-palm growing on the north side of Delian Mount Cynthus, delivered her of Apollo on the ninth day of labour. Delos, hitherto a floating island, became immovably fixed in the sea and by decree no one was allowed either to be born or to die there: sick folk and pregnant women were ferried over to Ortygia instead.

Finally, Zeus, disguised as a mortal, had a secret love affair with Semele ('moon'), daughter of King Cadmus of Thebes, and jealous Hera, disguising herself as an old neighbour, advised Semele, then already six months with child, to make her mysterious lover a request: that he would no longer deceive her, but reveal himself in his true nature and form. How, otherwise, could she know that he was not a monster? Semele followed his advice and, when Zeus refused her plea, denied him further access to her bed. Then, in anger, he appeared as thunder and lightning, and she was consumed. But Hermes saved her six-months' son; sewed him up inside Zeus's thigh, to mature there for three months longer; and, in due course of time, delivered him. Thus Dionysus is called 'twice-born', or 'the child of the double door'.

The Birth of Eros

Some argue that Eros, hatched from the world-egg, was the first of the gods since, without him, none of the rest could have been born. Others hold that he was Aphrodite's son Hermes, or by Ares, or by her own father, Zeus; or the son of Iris by the West Wind. He was a wild boy, who showed no respect for age or station but flew about on golden wings, shooting barbed arrows at random or wantonly setting hearts on fire with his dreadful torches.

2

THE OLYMPIANS

Poseidon's Nature and Deeds

WHEN ZEUS, POSEIDON, and Hades, after deposing their father Cronus, shook lots in a helmet, for the lordship of the sky, sea, and murky underworld, leaving the earth common to all, Zeus won the sky, Hades the underworld, and Poseidon the sea. Poseidon, who is equal to his brother Zeus in dignity, though not in power, and of a surly, quarrelsome nature, at once set about building his under-water palace off Aegze in Euboea. In its spacious stables he keeps white chariot horses and a golden chariot, at the approach of which storms instantly cease.

Needing a wife who would be at home in the sea-depths, he courted Thetis the Nereid; but when it was prophesied by Themis that any son born to Thetis would be greater than his father, he allowed her to marry a mortal named Peleus. Amphitrite, whom he next approached, fled to the Atlas Mountains to escape him; but he sent messengers after her, among them one Delphinus, who pleaded Poseidon's cause so winningly that she yielded. Poseidon set Delphinus's image among the stars as a constellation, the Dolphin.

Amphitrite bore Poseidon three children: Triton, Rhode, and Benthesicyme; but he caused her almost as much jealousy as Zeus did Hera by his love affairs with goddesses, nymphs and mortals.

Poseidon is greedy of earthly kingdoms, and once claimed possession of Attica by thrusting his trident into the acropolis at Athens, where a well of sea-water immediately gushed out and is still to be seen. Later, during the reign of Cecrops, Athene came and took possession in a gentler manner, by planting the first olive-tree beside the well. Poseidon, in a fury, challenged her to single combat, but Zeus interposed and ordered them to submit the dispute to arbitration. Zeus himself expressed no opinion, but while all the other gods supported Poseidon, all the goddesses supported Athene. Thus, by a majority of one, the court ruled that Athene had the better right

*Poseidon. Detail from a bronze statue (National
Archaeological Museum, Athens)*

23

to the land, because she had given it the better gift.

Poseidon also disputed Troezen with Athene; and on this occasion Zeus issued an order for the city to be shared equally between them. Next, he tried unsuccessfully to claim Aegina from Zeus, and Naxos from Dionysus; and in a claim for Corinth with Helius received the Isthmus only, while Helius was awarded the Acropolis. In fury, he tried to seize Argolis from Hera, refusing to appear before his Olympian peers who, he said, were prejudiced against him. Zeus, therefore, referred the matter to the River-gods, Inachus, Cephissus, and Asterion, who judged in Hera's favour.

Poseidon boasts of having created the horse, though some say that, when he was newly born, Rhea gave one to Cronus to eat; and of having invented the bridle, though Athene had done so before him; but his claim to have instituted horse-racing is not disputed. Certainly, horses are sacred to him, perhaps because of his amorous pursuit of Demeter. It is said that, wearied and disheartened by her search for her daughter, Persephone, and disinclined for passionate dalliance she transformed herself into a mare. She did not, however, deceive Poseidon, who transformed himself into a stallion and covered her, from which outrageous union sprang the nymph Despoena and the wild horse Arion.

Herme's Nature and Deeds.

When Hermes was born on Mount Cyllene his mother Maia laid him in swaddling bands on a winnowing fan, but he grew with astonishing quickness into a little boy, and as soon as her back was turned, slipped off and went looking for adventure. Arrived at Pieria, where Apollo was tending a fine herd of cows, he decided to steal them. But, fearing to be betrayed by their tracks, he quickly made shoes from the bark of a fallen oak and tied them to the feet of the cows, which he then drove off by night. Apollo discovered the loss, but Herme's trick deceived him, and he was forced to offer a reward for the apprehension of the thief. Silenus and his satyrs spread out in different directions to track him down, but without success until a party of them passed through Arcadia, and heard the muffled sound of music. The nymph Cyllene, from the mouth of a cave, told them that a most gifted child, to whom she was acting as nurse, had constructed an ingenious musical toy from the shell of a tortoise and some cow-gut, with which he had lulled his mother to sleep.

'And from whom did he get the cow-gut?' asked the alert satyrs, noticing two hides stretched outside the cave. 'Do you charge the poor child with theft?' asked Cyllene. Harsh words were exchanged.

At that moment Apollo came up, and entering the cave, he awakened Maia and told her severely that Hermes must restore the stolen cows. Maia pointed to the child, still wrapped in his swaddling bands and feigning sleep. 'What an absurd charge!' she cried. But Apollo had already recognized the hides. He picked up Hermes, carried him to Olympus, and there formally accused him of theft, offering the hides as evidence. Zeus, loth to believe that his own new-born son was a thief, encouraged him to plead not guilty, but Apollo would not be put off and Hermes, at last, confessed.

'Very well, come with me', he said, 'and you may have your herd. I slaughtered only two, and those I cut up into twelve equal portions as a sacrifice to the twelve gods.'

'*Twelve* gods?' asked Apollo. 'Who is the twelfth?'

'Your servant, sir,' replied Hermes modestly. 'I ate no more than my share, though I was very hungry, and duly burned the rest.'

Now, this was the first flesh-sacrifice ever made.

The two gods returned to Mount Cyllene, where Hermes retrieved something that he had hidden underneath a sheepskin.

'What have you there?' asked Apollo.

In answer, Hermes showed his newly-invented tortoise-shell lyre, and played such a ravishing tune on it with the plectrum he had also invented that he was forgiven at once. He led Apollo to Pylus, and there gave him the remainder of the cattle, which he had hidden in a cave.

'A bargain!' cried Apollo. 'You keep the cows, and I take the lyre.'

'Agreed,' said Hermes, and they shook hands on it.

While the hungry cows were grazing, Hermes cut reeds, made them into a shepherd's pipe, and played another tune. Apollo, again delighted, cried: 'A bargain! If you give me that pipe, I will give you this golden staff with which I herd my cattle; in future you shall be the god of all herdsmen and shepherds.'

'My pipe is worth more than your staff', replied Hermes. 'But I will make the exchange, if you teach me augury too.'

'I cannot do that,' Apollo said, 'but if you go to my old nurses, the Thriae, they will teach you.'

They again shook hands and Apollo, taking the child back to Olympus, told Zeus all that had happened. Zeus could not help being amused. 'You seem to be a very ingenious, eloquent, and persuasive godling,' he said.

'Then make me your herald, Father,' Hermes answered, 'and I will

The Rhodes Aphrodite (Rhodes Museum)

be responsible for the safety of all divine property, and never tell lies, though I cannot promise always to tell the whole truth.'

'That would not be expected of you,' said Zeus, with a smile. 'But your duties would include the making of treaties, the promotion of commerce, and the maintenance of free rights of way for travellers on any road in the world.' Zeus gave him a herald's staff which everyone was ordered to respect; a round hat against the rain, and winged golden sandals which carried him about with the swiftness of wind.

Afterwards, the Thriae showed Hermes how to foretell the future from the dance of pebbles in a basin of water; and he himself invented both the game of knuckle-bones and the art of divining by them. Hades also engaged him as his herald, to summon the dying gently and eloquently, by laying the golden staff upon their eyes.

He then assisted the Three Fates in the composition of the Alphabet, invented astronomy, the musical scale, the arts of boxing and gymnastics, weights and measures and the cultivation of the olive-tree.

Hermes had numerous sons, including Echion the Argonauts' herald; Autolycus the thief; and Daphnis the inventor of bucolic poetry.

Aphrodite's Nature and Deeds

Aphrodite could seldom be persuaded to lend the other goddesses her magic girdle which made everyone fall in love with its wearer; for she was jealous of her position. Zeus had given her in marriage to Hephaestus, the lame Smith-god; but the true father of the three children with whom she presented him — Phobus, Deiumus, and Harmonia — was Ares, the God of War. Hephaestus knew nothing of the deception until, one night, the lovers stayed too long together in bed at Ares's Thracian palace; then Helius, as he rose, saw them and told Hephaestus.

Hephaestus angrily retired to his forge, and hammered out a bronze hunting-net, as fine as gossamer but quite unbreakable, which he secretly attached to the posts and sides of his marriage-bed. He told Aphrodite: 'Dear wife, I am taking a short holiday on Lemnos, my

Marble statue of Aphrodite (Soli, Cyprus)

27

favourite island.' Aphrodite did not offer to accompany him and, when he was out of sight, sent hurriedly for Ares. The two went merrily to bed but, at dawn, found themselves entangled in the net, naked and unable to escape. Hephaestus surprised them there, and summoned all the gods to witness his dishonour. He then announced that he would not release his wife until the marriage-gifts which he had paid Zeus, were restored to him.

Up ran the gods, but the goddesses, from a sense of delicacy, stayed in their houses. Apollo, nudging Hermes, asked: 'You would not mind being in Ares's position, would you, net and all?'

Hermes swore that he would not, were there three times as many nets, and all the goddesses looking on. At this, both gods laughed uproariously, but Zeus was so disgusted that he refused to hand back the marriage-gifts, or to interfere. Poseidon pretended to sympathize with Hephaestus. 'Since Zeus refuses to help,' he said, 'I will undertake that Ares, as a fee for his release, pays the equivalent of the marriage-gifts in question.'

'That is all very well,' Hephaestus replied gloomily. 'But if Ares defaults, you will have to take his place under the net.'

'I cannot think that Ares will default,' Poseidon said nobly. 'But if he should do so, I am ready to pay the debt and marry Aphrodite myself.'

So Ares was set at liberty, and returned to Thrace; and Aphrodite went to Paphos, where she renewed her virginity in the sea.

Flattered by Hermes's frank confession of his love for her, Aphrodite presently spent a night with him, the fruit of which was Hermaphroditus, a double-sexed being; and, equally pleased by Poseidon's intervention on her behalf, she bore him two sons, Rhodis and Herophilus. Later, Aphrodite yielded to Dionysus, and bore him Priapus; an ugly child with enormous genitals. He is a gardener and carries a pruning-knife.

Though Zeus never lay with his adopted daughter Aphrodite, the magic of her girdle put him under constant temptation, and at last he decided to humiliate her by making her fall desperately in love with a mortal. This was the handsome Anchises, King of the Dardanians, a grandson of Ilus and, one night, when he was asleep in his herdsman's hut on Trojan Mount Ida, Aphrodite visited him in the guise of a Phrygian princess, and lay with him. When they parted at dawn, she revealed her identity, and made him promise not to tell anyone that she had slept with him. Anchises was horrified to learn that he had uncovered the nakedness of a goddess, and begged her to spare his life. She assured him that he had nothing to fear, and that their son, Aeneas, would be famous.

One day, the wife of King Cinyras the Cyprian foolishly boasted that her daughter Smyrna was more beautiful even than Aphrodite. The goddess avenged this insult by making Smyrna fall in love with her father and climb into his bed one dark night, when her nurse had made him too drunk to realize what he was doing. Later, Cinyras disovered that he was both the father and grandfather of Smyrna's unborn child, and wild with wrath, seized a sword. Aphrodite hurriedly changed Smyrna into a myrrh-tree, which the descending sword split in halves. Out tumbled the infant Adonis. Aphrodite concealed Adonis in a chest, which she entrusted to Persephone, Queen of the Dead.

Persephone had the curiosity to open the chest, and found Adonis. He was so lovely that she lifted him out and brought him up in her own palace. The news reached Aphrodite, who at once visited Tartarus to claim Adonis; and when Persephone would not assent, having by now made him her lover, she appealed to Zeus. Zeus, well aware that Aphrodite also wanted to lie with Adonis, refused to judge so unsavoury a dispute; and transferred it to a lower court, presided over by the Muse Calliope. Calliope's verdict was that Persephone and Aphrodite had equal claims on Adonis, but that he should be allowed a brief annual holiday from the amorous demands of both. She therefore divided the year into three equal parts, of which he was to spend one with Persephone, one with Aphrodite, and the third by himself.

Aphrodite did not play fair: by wearing her magic girdle all the time, she persuaded Adonis to give her his own share of the year, grudge the share due to Persephone, and disobey the court-order.

Persephone, justly aggrieved, went to Thrace, where she told her benefactor Ares that Aphrodite now preferred Adonis to himself. Ares grew jealous and, disguised as a wild boar, rushed at Adonis who was out hunting on Mount Lebanon, and gored him death before Aphrodite's eyes. Anemones sprang from his blood, and his soul descended to Tartarus. Aphrodite went tearfully to Zeus, and pleaded that Adonis should not have to spend more than the gloomier half of the year with Persephone, but might be her companion for the summer months. This Zeus magnanimously granted.

Ares's Nature and Deeds

Thracian Ares loves battle for its own sake, and his sister Eris is

above: *The Ptoan Apollo. Detail (National Museum of Athens)*

opposite: *The Piombino Apollo (Louvre)*

right: *The 'Todi' Ares. Detail of bronze statue (Vatican Museum)*

always stiring up occasions for war. Like her, he never favours one city or party more than another, delighting in the slaughter of men and the sacking of towns. All his fellow-immortals hate him, except Eris, and Aphrodite, and greedy Hades who welcomes the fighting-men slain in cruel wars.

Ares has not been consistently victorious. Athene has twice worsted him in battle; and once, the gigantic sons of Aloeus conquered and kept him imprisoned in a brazen vessel until he was released by Hermes; and, on another occasion, Heracles sent him running. He professes too deep a contempt for litigation ever to appear in court as a plaintiff, and has only once done so as a defendant: that was when charged with the murder of Poseidon's son Halirrhothius. He pleaded justification, claiming to have saved his daughter Alcippe from being violated. Since no one else had witnessed the incident, the court acquitted him. This was the first judgement ever pronounced in a murder trial; and the hill on which the proceedings took place became known as the Areiopagus.

Hestia's Nature and Deeds

It is Hestia's glory that, alone of the great Olympians, she never takes part in wars or disputes. Like Artemis and Athene, moreover, she has always resisted every amorous invitation offered her; for, after the dethronement of Cronus, when Poseidon and Apollo came forward as rival suitors, she swore by Zeus's head to remain a virgin for ever. At that, Zeus gratefully awarded her the first victim of every public sacrifice, because she had preserved the peace of Olympus.

She was the Goddess of the Hearth and in every private house and city hall protected suppliants who fled to her for protection. Universal reverence was paid Hestia, not only as the mildest, most upright and most charitable of all the Olympians, but as having invented the art of building houses; and her fire was so sacred that, if ever a hearth went cold, either by accident or in token of mourning, it was kindled afresh with the aid of a fire-wheel.

Apollo's Nature and Deeds

Apollo was Zeus's son by Leto. Themis fed him on nectar and ambrosia, and when he was four days old he called for bow and arrows, made straight for Mount Parnassus, where the serpent Python, his mother's enemy, was lurking. Severely wounded with arrows, Python fled to the Oracle of Mother Earth at Delphi, but Apollo dared follow him into the shrine, and there despatched him beside the sacred chasm.

Mother Earth reported this outrage to Zeus, who not only ordered Apollo to visit Tempe for purification, but instituted the Pythian Games in honour of Python. Quite unabashed, Apollo disregarded Zeus's command to visit Tempe. Instead, he went to Aigialiaea accompanied by Artemis; and then, disliking the place, to Tarrha in Crete, where King Carmanor performed the ceremony.

On his return to Greece, Apollo sought out Pan, and, having coaxed him to reveal the art of prophecy, seized the Delphic Oracle. Leto, on hearing the news, came with Artemis to Delphi, where she turned aside to perform some private rite in a sacred grove. The giant Tityus interrupted her devotions, and was trying to violate her, when Apollo and Artemis, hearing screams, ran up and killed him with a volley of arrows — a vengeance which Zeus, Tityus's father, was pleased to consider a pious one. In Tartarus, Tityus was stretched out for torment, his arms and legs securely pegged to the ground, while two vultures ate his liver.

Next, Apollo killed the satyr Marsyas. This was how it came about. One day, Athene made a double-flute from stag's bones, and played on it at a banquet of the gods. She could not understand, at first, why Hera and Aphrodite were laughing silently behind their hands, although her music seemed to delight the other deities; she therefore went away by herself into a Phrygian wood, took up the flute again beside a stream, and watched her image in the water, as she played. Realizing at once how ludicrous those swollen cheeks made her look, she threw down the flute, and laid a curse on anyone who picked it up.

Marsyas stumbled upon the flute, which he had no sooner put to his lips than it played of itself, inspired by the memory of Athene's music; and he went about Phrygia delighting the ignorant peasants. They cried out that Apollo himself could not have made better music, even on his lyre, and Marsyas was foolish enough not to contradict them. This of course, provoked the anger of Apollo, who invited him to a contest, the winner of which should inflict whatever punishment he pleased on the loser.

The contest proved an equal one, until Apollo cried out to Marsyas: 'I challenge you to do with your instrument as much as I can do with mine. Turn it upside down, and both play and sing at the same time.'

This, with the flute, was manifestly impossible, and Marsyas failed to meet the challenge. Then Apollo took a most cruel revenge on Marsyas, flaying him alive and nailing his skin to a pine near the

above: *Artemis of
Ephesus. Detail of statue
(Town Hall, Ephesus)*

right: *Hephaestus in his
smithy. Amphora (British
Museum)*

opposite: *Athene with
her chariot (Acropolis
Museum, Athens)*

source of the river which now bears his name.

Afterwards, Apollo won a second musical contest, at which King Midas presided. This time he beat Pan, becoming the acknowledged god of Music. Another of his duties was once to guard the herds and flocks of the gods, but he later delegated this task to Hermes.

Though Apollo refuses to bind himself in marriage, he has got many nymphs and mortal women with child; among them, Phthia, and Thalia the Muse, and Coronis, and Aria, and Cyrene. He also seduced the nymph Dryope, but was not invariably successful in love. On one occasion he tried to steal Marpessa from Idas, but she remained true to her husband. On another, he pursued Daphne, the mountain nymph, a priestess of Mother Earth, daughter of the river Peneius in Thessaly; but when he overtook her, she cried out to Mother Earth who, in the nick of time, spirited her away to Crete, where she became known as Pasiphaë. Mother Earth left a laurel-tree in her place, and from its leaves Apollo made a wreath to console himself.

There was also the case of the beautiful youth Hyacinthus, a Spartan prince, with whom not only the poet Thamyris fell in love — the first man who ever wooed one of his own sex — but Apollo himself, the first god to do so. But the West Wind had also taken a fancy to Hyacinthus, and became insanely jealous of Apollo, who was one day teaching the boy how to hurl a discus, when the West Wind caught it in mid-air, dashed it against Hyacinthus's skull, and killed him. From his blood sprang the hyacinth flower, on which his initials are still to be traced.

Apollo earned Zeus's anger only once after the famous conspiracy to dethrone him. This was when his son Asclepius, the physician, had the temerity to resurrect a dead man, and thus rob Hades of a subject; Hades naturally lodged a complaint on Olympus, Zeus killed Asclepius with a thunderbolt, and Apollo in revenge killed the Cyclopes. Zeus was enraged at the loss of his armourers, and would have banished Apollo to Tartarus for ever, had not Leto pleaded for his forgiveness. The sentence was reduced to one year's hard labour, which Apollo was to serve in the sheep-folds of King Admetus of Therae. Obeying Leto's advice, Apollo not only carried out the sentence humbly, but conferred great benefits on Admetus.

Artemis's Nature and Deeds

Artemis, Apollo's sister, goes armed with bow and arrows and, like him, has the power both to send plagues or sudden death among mortals, and to heal them. She is the protectress of little children, and of all sucking animals, but she also loves the chase.

One day, while still a child, her father Zeus asked her what presents she would like. Artemis answered: 'Pray give me eternal virginity; as many names as my brother Apollo; a bow and arrows like his; the office of bringing light; a hunting tunic reaching to my knees; sixty ocean nymphs, as my maids of honour; twenty river nymphs to take care of my buskins and feed my hounds; all the mountains in the world; and, lastly, any city you care to choose for me, but one will be enough, because I intend to live on mountains most of the time. Unfortunately, since my mother Leto bore me without pains, the Fates have made me patroness of childbirth.'

Zeus smiled proudly, saying: 'You shall have all this, and more besides: not one, but thirty cities, and a share in many others, and I appoint you guardian of their roads and harbours.'

Artemis thanked him and went first to Mount Leucus in Crete, and next to the Ocean stream, where she chose nymphs for her attendants. She then visited the Cyclopes on the Island of Lipara. Brontes, who had been instructed to make whatever she wanted, took her on his knee; but, disliking his endearments, she tore a handful of hair from his chest, where a bald patch remained to the day of his death. The nymphs were terrified at the wild appearance of the Cyclopes, and well they might be, for whenever a little girl is disobedient her mother threatens her with Brontes, Arges, or Steropes. But Artemis boldly told them to make her a silver bow, with a quiverful of arrows, in return for which they should eat the first prey she brought down. With these weapons she went to Arcadia, where Pan gave her three lop-eared hounds, two parti-coloured and one spotted, together capable of dragging live lions back to their kennels; and seven swift hounds from Sparta.

Once the River-god Alpheius, son of Thetis, dared fall in love with Artemis and pursue her across Greece; but she came to Letrini in Elis, where she daubed her face, and those of all her nymphs, with white mud, so that she became indistinguishable from the rest of the company. Alpheius was forced to retire, pursued by mocking laughter.

Artemis requires the same perfect chastity from her companions as she practises herself. When Zeus had seduced one of them, Callisto, daughter of Lycaon, Artemis noticed that she was with child. Changing her into a bear, she shouted to the pack, and Callisto would have been hunted to death had she not been caught up to Heaven by

Zeus who, later, set her image among the stars. Callisto's child, Arcas, was saved, and became the ancestor of the Arcadians.

Hephaestus's Nature and Deeds
Hephaestus, the ugly and ill-tempered Smith-god, was so weakly at birth that his disgusted mother, Hera, dropped him from the height of Olympus, to rid herself of the embarrassment. He survived this misadventure, however, without bodily damage, because he fell into the sea, where Thetis and Eurynome were at hand to rescue him. These gentle goddesses kept him with them in an underwater grotto, where he set up his first smithy and rewarded their kindness by making them all sorts of ornamental and useful objects.

When nine years had passed, Hera met Thetis, wearing a brooch of his workmanship, and asked: 'Where in the world did you find that wonderful jewel?'

Thetis hesitated, but Hera forced the truth from her. At once she fetched Hephaestus back to Olympus, where she set him up in a far finer smith, made much of him, and arranged that he should marry Aphrodite.

Hephaestus became so far reconciled with Hera that he dared reproach Zeus himself for hanging her by the wrists from Heaven when she rebelled against him. But angry Zeus only heaved him down from Olympus a second time. He was a whole day falling. On striking the earth of the island of Lemnos, he broke both legs and, though immortal, had little life left in his body when the islanders found him. Afterwards pardoned and restored to Olympus, he could walk only with golden leg-supports.

Demeter's Nature and Deeds
Though the priestesses of Demeter, goddess of the cornfield, initiate brides and bridegrooms into the secrets of the couch, she has no husband of her own. While still young and gay, she bore Core and the lusty Iacchus to Zeus, her brother, out of wedlock. She also bore Plutus to the Titan Iasius, with whom she fell in love at the wedding of Cadmus and Harmonia. Inflamed by the nectar, the lovers slipped out and lay together openly in a thrice-ploughed field. On their return, Zeus, guessing what they had been at, and enraged that Iasius should have dared to touch Demeter, struck him dead with a thunderbolt.

Demeter herself has a gentle soul, and Erysichthon, son of Tropias, was one of the few men with whom she ever dealt harshly.

*Persephone fleeing
from Hades
(Acropolis Museum,
Athens)*

Erysichthon dared invade a grove which the Pelasgians had planted for her at Dotium, and began cutting down the sacred trees, to provide timber for his new banqueting hall. Demeter assumed the form of Nicippe, priestess of the grove, and mildly ordered Erysichthon to desist. Only when he threatened her with his axe did she reveal herself in splendour and condemned him to suffer perpetual hunger. He grew hungrier and thinner the more he ate, until his parents could no longer afford to keep him supplied with food, and he became a beggar in the streets, eating filth.

Hades fell in love with Core, and went to ask Zeus's leave to marry her. Zeus feared to offend his eldest brother by a refusal, but knew that Demeter would not forgive him if Core were committed to Tartarus; he therefore answered that he could neither give nor withhold his consent. This emboldened Hades to abduct the girl, as she was picking flowers in a meadow. (It may have been anywhere in the widely separated regions which Demeter visited in her wandering search for Core, but her own priests say that it was at Eleusis.) She sought Core for nine days and nights, neither eating nor drinking, and calling fruitlessly all the while. The only news she could get came from old Hecate, who early one morning had heard Core crying 'A rape! A rape!' but, on hurrying to the rescue, found no sign of her.

On the tenth day, Demeter came in disguise to Eleusis, where King Celeus and his wife Metaneira entertained her; and she was invited to remain as wet-nurse to Demophoön, the newly-born prince. Their lame daughter Iambe tried to console Demeter and the dry-nurse, old Baubo, persuaded her to drink barley-water by a jest: she groaned as if in travail and, unexpectedly, produced from beneath her skirt Demeter's own son Iacchus, who leaped into his mother's arms and kissed her.

'Oh, how greedily you drink!' cried Abas, an elder son of Celeus's: Demeter metamorphosed him into a lizard. Somewhat ashamed of herself, Demeter now decided to do Celeus a service, by making Demophoön immortal. That night she held him over the fire, to burn away his mortality. Metaneira happened to enter the hall and broke the spell; so Demophoön died. 'Mine is an unlucky house!' Celius complained, 'Dry your tears,' said Demeter. 'You still have three sons on whom I intend to confer such great gifts that you will forget your double loss.'

For Triptolemus, who herded his father's cattle, had recognized Demeter and given her the news she needed: ten days before this his brothers Eumolpus, a shepherd, and Eubuleus, a swineherd, had been out in the fields, when the earth suddenly gaped open, engulfing Eubeleus's swine before his very eyes; then a chariot drawn by black horses appeared, and dashed down the chasm. The chariot-driver's face was invisible, but his right arm was tightly clasped around a shrieking girl.

Demeter summoned Hecate. Together they approached Helius, who sees everything, and forced him to admit that Hades had been the villain. Demeter was so angry that she continued to wander about the earth, forbidding the trees to yield fruit and the herbs to grow. Zeus sent her first a message by Iris and then a deputation of the Olympian gods, with conciliatory gifts, begging her to be reconciled to his will. But she would not return to Olympus, and swore that the earth must remain barren until Core had been restored.

Only one course of action remained for Zeus. He sent Hermes with a message to Hades: 'If you do not restore Core, we are all undone!' and with another to Demeter: 'You may have your daughter again, on the single condition that she has not yet tasted the food of the dead.'

Because Core had refused to eat so much as a crust of bread ever since her abduction, Hades was obliged to cloak his vexation, telling her mildly: 'My child, you seem to be unhappy here, and your mother weeps for you. I have therefore decided to send you home.'

Core's tears ceased to flow, but, just as she was setting off for Eleusis, one of Hades's gardeners, Ascalaphus, began to cry: 'Having seen the Lady Core pick a pomegranate and eat seven seeds, I am ready to bear witness that she has tasted the food of the dead!'

At Eleusis, Demeter joyfully embraced Core; but, on hearing about the pomegranate, grew more dejected than ever, and said again: 'I will neither return to Olympus, nor remove my curse from the land.' Zeus then persuaded Rhea to plead with her; and a compromise was at last reached. Core should spend three months of the year in Hades's company, as Queen of Tartarus, with the title of Persephone, and the remaining nine in Demeter's.

Demeter finally consented to return home. Before leaving Eleusis, she instructed Triptolemus, Eumolpus, and Celeus (together with Diocles, King of Pherae, who had been assiduously searching for Core all this while) in her worship and mysteries. Triptolemus she supplies with seed-corn, a wooden plough, and a chariot drawn by serpents; and sent him all over the world to teach mankind the art of agriculture. But she punished Ascalaphus for his tale-bearing.

Athene's Nature and Deeds
Athene invented the flute, the trumpet, the earthenware pot, the plough, the rake, the ox-yoke, the horse-bridle, the chariot, and the ship. She first taught the science of numbers, and all women's arts. Although goddess of war, she gets no pleasure from battle, but rather from settling disputes, and upholding the law by pacific means. She bears no arms in time of peace and, if ever she needs any, will usually borrow a set from Zeus. Her mercy is great: when the judges' votes are equal she always gives a casting vote to liberate the accused. Yet in battle she never loses, even against Ares himself, being better grounded in tactics and strategy, and wise captains always approach her for advice.

Many gods, Titans, and giants would gladly have married Athene, but she has repulsed all advances. Once, not wishing to borrow arms from Zeus, she asked Hephaestus to make her a set of her own. Hephaestus refused payment, saying that he would undertake the work for love. When, missing the implication of these words, she entered the smithy to watch him, he suddenly turned about and tried to outrage her. Hephaestus was the victim of a malicious joke: Poseidon informed him that Athene was on her way with Zeus's consent, expecting to have violent love made to her. As she tore herself away, Hephaestus ejaculated against her thigh. She wiped off the seed with a handful of wool, which she threw away in disgust; it fell to the ground near Athens and accidentally fertilized Mother Earth. Revolted at the prospect of bearing a child which Hephaestus had tried to father on Athene, Mother Earth declared that she would accept no responsibility for it.

'Very well,' said Athene, 'I will take care of it myself.' So she took charge of the infant, called him Erichthonius and, not wishing Poseidon to laugh at the success of his joke, hid him in a sacred basket; this she gave to Aglauros, eldest daughter of the Athenian King Cecrops, with orders to guard it carefully.

Cecrops, a son of Mother Earth, was the first king to recognize paternity. He also instituted monogamy, divided Attica into twelve communities, built temples to Athene, and abolished certain bloody sacrifices in favour of sober barley-cake offerings. His wife was named Agraulos; and his three daughters, Aglauros, Herse, and Pandrosos. One evening when the girls had returned from a festival, carrying Athene's sacred baskets on their heads, Hermes bribed Aglauros to give him access to Herse, with whom he had fallen violently in love. Aglauros kept Hermes's gold, but did nothing to earn it, because Athene had made her jealous of Herse's good fortune; so Hermes turned Aglauros to stone, and had his will of Herse. After Herse had borne Hermes two sons, Cephalus and Ceryx, she and Pandrosos and their mother Aglauros were curious enough to peep beneath the lid of the basket which Aglauros had carried. Seeing a child with a serpent's tail for legs, they screamed in fear and leaped from the Acropolis.

Athene was so grieved that she let fall the enormous rock which she had been carrying to the Acropolis as an additional fortification, and it became Mount Lycabettus. As for the crow that had brought her the news, she changed its colour from white to black, and forbade all crows ever again to visit the Acropolis. Erichthonius then took refuge in Athene's aegis, where she reared him to tenderly that some mistook her for his mother. His image was set among the stars as the constellation Auriga, since he had introduced the four-horse chariot.

Athene, though as modest as Artemis, is far more generous. When Teiresias, one day, was accidentally surprised in a bath, she laid her hands over his eyes and blinded him, but gave him inward sight by way of a compensation.

Pan's Nature and Deeds
Some say that Hermes fathered Pan on Dryope, daughter of Dryops, or on the nymph Oeneis. He is said to have been so ugly at birth that his mother ran away from him in fear, and Hermes carried him up to

Persephone holding a pomegranate. Terracotta (British Museum)

43

Olympus for the gods' amusement: but Pan was Zeus's foster-brother, and therefore far older than Hermes. Still others make him the son of Cronus and Rhea; or of Zeus by Hybris, which is the least improbable account.

He lived in Arcadia, where he guarded flocks, herds, and bee-hives, took part in the revels of the mountain-nymphs, and helped hunters to find their quarry. He was, on the whole, easy-going and lazy, loving nothing better than his afternoon sleep, and revenged himself on those who disturbed him with a sudden shout which made the hair bristle on their heads.

Pan seduced several nymphs, such as Echo, and Eupheme, nurse of the Muses, who bore him Crotus, the Bowman in the Zodiac. Once he tried to violate the chaste Pitys, who escaped him only by being metamorphosed into a fir-tree, a branch of which he afterwards wore as a chaplet. On another occasion he pursued the chaste Syrinx to the River Ladon, where she became a reed; there, since he could not distinguish her from among all the rest, he cut several reeds at random, and made them into a Pan-pipe. His greatest success in love was the seduction of Selene, which he accomplished by disguising his hairy black goatishness with well-washed white fleeces. Not realizing who he was, Selene consented to ride on his back, and let him do as he pleased with her.

The Olympian gods, while despising Pan, exploited his powers. Apollo wheedled the art of prophecy from him, and Hermes copied his pipe, claimed it as his own invention, and sold it to Apollo.

Pan is the only god who has died. To one Thamus, a sailor in a ship bound for Italy, a divine voice shouted across the sea: 'Thamus, when you reach Palodes, proclaim that the great god Pan is dead!', which Thamus did; and the news was greeted from the shore with groans.

Dionysus's Nature and Deeds

At Hera's orders the Titans seized Zeus's newly-born son Dionysus and tore him into shreds. These they boiled in a cauldron, but he was rescued and reconstituted by his grandmother Rhea. Persephone, now entrusted with his charge by Zeus, brought him to King Athamas of Orchomenus and his wife Ino, whom she persuaded to rear the child in the women's quarters, disguised as a girl. But Hera could not be deceived, and punished the royal pair with madness.

Then Hermes temporarily transformed Dionysus into a kid or a ram, and presented him to the nymphs Macris, Nysa, Erato, Bromie, and Bacche, of Mount Nysa. They tended Dionysus, for which service Zeus subsequently placed their images among the stars, as the Hyades. On Mount Nysa Dionysus invented wine, for which he is chiefly celebrated.

When he grew to manhood Hera recognized him as Zeus's son, and drove him mad also. He went wandering all over the world, accompanied by his tutor Silenus and a wild army of Satyrs and Maenads, whose weapons were the ivy-twined staff tipped with a pine-cone, called the *thyrsus*, and swords and serpents and bullroarers. He sailed to Egypt, bringing the vine with him; and at Pharos King Proteus received him hospitably.

Among the Libyans of the Nile Delta, opposite Pharos, were certain Amazon queens whom Dionysus invited to march with him against the Titans. Dionysus's defeat of the Titans and restoration of King Ammon was the earliest of his many military successes. He then turned east and made for India and conquered the whole country, which he taught the art of viniculture, also giving it laws and founding great cities. On his return he was opposed by the Amazons, a horde of whom he chased as far as Ephesus. Others fled to Samos, and Dionysus followed them in boats, killing many.

Next, Dionysus returned to Europe by way of Phrygia, where his grandmother Rhea purified him of the many murders he had committed during his madness, and initiated him into her Mysteries. He then invaded Thrace; but no sooner had his people landed at the mouth of the river Strymon than Lycurgus, King of the Edonians, captured the entire army, except Dionysus himself, who plunged into the sea and took refuge in Thetis's grotto. Rhea helped the prisoners to escape, and drove Lycurgus mad: he struck his own son Dryas dead with an axe, in the belief that he was cutting down a vine, and the whole land of Thrace grew barren in horror of his crime. When Dionysus announced that this barrenness would continue unless Lycurgus were put to death, the Edonians led him to Mount Pangaeum, where wild horses pulled his body apart.

Dionysus met with no further opposition in Thrace, but travelled on to Thebes, and invited the women to join his revels on Mount Cithaeron. Pentheus, King of Thebes, disliking Dionysus's dissolute appearance, arrested him, together with all his Maenads, but went mad and, instead of shackling Dionysus, shackled the bull. The Maenads escaped again, and went raging out upon the mountain. Pentheus attempted to stop them; but, inflamed by wine and religious ecstasy, they rent him limb from limb. His mother Agave led the riot, and it was she who wrenched off his head.

Pan and his pipes.
Bronze statuette
(British Museum)

At Orchomenus the three daughters of Minyas, by name Alcithoë, Leucippe, and Arsippe, refused to join in the revels, though Dionysus himself invited them, appearing in the form of a girl. He then changed his shape, becoming successively a lion, a bull, and a panther, and drove them insane. Leucippe offered her own son Hippasus as sacrifice, and the three sisters, having torn him to pieces and devoured him, skimmed the mountains in a frenzy until at last Hermes changed them into birds.

When all Boeotia had acknowledged Dionysus's divinity, he made a tour of the Aegean Islands, spreading joy and terror wherever he went. Arriving at Icaria, he found that his ship was unseaworthy, and hired another from certain Tyrrhenian sailors who claimed to be bound for Naxos. But they proved to be pirates and, unaware of his godhead, steered for Asia to sell him as a slave. Dionysus made a vine grow from the deck and enfold the mast, while ivy twined about the rigging; he also turned the oars into serpents, and became a lion himself, filling the vessel with phantom beasts and the sound of flutes, so that the terrified pirates leaped overboard and became dolphins.

It was at Naxos that Dionysus met the lovely Ariadne whom Theseus had deserted, and married her without delay. She bore him Oenopion, Thoas, Staphylus, Latromis, Euanthes, and Tauropolus. Later, he placed her bridal chaplet among the stars.

From Naxos he came to Argos and punished Perseus, who at first opposed him and killed many of his followers, by inflicting a madness on the Argive women. Perseus hastily admitted his error, and appeased Dionysus by building a temple in his honour.

Finally, having established his worship throughout the world, Dionysus ascended to Heaven, and now sits at the right hand of Zeus as one of the Twelve Great Ones.

The Gods of the Underworld

When ghosts descend to Tartarus, each is supplied by pious relatives with a coin laid under the tongue of its corpse. They are thus able to pay Charon, the miser who ferries them in a crazy boat across the Styx. Penniless ghosts must wait for ever on the near bank; unless they have evaded Hermes, their conductor, and crept down by a back entrance. A three-headed dog named Cerberus guards the opposite shore of Styx.

The first region of Tartarus contains the cheerless Asphodel Fields, where souls of heroes stray without purpose among the throngs of less distinguished dead that twitter like bats. Their one delight is in

Hades and Persephone in the Underworld. Detail of an Apulian amphora (British Museum)

libations of blood poured to them by the living: when they drink they feel themselves almost men again. Beyond these meadows lie Erebus and the palace of Hades and Persephone. Close by, newly arrived ghosts are daily judged by Minos, Rhadamanthys, and Aeacus at a place where three roads meet. As each verdict is given the ghosts are directed along one of the three roads: that leading back to the Asphodel Meadows, if they are neither virtuous nor evil; that leading to the punishment-field of Tartarus, if they are evil; that leading to the orchards of Elysium, if they are virtuous.

Elysium, ruled over by Cronus, lies near Hades's dominions, but forms no part of them; it is a happy land of perpetual day, without cold or snow, where games, music, and revels never cease, and where the inhabitants may elect to be reborn on earth whenever they please. Near by are the Fortunuate Islands, reserved for those who have been three times born, and three times attained Elysium.

Hades seldom visits the upper air, except on business or when he is overcome by sudden lust. Once he dazzled the Nymph Minthe with the splendour of his golden chariot and its four black horses, and would have seduced her without difficulty had not Queen Persephone metamorphosed Minthe into sweet-smelling mint. He willingly allows none of his subjects to escape, and few who visit Tartarus return alive to describe it.

Hades never knows what is happening in the world above, or in Olympus, except for fragmentary information which comes to him when mortals strike their hands upon the earth and invoke him with oaths and curses. His most prized possession is the helmet of invisibility, given him as a mark of gratitude by the Cyclopes when he consented to release them at Zeus's order. All the riches of gems and precious metals hidden beneath the earth are his, but he owns no property above ground, except for certain gloomy temples in Greece.

Queen Persephone. however, can be both gracious and merciful. She is faithful to Hades, but has had no children by him and prefers the company of Hecate, goddess of witches, to his.

Tisiphone, Alecto, and Megaera, the Erinnyes or Furies, live in Erebus, and are older than Zeus or any of the other Olympians. Their task is to hear complaints brought by mortals against the insolence of the young to the aged, of children to parents, of hosts to guests, and of householders or city councils to suppliants — and to punish such crimes by hounding the culprits relentlessly. These Erinnyes are crones, with snakes for hair, dog's heads, coal-black bodies, bat's

Coin of Dionysus (Archaeological Museum, Syracuse, Sicily)

wings, and bloodshot eyes. In their hands they carry brass-studded scourges, and their victims die in torment. It is unwise to mention them by name in conversation; hence they are usually styled the Eumenides, which means 'The Kindly Ones' — as Hades is styled Pluton, or Pluto, 'The Rich One'.

Tyche and Nemesis

Tyche is a daughter of Zeus, to whom he has given power to decide what the fortune of this or that mortal shall be. On some she heaps gifts from a horn of plenty, others she deprives of all that thay have. Tyche is altogether irresponsible in her awards, and runs about juggling with a ball to exemplify the uncertainty of chance. But if it ever happens that a man, whom she has favoured, boasts of his abundant riches and neither sacrifices a part of them to the gods, nor alleviates the poverty of his fellow-citizens, then the ancient goddess Nemesis steps in to humiliate him. Nemesis carries an apple-bough in one hand, and a wheel in the other, and wears a silver crown adorned with stags; the scourge hangs at her girdle.

3

OF HEROES, GODS AND MEN

Orpheus

ORPHEUS, SON OF THE Thracian King Oeagrus and the Muse Calliope, was the most famous poet and musician who ever lived. Apollo presented him with a lyre, and the muses taught him its use, so that he not only enchanted wild beasts, but made the trees and rocks move from their places to follow the sound of his music.

After a visit to Egypt, Orpheus joined the Argonauts, with whom he sailed to Colchis, his music helping them to overcome many difficulties — and, on his return, married Eurydice, and settled among the savage Cicones of Thrace.

One day, near Tempe, in the valley of the river Peneius, Eurydice met Aristaeus, who tried to force her. She trod on a serpent as she fled, and died of its bite; but Orpheus boldly descended into Tartarus, hoping to fetch her back. On his arrival, he not only charmed the ferryman Charon, the Dog Cerberus, and the three Judges of the Dead with his plaintive music, but temporarily suspended the tortures of the damned; and so far soothed the savage heart of Hades that he won leave to restore Eurydice to the upper world. Hades made a single condition: that Orpheus might not look behind him until she was safely back under the light of the sun. Eurydice followed Orpheus up through the dark passage, guided by the sounds of his lyre, and it was only when he reached the sunlight again that he turned to see whether she were still behind him, and so lost her for ever.

When Dionysus invaded Thrace, Orpheus neglected to honour him, but taught other sacred mysteries and preached the evil of sacrificial murder to the men of Thrace. In vexation, Dionysus set the Maenads upon him at Deium in Macedonia. First waiting until their husbands had entered Apollo's temple, where Orpheus served as priest, they seized the weapons stacked outside, burst in, murdered their husbands, and tore Orpheus limb from limb. His head they threw into the river Hebrus, but it floated, still singing, down to the sea, and was carried to the island of Lesbos.

Tearfully, the Muses collected his limbs and buried them at Leibethra, at the foot of Mount Olympus, where the nightingales now sing sweeter than anywhere else in the world. As for Orpheus's head: after being attacked by a jealous Lemnian serpent (which Apollo at once changed into a stone) it was laid to rest in a cave at Antissa, sacred to Dionysus. There it prophesied day and night until Apollo, finding that his oracles at Delphi, Gryneium, and Clarus were deserted, came and stood over the head, crying: 'Cease from interference in my business'. Thereupon the head fell silent. Orpheus's lyre had likewise drifted to Lesbos and been laid up in a temple of Apollo, at whose intercession, and that of the Muses, the lyre was placed in heaven as a constellation.

Ganymedes

Ganymedes, the son of King Tros who gave his name to Troy, was the most beautiful youth alive and therefore chosen by the gods to be Zeus's cup-bearer. It is said that Zeus, desiring Ganymedes also as his bedfellow, disguised himself in eagle's feathers and abducted him from the Trojan plain.

Afterwards, on Zeus's behalf, Hermes presented Tros with a golden vine, the work of Hephaestus, and two fine horses, in compensation for his loss, assuring him at the same time that Ganymedes had become immortal, exempt from the miseries of old age, and was now smiling, golden bowl in hand, as he dispensed bright nectar to the Father of Heaven.

The Giants' Revolt

Enraged because Zeus had confined their brothers, the Titans, in Tartarus, certain tall and terrible giants plotted an assault on Heaven. They had been born from Mother Earth at Thracian Phlegra, twenty-four in number.

Without warning, they seized rocks and fire-brands and hurled them upwards from their mountain tops, so that the Olympians were hard pressed. Hera prophesied that the giants could never be killed by any god, but only by a single, lion-skinned mortal; and that even he could do nothing unless the enemy were anticipated in their search for a certain herb of invulnerability, which grew in a secret place on earth. Zeus at once took counsel with Athene; sent her off to warn Heracles, the lion-skinned mortal; and forbade Eos, Selene, and

Helius to shine for a while. Under the light of the stars, Zeus groped about, found the herb, and brought it safely to Heaven.

The Olympians could not join battle with the giants. Heracles let loose his first arrow against Alcyoneus, the enemy's leader. He fell, but sprang up again revived, because this was his native soil of Phlegra. 'Quick!' cried Athene. 'Drag him away to another country!' Heracles caught Alcyoneus and dragged him over the Thracian border, where he despatched him with a club.

Then Porphyrion leaped into Heaven from the great pyramid of rocks which the giants had piled up, and none of the gods stood his ground. He made for Hera, whom he tried to strangle; but, wounded in the liver by an arrow from Eros's bow, he turned from anger to lust. Zeus, seeing that his wife was about to be outraged, felled Porphyrion with a thunderbolt. Up he sprang again, but Heracles, returning in the nick of time, mortally wounded hims with an arrow. Meanwhile, Ephialtes had beaten Ares to his knees; however, Apollo shot the wretch in the left eye and Heracles planted another arrow in the right. Thus died Ephialtes.

Now, whenever a god wounded a giant, it was Heracles who had to deal the death blow. The peace-loving goddesses Hestia and Demeter took no part in the conflict, but stood dismayed, wringing their hands.

Discouraged, the remaining giants fled to earth, pursued by the Olympians. Athene threw a vast missile at Enceladus, which crushed him flat and became the island of Sicily. And Poseidon broke off part of Cos with his trident and threw it at Polybutes; this became the nearby islet of Nisyros, beneath which he lies buried.

The remaining giants made a last stand at Bathos, near Arcadian Trapezus. Hermes, borrowing Hades's helmet of invisibility, struck down Hippolytus, and Artemis pierced Gration with an arrow; while the Fates' pestles broke the heads of Agrius and Thoas. Ares, with his spear, and Zeus, with his thunderbolt, now accounted for the rest, though Heracles was called upon to despatch each giant as he fell.

Typhon
In revenge for the destruction of the giants, Mother Earth lay with Tartarus, and presently brought forth her youngest child, Typhon: the largest monster ever born. From the thighs downward he was coiled serpents, and his arms, which reached a hundred leagues in either direction, had countless serpents' heads instead of hands. His brutish ass-head touched the stars, his vast wings darkened the sun,

fire flashed from his eyes, and flaming rocks hurtled from his mouth. When he came rushing towards Olympus, the gods fled in terror to Egypt, where they disguised themselves as animals.

Athene alone stood her ground, and taunted Zeus with cowardice until, resuming his true form, he let fly a thunderbolt at Typhon, and follwed this up with a sweep of the same flint sickle that had served to castrate his father Uranus. Typhon fled to Mount Casius, and there the two grappled. Typhon twined his myriad coils about Zeus, disarmed him of his sickle and, after severing the sinews of his hands and feet with it, dragged him into the Corycian Cave. Zeus now could not move a finger, and Typhon had hidden the sinews in a bear-skin, over which Delphyne, a serpent-tailed sister-monster, stood guard.

Zeus's defeat spread dismay among the gods, but Hermes and Pan went secretly to the cave, where Pan frightened Delphyne with a sudden shout, while Hermes abstracted the sinews and replaced them on Zeus's limbs.

Zeus returned to Olympus and, mounted upon a chariot drawn by winged horses, once more pursued Typhon with thunderbolts. Typhon reached Mount Haemus in Thrace and, picking up whole mountains, hurled them at Zeus, who interposed his thunderbolts, so that they rebounded on the monster, wounding him frightfully. He fled towards Sicily, where Zeus ended the running fight by hurling Mount Aetna upon him, and fire belches from its cone to this day.

Deucalion's Flood

Deucalion's Flood, so called to distinguish it from the Ogygian and other floods, was caused by Zeus's anger against the impious sons of Lycaon, the son of Pelasgus. News of their crimes reached Olympus, and Zeus himself visited them, disguised as a poor traveller. They had the effrontery to set umble soup before him, mixing the guts of their brother Nyctimus with the umbles of sheep and goats that it contained. Zeus was undeceived and, thrusting away the table changed all of them except Nyctimus, whom he restored to life, into wolves.

On his return to Olympus, Zeus in disgust let loose a great flood on the earth, meaning to wipe out the whole race of man; but Deucalion, King of Phthia, warned by his father Prometheus the Titan, built an ark, victualled it, and went aboard with his wife Pyrrha. Then the South Wind blew, the rain fell, and the rivers roared down to the sea which, rising with astonishing speed, washed away every city of the coast and plain; until the entire world was flooded, but for a few

The three-headed monster Typhon. A sculpture from Naxos (Acropolis Museum, Athens)

mountain peaks, and all mortal creatures seemed to have been lost, except Deucalion and Pyrrha. The ark floated about for nine days until, at last, the waters subsided, and it came to rest on Mount Parnassus.

Disembarking, they offered a sacrifice to Father Zeus, and went down to pray at the shrine of Themis, beside the river Cephissus. They pleaded humbly that mankind should be renewed, and Zeus, hearing their voices from afar, sent Hermes to assure them that whatever request they might make would be granted forthwith. Themis appeared in person, saying: 'Shroud your heads, and throw the bones of your mothers behind you!' Since Deucalion and Pyrrha had different mothers, both now deceased, they decided that the Titaness meant Mother Earth, whose bones were the rocks lying on the river bank. Therefore, stooping with shrouded heads, they picked up rocks and threw them over their shoulders; these became either men or women, according as Deucalion or Pyrrha had handled them.

However, as it proved, Deucalion and Pyrrha were not the sole survivors of the Flood, for Megarus, a son of Zeus, had been roused from his couch by the scream of cranes that summoned him to the peak of Mount Gerania, which remained above water. Similarly, the inhabitants of Parnassus were awakened by the howling of wolves and followed them to the mountain top. They named their new city Lycorea, after the wolves. Thus the flood proved of little avail, for some of the Parnassians migrated to Arcadia, and revived Lycaon's abominations.

This Deucalion was the brother of Cretan Ariadne and the father of Orestheus, King of the Ozolian Locrians, in whose time a white bitch littered a stick, which Orestheus planted, and which grew into a vine. Another of his sons, Amphictyon, entertained Dionysus, and was the first man to mix wine with water. But his eldest and most famous son was Hellen, father of all Greeks.

Atlas and Prometheus

Prometheus, the creator of mankind, whom some include among the seven Titans, was the son either of the Titan Eurymedon, or of Iapetus by the nymph Clymene; and his brothers were Epimetheus, Atlas, and Menoetius.

Atlas and Menoetius joined Cronus and the Titans in their unsuccessful war agains the Olympian gods. Zeus killed Menoetius with a thunderbolt, but spared Atlas, whom he condemned to support Heaven on his shoulders for all eternity.

Atlas was the father of the Pleiades, the Hyades, and the Hesperides; and has held up the Heavens ever since, except when Heracles temporarily relieved him of the task. Some say that Perseus petrified Atlas into Mount Atlas by showing him the Gorgon's head.

Prometheus, being wiser than Atlas, foresaw the issue of the rebellion against Cronus, and therefore preferred to fight on Zeus's side, persuading Epimetheus to do the same. He was, indeed, the wisest of his race, and Athene taught him architecture, astronomy, mathematics, navigation, medicine, metallurgy, and other useful arts, which he passed on to mankind. But Zeus, who had decided to extirpate the whole race of man, and spared them only at Prometheus's urgent plea, grew angry at their increasing powers and talents.

One day, when a dispute took place at Sicyon, as to which portions of a sacrificial bull should be offered to the gods, and which should be reserved for men, Prometheus was invited to act as arbiter. He therefore flayed and jointed a bull, and sewed its hide to form two open-mouthed bags, filling these with what he had cut up. One bag contained all the flesh, but this he concealed beneath the stomach, and the other contained the bones, hidden beneath a rich layer of fat. When he offered Zeus the choice of either, Zeus chose the bag containing the bones and fat (still the divine portion); but punished Prometheus by withholding fire from mankind.

Prometheus at once went to Athene, with a plea for a backstairs admittance to Olympus, and this she granted. On his arrival, he lighted a torch at the fiery chariot of the Sun and presently broke from it a fragment of glowing charcoal, which he thrust into the pithy hollow of a giant fennel-stalk. Then, extinguishing his torch, he stole away undiscovered, and gave fire to mankind.

Zeus swore revenge. He ordered Hephaestus to make a clay woman, and the four Winds to breathe life into her, and all the goddesses to adorn her. This woman, Pandora, the most beautiful ever created, Zeus sent as a gift to Epimetheus, but Epimetheus, having been warned by his brother to accept no gift from Zeus, respectfully excused himself. Now angrier even than before, Zeus had Prometheus chained naked to a pillar in the Caucasian mountains, where a greedy vulture tore at his liver all day, and there was no end to the pain, because every night his liver grew whole again.

But Zeus excused his savagery by circulating a falsehood: Athene, he said, had invited Prometheus to Olympus for a secret love affair.

Epimetheus, alarmed by his brother's fate, hastened to marry Pandora, whom Zeus had made as foolish, mischievous, and idle as she was beautiful. Presently she opened a jar, which Prometheus had warned Epimetheus to keep closed, and in which he had been at pains to imprison all the Spites that might plague mankind: such as Old Age, Labour, Sickness, Insanity, Vice and Passion. Out these flew in a cloud, stung Epimetheus and Pandora and then attacked the race of mortals. Delusive Hope, however, whom Prometheus had also shut in the jar, discouraged them by her lies from a general suicide.

Eos

At the close of every night, Eos, a daughter of the Titans Hyperion and Theia, rises from her couch in the east, mounts her chariot and rides to Olympus, where she announces the approach of her brother Helius. When Helius appears, she accompanies him on his travels until she announces their safe arrival on the western shores of Ocean.

Aphrodite was once vexed to find Ares in Eos's bed, and cursed her with a constant longing for young mortals, whom thereupon she secretly and shamefacedly began to seduce. First, Orion; next, Cephalus; then Cleitus; though she was married to Astraeus, who came of Titan stock.

Lastly, Eos carried off Ganymedes and Tithonus, sons of Tros,

above: *Hermes, Eurydice and Orpheus in the Underworld (Louvre)*

opposite above: *Ganymedes and Zeus (Hermitage Museum, Leningrad)*

right: *Apollo and Artemis in the battle of the gods and giants (Archaeological Museum, Delphi)*

When Zeus robbed her of Ganymedes she begged him to grant Tithonus immortality, and to this he assented. But she forgot to ask also for perpetual youth, and Tithonus became daily older, his voice grew shrill, and, when Eos tired of nursing him, he turned into a cicada.

Orion

Orion, a hunter of Boeotian Hyria, and the handsomest man alive, was the son of Poseidon and Euryale. Coming one day to Hyria in Chios, he fell in love with Merope, daughter of Dionysus's son Oenopion. Oenopion had promised Merope to Orion in marriage, if he would free the island from the dangerous wild beasts that infested it; and this he set himself to do. But when the task was at last accomplished, and he claimed her as his wife, Oenopion brought him rumours of lions, bears, and wolves still lurking in the hills, and refused to give her up.

One night Orion, in disgust, drank a skinful of Oenopion's wine, which so inflamed him that he broke into Merope's bedroom, and forced her to lie with him. When dawn came, Oenopion invoked his father, Dionysus, who sent satyrs to ply Orion with still more wine, until he fell fast asleep; whereupon Oenopion put out both his eyes and flung him on the seashore. An oracle announced that the blind man would regain his sight, if he travelled to the east and turned his eye-sockets towards Helius at the point where he first rises from Ocean. Orion at once rowed out to sea in a small boat and, following the sound of a Cyclops's hammer, reached Lemnos. There he entered the smithy of Hephaestus, snatched up an apprentice named Cedalion, and carried him off on his shoulders as a guide. Cedalion led Orion over land and sea, until he came to the farthest Ocean, where Eos fell in love with him, and her brother Helius restored his sight.

After visiting Delos in Eos's company, Orion returned to avenge himself on Oenopion, whom he could not, however, find anywhere in Chios, because he was hiding in an underground chamber made for him by Hephaestus. Sailing on to Crete, where he thought that Oenopion might have fled for protection to his grandfather Minos, Orion met Artemis, who shared his love of the chase. She soon persuaded him to forget his vengeance, and, instead, come hunting with her.

Now, Apollo was aware that Orion had not refused Eos's invitation to her couch in the holy island of Delos. Fearing that his sister Artemis might prove as susceptible as Eos, Apollo went to Mother Earth and, repeating Orion's boast that he would rid the whole earth of wild beasts and monsters, arranged for a monstrous scorpion to pursue him. Orion attacked the scorpion, but, finding that its armour was proof against any mortal weapon, dived into the sea and swam away in the direction of Delos where, he hoped, Eos would protect him. Apollo then called to Artemis: 'Do you see the black object bobbing about in the sea, far away, close to Ortygia? It is the head of a villain called Candaon, who has just seduced Opis, one of your Hyperborean priestesses. I challenge you to transfix it with an arrow!' Now, Candaon was Orion's Boeotian nickname, though Artemis did not know this. She took careful aim, let fly, and, swimming out to retrieve her quarry, found that she had shot Orion through the head. In great grief she implored Apollo's son Asclepius to revive him, and he consented; but was destroyed by Zeus's thunderbolt before he could accomplish his task. Artemis then set Orion's image among the stars, eternally pursued by the Scorpion; his ghost had already descended to the Asphodel Fields.

Helius

Helius is a brother of Selene and Eos. Roused by the crowing of the cock, and heralded by Eos, he drives his four-horse chariot daily across the Heavens from a palace in the far east, near Colchis, to an equally magnificent far-western palace, where his horses pasture in the Islands of the Blessed. He sails home along the Ocean stream, which flows around the world, embarking his chariot and team on a golden ferry-boat.

Helius can see everything that happens on earth, but is not particularly observant — once he even failed to notice the robbery of his sacred cattle by Odysseus's companions. Rhodes is his freehold. It happend that, when Zeus was allotting islands and cities to the various gods, he forgot to include Helius among these, and 'Alas!' he said, 'now I shall have to begin all over again.'

'No, Sire,' replied Helius politely, 'today I noticed signs of a new island emerging from the sea, to the south of Asia Minor. I shall be well content with that.'

Zeus called the Fate Lachesis to witness that any such new island should belong to Helius; and, when Rhodes had risen well above the waves, Helius claimed it and begot seven sons and a daughter there on the Nymph Rhode. Some say that Rhodes had existed before this time, and was re-emerging from the great flood which Zeus sent. The

above: *Helius riding across the sky in his chariot. Detail from a two-handed bowl (British Museum)*

opposite above: *Pandora. Vase (British Museum)*

opposite below: *Atlas watching the vulture attacking the chained Prometheus. From a black-figured vase (Vatican Museum)*

Telchines were its aboriginal inhabitants and Poseidon fell in love with one of them, the nymph Halia, on whom he begot Rhode. The Telchines, foreseeing the flood, sailed away in all directions, and abandoned their claims on Rhodes. Rhode was thus left the sole heiress, and her seven sons by Helius ruled in the island after its re-emergence. They became famous astronomers, and when one of them, by name Actis, was banished for fratricide, he fled to Egypt. There he founded the city of Heliopolis, and first taught the Egyptians astrology, inspired by his father Helius. The Rhodians built the Colossus, seventy cubits high, in his honour.

One morning Helius yielded to his son Phaëthon who had been constantly plaguing him for permission to drive the sun-chariot. Phaëthon wished to show his sisters Prote and Clymene what a fine fellow he was: and his fond mother Rhode encouraged him. But, not being strong enough to check the career of the white horses, Phaëthon drove them first so high above the earth that he scorched the fields. Zeus, in a fit of rage, killed him with a thunderbolt, and he fell into the river Po. His grieving sisters were changed into poplar trees on its banks.

Tereus

Tereus, a son of Ares, ruled over the Thracians then occupying Phocian Daulis and, having acted as mediator in a boundary dispute for Pandion, King of Athens and father of the twins Butes and Erechtheus, married their sister Procne, who bore him a son, Itys.

Unfortunately Tereus had fallen in love with Pandion's younger sister Philomela. A year later, concealing Procne in a rustic cabin near his palace at Daulis, he reported her death to Pandion, who offered him Philomela in Procne's place. When Philomela reached the palace, Tereus forced her to lie with him. Procne soon heard the news, but Tereus cut out her tongue and confined her to the slaves' quarters, where she could communicate with Philomela only by weaving a secret message into the pattern of a bridal robe — 'Procne is among the slaves.'

Meanwhile, an oracle had warned Tereus that Itys would die by the hand of a blood relative and, suspecting his brother Dryas of a murderous plot to seize the throne, struck him down unexpectedly with an axe. The same day, Philomela read the message woven into the robe. She hurried to the slaves' quarters, and released Procne.

'Oh, to be revenged on Tereus, who pretended that you were dead, and seduced me!' wailed Philomela, aghast.

Procne, being tongueless, could not reply, but flew out and, seizing her son Itys, killed him, gutted him, and then boiled him in a copper cauldron for Tereus to eat on his return.

When Tereus realized what flesh he had been tasting, he grasped the axe with which he had killed Dryas and pursued the sisters as they fled from the palace. He soon overtook them and was on the point of committing a double murder when the gods changed all three into birds; Procne became a swallow; Philomela, a nightingale; Tereus, a hoopoe.

Boreas

Oreithyia, daughter of Erechtheus, King of Athens, and his wife Praxithea, was one day whirling in a dance beside the river Ilissus, when Boreas, son of Astraeus and Eos, and brother of the South and West Winds, carried her off. Wrapped in a mantle of dark clouds, he ravished her.

Boreas had long loved Oreithyia and repeatedly sued for her hand, but Erechtheus put him off until at length, complaining that he had wasted too much time in words, he resorted to his natural violence.

He took her to the city of the Thracian Cicones, where she became his wife, and bore him two sons, Calais and Zetes, who grew wings when they reached manhood; also two daughters, namely Chione and Cleopatra.

Once, disguising himself as a dark-maned stallion, he covered twelve of the three thousand mares belonging to Erichthonius, son of Dardanus, which used to graze in water-meadows beside the river Scamander. Twelve fillies were born from this union; they could race over ripe ears of standing corn without bending them, or over the crests of waves.

The Athenians regard Boreas as their brother-in-law and, having once successfully invoked him to destroy King Xerxes's fleet, they built him a fine temple on the banks of the river Ilissus.

Io

Io, daughter of the River-god Inachus, was a priestess of Argive Hera. Zeus, over whom Iynx, daughter of Pan and Echo, had cast a spell, fell in love with Io, and when Hera charged him with infidelity and turned Iynx into a wryneck as a punishment, lied: 'I have never touched Io.' He then turned her into a white cow, which Hera claimed as hers and handed over for safe keeping to Argus Panoptes, ordering him: 'Tether this beast secretly to an olive-tree at Nemea.' But Zeus sent Hermes to fetch her back, and himself led the way to Nemea dressed in woodpecker disguise. Hermes, though the cleverest of thieves, knew that he could not steal Io without being detected by one of Argus's hundred eyes; he therefore charmed him asleep by playing the flute, crushed him with a boulder, cut off his head, and released Io. Hera, having placed Argus's eyes in the tail of a peacock, as a constant reminder of his foul murder, set a gadfly to sting Io and chase her all over the world.

Io first went to Dodona, and presently reached the sea called the Ionian after her, but there turned back and travelled north to Mount Haemus and then, by way of the Danube's delta, coursed sun-wise around the Black Sea, crossing the Crimean Bosphorus, and following the River Hybristes to its source in the Caucasus, where Prometheus still languished on his rock. She regained Europe by way of Colchis, the land of the Chalybes, and the Thracian Bosphorus; then away she galloped through Asia Minor to Tarsus and Joppa, thence to Media, Bactria, and India and, passing south-westward through Arabia, across the Indian Bosphorus, reached Ethiopia. Thence she travelled down from the sources of the Nile, where the pygmies make perpetual war with the cranes, and found rest at last in Egypt. There Zeus restored her to human form and, having married Telegonus, she gave birth to Epaphus — her son by Zeus, who had *touched* her to some purpose — and founded the worship of Isis, as she called Demeter. Epaphus, who was rumoured to be the divine bull Apis, reigned over Egypt, and had a daughter, Libya, the mother by Poseidon of Agenor and Belus.

Europe and Cadmus

Agenor, Libya's son by Poseidon and twin to Belus, left Egypt to settle in the Land of Canaan, where he married Telephassa, who bore him Cadmus, Phoenix, Cilix, Thasus, Phineus, and one daughter, Europe.

Helius, the sun-god. A silver-gilt disc (British Museum)

Europe and the Bull. Metope (Seljuk Museum, Konya, Turkey)

Zeus, falling in love with Europe, sent Hermes to drive Agenor's cattle down to the seashore at Tyre, where she and her companions used to walk. He himself joined the herd, disguised as a snow-white bull. Europe was struck by his beauty and, on finding him gentle as a lamb, mastered her fear and began to play with him; in the end, she climbed upon his shoulders, and let him amble down with her to the edge of the sea. Suddenly he swam away, while she looked back in terror at the receding land. Wading ashore near Cretan Gortyna, Zeus became an eagle and ravished Europe. She bore him three sons: Minos, Rhadamanthys, and Sarpedon.

Agenor sent his sons in search of their sister, forbidding them to return without her. They set sail at once but, having no notion where the bull had gone, each steered a different course. Phoenix travelled westward to what is now Carthage; Cilix went to the Land of the

Hypachaens, which took his name, Cilicia; and Phineus to Thynia, a peninsula separating the Sea of Marmara from the Black Sea. Thasus and his followers, first making for Olympia, then set off to colonize the island of Thasos and work its rich gold mines.

Cadmus sailed with Telephassa to Rhodes, where he dedicated a brazen cauldron to Athene of Lindus, and built Poseidon's temple. They next touched at Thera, and built a similar temple, finally reaching the land of the Thracian Edonians. Here Telephassa died and Cadmus and his companions proceeded on foot to the Delphic Oracle. When he asked where Europe might be found, the Pythoness advised him to give up his search and, instead, follow a cow and build a city wherever she should sink down from weariness.

Departing, Cadmus came upon some cowherds in the service of King Pelagon, who sold him a cow. He drove her eastward through Boetia, never allowing her to pause until, at last, she sank down where the city of Thebes now stands, and here he erected an image of Athene.

Cadmus, warning his companions that the cow must be sacrificed to Athene without delay, sent them to fetch lustral water from the Castalian Spring, but did not know that it was guarded by a great serpent. This serpent killed most of Cadmus's men, and he took vengeance by crushing its head with a rock. No sooner had he offered Athene the sacrifice, than she appeared, ordering him to sow the serpent's teeth, in the soil. When he obeyed her, armed Sown Men at once sprang up. Cadmus tossed a stone among them and they began to brawl, each accusing the other of having thrown it, and fought so fiercely that only five survived: Echion, Udaeus, Chthonius, Hyperenor, and Pelorus, who offered Cadmus their services.

Cadmus and Harmonia

When Cadmus had served eight years in bondage to expiate the murder of the Castalian serpent, Athene secured him the land of the Boeotia. With the help of his Sown Men, he built the Theban acropolis, named 'The Cadmea' in his own honour and, after being initiated into the mysteries which Zeus had taught Iasion, married Harmonia, the daughter of Aphrodite and Ares.

This was the first mortal wedding ever attended by the Olympians. Twelve golden thrones were set up for them in Cadmus's house, and they all brought gifts. Aphrodite presented Harmonia with the famous golden necklace made by Hephaestus which conferred irresistible beauty on its wearer. Athene gave her a golden robe, which similarly conferred divine dignity on its wearer, and Hermes a lyre. Cadmus's own present to Harmonia was another rich robe; and Electra, Iasion's mother, taught her the rites of the Great Goddess; while Demeter assured her a prosperous barley harvest by lying with Iasion in a thrice-ploughed field during the celebrations.

In his old age, Cadmus resigned the Theban throne in favour of his grandson Pentheus, whom his daughter Agave had borne to Echion, and lived quietly in the city. But when Pentheus was done to death by his mother, Dionysus foretold that Cadmus and Harmonia would rule over barbarian hordes. These same barbarians, he said, would sack many Greek cities until, at last, they plundered a temple of Apollo, whereupon they would suffer just punishment; but Ares would turn Cadmus and Harmonia into serpents and they would live happily for all time in the Islands of the Blessed.

Cadmus and Harmonia therefore emigrated to the land of the Encheleans who, when attacked by the Illyrians, chose them as their rulers. Agave was now married to Lycotherses, King of Illyria, but on hearing that her parents commanded the Enchelean forces, she murdered Lycotherses too, and gave the kingdom to Cadmus. In their old age, when the prophecy had been wholly fulfilled, Cadmus and Harmonia duly became blue-spotted black serpents, and were sent by Zeus to the Islands of the Blessed.

Belus and the Danaids

King Belus, who ruled at Chemmis in the Thebaid, was the son of Libya by Poseidon, and twin-brother of Agenor. His wife Achinoë, daughter of Nilus, bore him the twins Aegyptus and Danaus, and a third son, Cepheus. Aegyptus was given Arabia as his kingdom; but also subdued the country of the Melampodes, and named it Egypt after himself. Fifty sons were born to him of various mothers: Danaus, sent to rule Libya, had fifty daughters, called the Danaids, also born of various mothers.

On Belus's death, the twins quarrelled over their inheritance, and as a conciliatory gesture Aegyptus proposed a mass-marriage between the fifty princes and the fifty princesses. Danaus would not consent and, when an oracle confirmed his fears that Aegyptus had it in his mind to kill all the Danaids, prepared to flee from Libya.

With Athene's assistance, he built a ship for himself and his daughters and they sailed towards Greece together, by way of Rhodes. There Danaus dedicated an image to Athene in a temple raised for her by the Danaids.

69

From Rhodes they sailed to the Peloponnese and landed near Lerna, where Danaus announced that he was divinely chosen to become King of Argos. Gelanor the Argive king, would doubtless have kept the throne, despite Danaus's declaration that Athene was supporting him, had not a wolf come boldly down from the hills, attacked the herd of cattle grazing near the city walls, and killed the leading bull. This was read as an omen that Danaus would take the throne by violence if he were opposed, and therefore persuaded Gelanor to resign it peacefully.

Danaus, convinced that the would had been Apollo in disguise, dedicated the famous shrine to Wolfish Apollo at Argos, and became so powerful a ruler that all the Pelasgians of Greece called themselves Danaans. He also built the citadel of Argos, and his daughters brought the Mysteries of Demeter from Egypt, and taught these to the Pelasgian women.

Danaus had found Argolis suffering from a prolonged drought, since Poseidon had dried up all the rivers and streams. He sent his daughters in search of water, with orders to placate Poseidon. One of them, by name Amymone, while chasing a deer in the forest, happened to disturb a sleeping satyr. He sprang up and tried to ravish her; but Poseidon, whom she invoked, hurled his trident at the satyr. The fleeing satyr dodged, the trident stuck quivering in a rock, and Poseidon himself lay with Amymone, who was glad that she could carry out her father's instructions so pleasantly. On learning her errand, Poseidon told her to pull his trident from the rock. When she did so, three streams of water jetted up from the three tine-holes. This spring, now named Amymone, is the source of the river Lerna, which never fails, even at the height of summer.

Aegyptus now sent his sons to Argos, forbidding them to return until they had punished Danaus and his whole family. On their arrival, they begged Danaus to reverse his former decision and let them marry his daughters — intending, however, to murder them on the wedding night. When he still refused, they laid siege to Argos. Now, the Argive citadel was waterless at the time in question. Seeing that thirst would soon force him to capitulate, Danaus promised to do what the sons of Aegyptus asked, as soon as they raised the siege.

A mass-marriage was arranged, and Danaus paired off the couples; but during the wedding-feast he secretly doled out sharp pins which his daughters were to conceal in their hair; and at midnight each stabbed her husband through the heart. There was only one survivor: on Artemis's advice, Hypermnestra saved the life of Lynceus, because

Leda and the Swan (Heraklion Museum, Crete)

he had spared her maidenhead, and helped him in his flight. At dawn, Danaus learned of Hypermnestra's disobedience, and she was tried for her life; but acquitted by the Argive judges.

The murdered men's heads were buried at Lerna, and their bodies given full funeral honours below the walls of Argos; but, although Athene and Hermes purified the Danaids in the Lernaean Lake with Zeus's permission, the Judges of the Dead have condemned them to the endless task of carrying water in jars perforated like sieves.

Lynceus and Hypermnestra were reunited, and Danaus, deciding to marry off the other daughters before noon on the day of their purification, called for suitors. He proposed a marriage race, the winner to have first choice of a wife, and the others the next choices, in their order of finishing the race. Since he could not find enough men who would risk their lives by marrying murderesses, only a few ran;

but when the wedding night passed without disaster to the new bridegrooms, more suitors appeared, and another race was run on the following day. Lynceus later killed Danaus, and reigned in his stead. Meanwhile, Aegyptus had come to Greece, but when he learned of his sons' fate, fled to Aroe, where he died, and was buried at Patrae, in a sanctuary of Serapis.

Leda

Some say that when Zeus fell in love with Nemesis, she fled from him into the water and became a fish; he pursued her as a beaver. She leaped ashore, and transformed herself into this wild beast or that, but could not shake Zeus off, because he borrowed the form of even fiercer and swifter beasts. At last she took to the air as a wild goose; he became a swan, and trod her triumphantly at Rhamnus in Attica. Nemesis came to Sparta, where Leda, wife of King Tyndareus, presently found a hyacinth-coloured egg lying in a marsh, which she brought home and hid in a chest: from it Helen of Troy was hatched.

The most usual account, however, is that it was Leda herself with whom Zeus companied in the form of a swan beside the river Eurotas; that she laid an egg from which were hatched Helen, Castor, and Polydeuces; and that she was consequently deified as the goddess Nemesis. Now, Leda's husband Tyndareus had also lain with her the same night and, though some hold that all these three were Zeus's children — and Clytaemnestra too, who had been hatched, with Helen, from a second egg — others record that Helen alone was a daughter of Zeus, and that Castor and Clytaemnestra were children of Tyndareus, while Helen and Polydeuces were children of Zeus.

Ixion

Ixion, a son of Phlegyas, the Lapith king, agreed to marry Dia, daughter of Eioneus. Inviting Eioneus to a banquet, he laid a pitfall in front of the palace, with a great charcoal fire underneath, into which the unsuspecting Eioneus fell and was burned. Zeus, having behaved equally ill himself when in love, not only purified Ixion but brought him to eat at his table.

Ixion was ungrateful, and planned to seduce Hera: Zeus, however, reading Ixion's intentions, shaped a cloud into a false Hera with whom Ixion, being far too gone in drink to notice the deception, duly took his pleasure. He was surprised in the act by Zeus, who ordered Hermes to scourge him mercilessly and then bind him to a fiery wheel which rolled without cease through the sky.

The false Hera bore Ixion the outcast child Centaurus who, when he grew to manhood, is said to have sired horse-centaurs on Magnesian mares, of whom the most celebrated was the learned Cheiron.

Sisyphus
Sisyphus, son of Aeolus, married Atlas's daughter Merope, the Pleiad, who bore him Glaucus, Ornytion, and Sinon, and owned a fine herd of cattle on the Isthmus of Corinth.

*Sisyphus in Hades.
Black-figured
Attic vase*

Near him lived Autolycus, son of Chione, whose twin-brother Philammon was begotten by Apollo, though Autolycus himself claimed Hermes as his father.

Now, Autolycus was a past master in theft, Hermes having given him the power of metamorphosing whatever beasts he stole. Thus, although Sisyphus noticed that his own herds grew steadily smaller, while those of Autolycus increased, he was unable at first to convict him of theft; and therefore, one day, engraved the inside of all his cattle's hooves with the monogram SS. That night Autolycus helped himself as usual, and at dawn hoof-prints along the road provided Sysyphus with sufficient evidence to summon neighbours in witness of the theft. He visited Autolycus's stable, recognized his stolen beasts by their marked hooves and, leaving his witnesses to remonstrate with the thief, hurried around the house and, while the argument was in progress outside, seduced Autolycus's daughter Anticleia. She bore him Odysseus, the manner of whose conception is enough to account for his habitual cunning.

Sisyphus founded Ephyra, afterwards known as Corinth, and peopled it with men sprung from mushrooms.

After Zeus's abduction of Aegina, her father the River-god Asopus came to Corinth in search of her. Sisyphus knew well what had happened to Aegina but would not reveal anything unless Asopus undertook to supply the citadel of Corinth with a perennial spring. Asopus accordingly made the spring Peirene rise: then Sisyphus told him all he knew.

Zeus, who had narrowly escaped Asopus's vengeance, ordered his brother Hades to fetch Sisyphus down to Tartarus and punish him everlastingly for his betrayal of divine secrets. Yet Sisyphus would not be daunted: he cunningly put Hades himself in handcuffs by persuading him to demonstrate their use, and then quickly locking them. Thus Hades was kept a prisoner in Sisyphus's house for some days, until at last Ares, whose interests were threatened, came hurrying up, set him free, and delivered Sisyphus into his clutches.

Sisyphus, however, kept another trick in reserve. Before descending to Tartarus, he instructed his wife Merope not to bury him; and, on reaching the Palace of Hades went straight to Persephone, and told her that, as an unburied person, he had no right to be there but should have been left on the far side of the river Styx. 'Let me return to the upper world,' he pleaded, 'arrange for my burial, and avenge the neglect shown me. My presence here is most irregular. I will be back within three days.' Persephone was deceived and granted his request; but as soon as Sisyphus found himself once again under the light of the sun, he repudiated his promise to Persephone. Finally, Hermes was called upon to hale him back by force.

Sisyphus was now given an exemplary punishment. The Judges of the Dead showed him a huge block of stone — identical in size with that into which Zeus had turned himself when fleeing from Asopus — and ordered him to roll it up the brow of the hill and topple it down the farther slope. He has never yet succeeded in doing so. As soon as he has almost reached the summit, he is forced back by the weight of the shameless stone, which bounces to the very bottom once more; where he wearily retrieves it and must begin all over again, though sweat bathes his limbs, and a cloud of dust rises above his head.

Merope, ashamed to find herself the only Pleiad with a husband in the Underworld — and a criminal too — deserted her six starry sisters in the night sky and has never been seen since.

Alcestis

Alcestis, the most beautiful of Pelias's daughters, was asked in marriage by many kings and princes. Not wishing to endanger his political position by refusing any of them, and yet clearly unable to satisfy more than one, Pelias let it be known that he would marry Alcestis to the man who could yoke a wild boar and a lion to his chariot and drive them around the race-course. At this, Admetus King of Pherae summoned Apollo, whom Zeus had bound to him for one year as a herdsman, and asked: 'Have I treated you with the respect due to your godhead?' 'You have indeed,' Apollo assented. 'Then,' pleaded Admetus, 'pray help me to win Alcestis, by enabling me to fulfil Pelias's conditions.' 'I shall be pleased to do so,' replied Apollo. Heracles lent him a hand and presently Admetus was driving his chariot around the race-course drawn by this savage team.

It is not known why Admetus omitted the customary sacrifice to Artemis before marrying Alcestis, but the goddess was quick enough to punish him. When he entered the bridal chamber that night, he recoiled in horror. No lovely naked bride awaited him, but a tangled knot of hissing serpents. Admetus ran shouting for Apollo, who kindly intervened with Artemis on his behalf. The neglected sacrifice having been offered at once, all was well, Apollo even obtaining Artemis's promise that, when Admetus's death came, he should be spared on condition that a member of his family died voluntarily for love of him.

This fatal day came sooner than Admetus expected. Hermes flew into the palace one morning and summoned him to Tartarus. General consternation prevailed; Admetus ran in haste to his old parents, and begged each of them in turn to surrender him the butt-end of existence. Both roundly refused, saying that he should be content with his appointed lot, like everyone else.

Then, for love of Admetus, Alcestis took poison and her ghost descended to Tartarus; but Heracles arrived unexpectedly with a new wild-olive club, and rescued her.

Athamas

Athamas the Aeolian, brother of Sisyphus and Salmoneus, ruled over Boeotia. At Hera's command, he married Nephele, a phantom whom Zeus created in her likeness when he wished to deceive Ixion the Lapith, and who was now wandering disconsolately about the halls of Olympus. She bore Athamas two sons: Phrixus and Leucon, and a daughter, Helle. But Athamas resented the disdain in which Nephele held him and, falling in love with Ino, daughter of Cadmus, brought her secretly to his palace at the foot of Mount Laphystium, where he begot Learchus and Melicertes on her.

Learning about her rival from the palace servants, Nephele returned in fury to Olympus, complaining to Hera that she had been insulted. Hera took her part, and vowed: 'My eternal vengeance shall fall upon Athamas and his House!'

Nephele thereupon went back to Mount Laphystium, where she publicly reported Hera's vow, and demanded that Athamas should die. But the men of Boeotia, who feared Athamas more than Hera, would not listen to Nephele; and the women of Boeotia were devoted to Ino, who now persuaded them to parch the seed-corn, without their husbands' knowledge, so that the harvest would fail. Ino foresaw that when the grain was due to sprout, but no blade appeared, Athamas would send to ask the Delphic Oracle what was amiss. She had already bribed Athamas's messengers to bring back a false reply: that the land would regain its fertility only if Nephele's son Phrixus were sacrificed to Zeus on Mount Laphystium.

This Phrixus was a handsome young man, with whom his aunt Biadice, Cretheus's wife, had fallen in love, and whom, when he rebuffed her advances, she accused of trying to ravish her. The men of Boeotia, believing Biadice's story, applauded Apollo's wise choice of a sin-offering and demanded that Phrixus should die; whereupon Athamas, loudly weeping, led Phrixus to the mountain top. He was on the point of cutting his throat when Heracles, who happened to be in the neighbourhood, came running up and wrested the sacrificial flint from his hand. 'My father Zeus,' Heracles exclaimed, 'loathes human sacrifices!' Nevertheless, Phrixus would have perished despite his plea, had not a winged golden ram, supplied by Hermes at Hera's order — or, some say, by Zeus himself — suddenly flown down to the rescue from Olympus.

'Climb on my back!' cried the ram, and Phrixus obeyed.

'Take me too!' pleaded Helle. 'Do not leave me to the mercy of my father.'

So Phrixus pulled her up behind him, and the ram flew eastwards, making for the land of Colchis, where Helius stables his horses. Before long, Helle felt giddy and lost her hold; she fell into the straits between Europe and Asia, now called Hellespont in her honour; but Phrixus reached Colchis safely, and there sacrificed the ram to Zeus the Deliverer. Its golden fleece became famous a generation later when the Argonauts came in search of it.

Overawed by the miracle of Mount Laphystium, Athamas's messengers confessed that they had been bribed by Ino to bring back a false reply from Delphi; and presently all her wiles, and Biadice's, came to light. Nephele thereupon again demanded that Athamas should die, and the sacrificial fillet, which Phrixus had worn, was placed on his head; only Heracles's renewed intervention saved him from death.

But Hera was incensed with Athamas and drove him mad, not only on Nephele's account, but because he had connived at Ino's harbouring of the infant Dionysus, Zeus's bastard by her sister Semele, who was living in the palace disguised as a girl. Seizing his bow, Athamas suddenly yelled: 'Look, a white stag! Stand back while I shoot!' So saying, he transfixed Learchus with an arrow, and proceeded to tear his still-quivering body into pieces.

Ino snatched up Melicertes, her younger son, and fled; but would hardly have escaped Athamas's vengeance, had not the infant Dionysus temporarily blinded him, so that he began to flog a she-goat

Bronze statuette of Hermes with a ram (National Archaeological Museum, Athens)

in mistake for her. Ino ran to the Molurian Rock, where she leaped into the sea and was drowned — this rock afterwards became a place of ill-repute, because the savage Sciron used to hurl strangers from it. But Zeus, remembering Ino's kindness to Dionysus, would not send her ghost down to Tartarus and deified her instead as the Goddess Leucothea. He also deified her son Melicertes as the God Palaemon, and sent him to the Isthmus of Corinth riding on dolphin-back; the Isthmian Games, founded in his honour by Sisyphus, were celebrated there every fourth year.

Athamas, now banished from Boeotia, and childless because his remaining son, Leucon, had sickened and died, enquired from the Delphic Oracle where he should settle, and was told: 'Wherever wild beasts entertain you to dinner.' Wandering aimlessly northward, without food or drink, he came on a wolf-pack devouring a flock of sheep in a desolate Thessalian plain. The wolves fled at his approach, and he and his starving companions ate what mutton had been left. Then he recalled the oracle and, having adopted Haliartus and Coronea, his Corinthian grand-nephews, founded a city which he called Alos, from his wanderings, or from his serving-maid Alos; and the country was called Athamania; afterwards he married Themisto and raised a new family.

The Mares of Glaucus

Glaucus, son of Sisyphus and Merope, and father of Bellerophon, lived at Potniae near Thebes where, scorning the power of Aphrodite, he refused to let his mares breed. He hoped by this means to make them more spirited than other contestants in the chariot races which were his chief interest. But Aphrodite was vexed; and complained to Zeus that he had gone so far as to feed the mares on human flesh. When Zeus permitted her to take what action she pleased against Glaucus, she led the mares out by night to drink from a well sacred to herself, and graze on a herb called hippomanes which grew at its lip. This she did just before Jason celebrated the funeral games of Pelias on the seashore at Iolcus; and no sooner had Glaucus yoked the mares to his chariot pole than they bolted, overthrew the chariot, dragged him along the ground, entangled in the reins, for the whole length of the stadium, and then ate him alive.

Glaucus's ghost, called the Taraxippus, or Horse-scarer, then haunted the Isthmus of Corinth, where his father Sisyphus first taught him the charioteer's art, and delighted in scaring the horses at the Isthmian Games, thus causing many deaths.

Perseus

Abas, King of Argolis and grandson of Danaus, married Aglaia, to whose twin sons, Proteus and Acrisius, he bequeathed his kingdom, bidding them rule alternately. Their quarrel, which began in the womb, became more bitter than ever when Proteus lay with Acrisius's daughter Danaë, and barely escaped alive. Since Acrisius now refused to give up the throne at the end of his term, Proteus fled to the court of Iobates, King of Lycia, whose daughter Anteia he

Detail taken from a vase showing a Gorgoneion, primitively executed, with curls, tusks and protruding tongue.

married; returning presently at the head of a Lycian army. A bloody battle was fought, but since neither side gained the advantage, Proetus and Acrisius's share was to be Argos and its environs; Proetus's was to be Tiryns, the Heraeum, Midea, and the coast of Argolis.

Acrisius, who was married to Aganippe, had no sons, but only this one daughter Danaë whom Proteus had seduced; and, when he asked an oracle how to procure a male heir, was told: 'You will have no sons, and your grandson must kill you.' To forestall this fate, Acrisius imprisoned Danaë in a dungeon with brazen doors, guarded by savage dogs; but, despite these precautions, Zeus came upon her in a shower of gold, and she bore him a son named Perseus. When Acrisius learned of Danaë's condition, he would not believe that Zeus was the father, and suspected his brother Proteus but, not daring to kill his own daughter, locked her and the infant Perseus in a wooden ark, which he cast into the sea. This ark was washed towards the island of Seriphos, where a fisherman named Dictys hauled it ashore, and found both Danaë and Perseus still alive. He took them at once to his brother, King Polydectes, who reared Perseus in his own house.

Some years passed, and Perseus, grown to manhood, defended Danaë against Polydectes who had tried to force marriage upon her. Polydectes then assembled his friends and, pretending that he was about to sue for the hand of Hippodameia, daughter of Pelops, asked them to contribute one horse apiece as his love-gift.

'Alas,' answered Perseus, 'I possess no horse, nor any gold to buy one. But if you intend to marry Hippodameia, and not my mother, I will contrive to win whatever gift you name.' He added rashly: 'Even the Gorgon Medusa's head, if need be.'

'That would indeed please me more than any horse in the world,' replied Polydectes at once. Now, the Gorgon Medusa had serpents for hair, huge teeth, protruding tongue, and altogether so ugly a face that all who gazed at it were petrified with fright.

Athene overheard the conversation and, being a sworn enemy of Medusa's, accompanied Perseus on his adventure. First she led him to the city of Deicterion in Samos, where images of all the three Gorgons are displayed, thus enabling him to distinguish Medusa from her immortal sisters Stheno and Euryale; then she warned him never to look at Medusa directly, but only at her reflection, and presented him with a brightly-polished shield.

Hermes also helped Perseus, giving him an adamantine sickle with which to cut off Medusa's head. But Perseus still needed a pair of winged sandals, a magic wallet to contain the decapitated head, and the dark helmet of invisibility which belonged to Hades. All these things were in the care of the Stygian Nymphs, from whom Perseus had to fetch them; but their whereabouts were known only to the Gorgon's sisters, the three swan-like Graeae, who had a single eye and tooth among the three of them. Perseus accordingly sought out the Graeae on their thrones at the foot of Mount Atlas. Creeping up behind them, he snatched the eye and tooth, as they were being passed from one sister to another, and would not return either until he had been told where the Stygian Nymphs lived.

Perseus then collected the sandals, wallet, and helmet from the nymphs, and flew westwards to the Land of the Hyperboreans, where he found the Gorgons asleep, among rain-worn shapes of men and wild beasts petrified by Medusa. He fixed his eyes on the reflection in the shield, Athene guided his hand, and he cut off Medusa's head with one stroke of the sickle; whereupon, to his surprise, the winged horse Pegasus, and the warrior Chrysaor grasping a golden falchion, sprang fully-grown from her dead body. Hurriedly thrusting the head into his wallet, he took flight; and though Stheno and Euryale, awakened by their new nephews, rose to pursue him, the helmet made Perseus invisible, and he escaped safely southward.

At sunset, Perseus alighted near the palace of the Titan Atlas to whom, as a punishment for his inhospitality, he showed the Gorgon's head and thus transformed him into a mountain; and on the following day turned eastward and flew across the Libyan desert, Hermes helping him to carry the weighty head. By the way he dropped the Graeae's eye and tooth into Lake Triton; and some drops of Gorgon blood fell on the desert sand, where they bred a swarm of venomous serpents.

Perseus paused for refreshment at Chemmis in Egypt, and then flew on. As he rounded the coast of Philistia he caught sight of a naked woman chained to a sea-cliff, and instantly fell in love with her. This was Andromeda, daughter of Cepheus, the Ethiopian King of Joppa, and Cassiopeia. Cassiopeia had boasted that both she and her daughter were more beautiful than the Nereids, who complained of this insult to their protector Poseidon. Poseidon sent a flood and a female sea-monster to devastate Philistia; and when Cepheus consulted the Oracle of Ammon, he was told that his only hope of deliverance lay in sacrificing Andromeda to the monster. His subjects had therefore obliged him to chain her to a rock, naked except for certain jewels, and leave her to be devoured.

As Perseus flew towards Andromeda, he saw Cepheus and Cassiopeia watching anxiously from the shore near by, and alighted beside them. On condition that, if he rescued her, she should be his wife and return to Greece with him, Perseus took to the air again, grasped his sickle and, diving from above, beheaded the approaching monster.

Cepheus and Cassiopeia grudgingly welcomed him as their son-in-law and, on Andromeda's insistence, the wedding took place at once; but the festivities were rudely interrupted when Agenor, King Belus's twin brother, entered at the head of an armed party, claiming Andromeda for himself. He was doubtless summoned by Cassiopeia, since she and Cepheus at once broke faith with Perseus, pleading that the promise of Andromeda's hand had been forced from them by circumstances, and that Agenor's claim was the prior one.

'Perseus must die!' cried Cassiopeia fiercely.

In the ensuing fight, Perseus struck down many of his opponents but, being greatly outnumbered, was forced to snatch the Gorgon's head and turn the remaining two hundred of them to stone. Poseidon set the images of Cepheus and Cassiopeia among the stars; but Athene afterwards placed Andromeda's image in a more honourable constellation, because she had insisted on marrying Perseus, despite her parents' ill faith.

Perseus returned hurriedly to Seriphos, taking Andromeda with him, and found that Danaë and Dictys, threatened by the violence of Polydectes, had taken refuge in a temple. He therefore went straight to the palace where Polydectes was banqueting and announced that he had brought the promised love-gift. Greeted by a storm of insults, he displayed the Gorgon's head and turned them all to stone. He then gave the head to Athene, who fixed it on her aegis; and Hermes returned the sandals, wallet, and helmet to the guardianship of the Stygian nymphs.

After raising Dictys to the throne of Seriphos, Perseus set sail for Argos. Acrisius, hearing of his approach, fled to Pelasgian Larissa; but Perseus happened to be invited there for the funeral games and competed in the fivefold contest. When it came to the discus-throw, his discus, carried out of its path by the wind and the will of the Gods, struck Acrisius's foot and killed him. Greatly grieved, Perseus buried his grandfather in the temple of Athene which crowned the local acropolis and then, being ashamed to reign in Argos, went to Tiryns, where Proetus had been succeeded by his son Megapenthes, and arranged to exchange kingdoms with him.

The Rival Twins

When the male line of Polycaon's House had died out after five generations, the Messenians invited Perieres, the son of Aeolus, to be their king, and he married Perseus's daughter Gorgophone. She survived him and was the first widow to remarry, her new husband being Oebalus the Spartan. Hitherto it had been customary for women to commit suicide on the death of their husbands.

Aphareus and Leucippus were Gorgophone's sons by Perieres, whereas Tyndareus and Icarius were her sons by Oebalus. Tyndareus succeeded his father on the throne of Sparta, Icarius acting as his co-king; but Hippocoön and his twelve sons expelled both of them. Taking refuge with King Thestius in Aetolia, Tyndareus married his daughter Leda, who bore him Castor and Clytaemnestra, at the same time bearing Helen and Polydeuces to Zeus. Later, having adopted Polydeuces, Tyndareus regained the Spartan throne.

Meanwhile, his half-brother Aphareus had succeeded Perieres on the throne of Messene, where Leucippus acted as his co-king and enjoyed the lesser powers. Aphareus took to wife his half-sister Arene, who bore him Idas and Lynceus; though Idas was, in truth, Poseidon's son. Now, Leucippus's daughters, the Leucippides, namely Phoebe, a priestess of Athene, and Hilaeria, a priestess of Artemis, were betrothed to their cousins, Idas and Lyceus; but Castor and Polydeuces, who are commonly known as the Dioscuri, carried them off, and had two sons by them; which occasioned a bitter rivalry between the two sets of twins.

The Dioscuri, who were never separated from one another in any adventure, became the pride of Sparta. Castor was famous as a soldier and tamer of horses, Polydeuces as the best boxer of his day; both won prizes at the Olympic Games. Their cousins and rivals were no less devoted to each other; Idas had greater strength than Lynceus, but Lynceus such sharp eyes that he could see in the dark or divine the whereabouts of buried treasure.

Now, Evenus, a son of Ares, had married Alcippe, by whom he became the father of Marpessa. In an attempt to keep her a virgin, he invited each of her suitors in turn to run a chariot race with him; the victor would win Marpessa, the vanquished would forfeit his head. Soon many heads were nailed to the walls of Evenus's house and Apollo, falling in love with Marpessa, expressed his disgust of so barbarous a custom; and said that he would soon end it by challenging Evenus to a race. But Idas had also set his heart on Marpessa, and begged a winged chariot from his father Poseidon.

Before Apollo could act, he had driven to Aetolia, and carried Marpessa away from the midst of a band of dancers. Evenus gave chase, but could not overtake Idas, and felt such mortification that, after killing his horses, he drowned himself in the river Lycormas, ever since called the Evenus.

When Idas reached Messene, Apollo tried to take Marpessa from him. They fought a duel, but Zeus parted them, and ruled that Marpessa herself should decide whom she preferred to marry. Fearing that Apollo would cast her off when she grew old, as he had done with many another of his loves, she chose Idas for her husband.

Idas and Lynceus were among the Calydonian hunters, and sailed in the *Argo* to Colchis. One day, after the death of Aphareus, they and the Dioscuri patched up their quarrel sufficiently to join forces in a cattle-raid on Arcadia. The raid proved successful, and Idas was chosen by lot to divide the booty among the four of them. He therefore quartered a cow, and ruled that half the spoil should go to the man who ate his share first, the remainder to the next quickest. Almost before the others had settled themselves to begin the contest, Idas bolted his own share and then helped Lyceus to bolt his; soon down went the last gobbet, and he and Lyceus drove the cattle away towards Messene. The Dioscuri remained, until Polydeuces, the slower of the two, had finished eating; whereupon they marched against Messene, and protested to the citizens that Lynceus had forfeited his share by accepting help from Idas, and that Idas had forfeited his by not waiting until all the contestants were ready. Idas and Lynceus happened to be away on Mount Taygetus, sacrificing to Poseidon; so the Dioscuri seized the disputed cattle, and other

plunder as well, and then hid inside a hollow oak to await their rival's return. But Lynceus had caught sight of them from the summit of Taygetus; and Idas, hurrying down the mountain slope, hurled his spear at the tree and transfixed Castor. When Polydeuces rushed out to avenge his brother, Idas tore the carved headstone from Aphareus's tomb, and threw it at him. Although badly crushed, Polydeuces contrived to kill Lynceus with his spear; and at this point Zeus intervened on behalf of his son, striking Idas dead with a thunderbolt.

After setting up a trophy beside the Spartan race-course to celebrate his victory over Lyceus, Polydeuces prayed to Zeus: 'Father, let me not outlive my dear brother!' Since, however, it was fated that only one of Leda's sons should die, and since Castor's father Tyndareus had been a mortal, Polydeuces, as the son of Zeus, was duly carried up to Heaven. Yet he refused immortality unless Castor might share it, and Zeus therefore allowed them both to spend their days alternately in the upper air, and under the earth at Therapne. In further reward of their brotherly love, he set their images among the stars as the Twins.

Poseidon made Castor and Polydeuces the saviours of shipwrecked sailors, and granted them power to send favourable winds; in response to a sacrifice of white lambs offered on the prow of any ship, they would come hastening through the sky, followed by a train of sparrows. They presided at the Spartan Games, and because they invented the war-dance and war-like music were the patrons of all bards who sang of ancient battles.

Bellerophon
Bellerophon, son of Glaucus and grandson of Sisyphus, left Corinth under a cloud, having first killed one Bellerus and then his own brother. He fled as a suppliant to Proetus, King of Tiryns; but (so ill luck would have it) Anteia, Proetus's wife, fell in love with him at sight. When he rejected her advances, she accused him of having tried to seduce her, and Proetus believed the story. Yet he dared not risk the Furies' vengeance by the murder of a suppliant, and therefore sent

opposite: *Zeus with a thunderbolt. Bronze miniature (National Archaeological Museum, Athens)*

85

him to Anteia's father Iobates, King of Lycia, carrying a sealed letter, which read: 'Pray remove the bearer from this world; he has tried to violate my wife, your daughter.'

Iobates, equally loth to ill-treat a royal guest, asked Bellerophon to do him the service of destroying the Chimaera, a fire-breathing she-monster with lion's head, goat's body, and serpent's tail. Before setting about this task, Bellerophon consulted the seer Polyeidus, and was advised to catch and tame the winged horse Pegasus.

Bellerophon found Pegasus drinking at Peirene, on the Acropolis of Corinth, and threw over his head a golden bridle, Athene's timely present. Bellerophon then overcame the Chimaera by flying above her on Pegasus's back, riddling her with arrows, and then thrusting between her jaws a lump of lead fixed to the point of his spear. The Chimaera's fiery breath melted the lead, which trickled down her throat, searing her vitals.

Iobates, however, far from rewarding Bellerophon, sent him at once against the warlike Solymians and their allies, the Amazons; both of whom he conquered by soaring above them, well out of bowshot, and dropping large boulders on their heads. Next, he beat off a band of Carian pirates; but when Iobates showed no gratitude even then but, on the contrary, sent the palace guards to ambush him on his return Bellerophon prayed that, while he advanced on foot, Poseidon would flood the Xanthian Plain behind him. Poseidon heard his prayer, and set great waves rolling slowly forward and, because no man could persuade him to retire, the Xanthian women hoisted their skirts to the waist and came rushing towards him. Bellerophon's modesty was such that he turned tail and ran; and the waves retreated with him.

Convinced now that Proetus must have been mistaken about the attempt on Anteia's virtue, Iobates produced the letter, and demanded an exact account of the affair. On learning the truth, he implored Bellerophon's forgiveness, gave him his daughter Philonoë in marriage, and made him heir to the Lycian throne.

Bellerophon, at the height of his fortune, presumptuously undertook a flight to Olympus, as though he were an immortal; but Zeus sent a gadfly, which stung Pegasus under the tail, making him rear and fling his rider ingloriously to earth. Bellerophon, who had fallen into a thorn-bush, wandered about the earth, lame, blind, lonely and accursed, always avoiding the paths of men, until death overtook him.

The Calydonian Boar

Oeneus, King of Calydon in Aetolia, married Althaea. She first bore him Toxeus, and then Meleager, said to have been, in reality, her son by Ares. When Meleager was seven days old, the Fates announced that he could live only so long as a certain brand on the hearth remained unburned. Althaea at once snatched the brand from the fire, extinguished it with a pitcherful of water, and then hid it in a chest.

Meleager grew up to be the best javelin-thrower in Greece. He might still be alive but for Oeneus who forgot to include Artemis in his yearly sacrifices to the gods. Artemis, informed of this, sent a huge boar to ravage Calydon; but Oeneus despatched heralds, inviting all the bravest fighters of Greece to hunt the boar, and promising that whoever killed it should have its pelt and tusks.

Perseus cutting off Medusa's head (Archaeological Museum, Palermo, Sicily)

Many answered the call, among them the chaste, swift-footed Atalanta, only daughter of Iasus and Clymene. Iasus had wished for a male heir and Atalanta's birth disappointed him so cruelly that he exposed her on the Parthenian Hill near Calydon, where she was suckled by a bear which Artemis sent to her aid. Atalanta grew to womanhood among a clan of hunters who found and reared her, but remained a virgin, and always carried arms.

Oeneus entertained the huntsmen royally; and though Ancaeus and Cepheus at first refused to hunt in company with a woman, Meleager declared that unless they withdrew their objection he would cancel the chase altogether. The truth was that Meleager now felt a sudden love for Atalanta and wished to ingratiate himself with her. His uncles, Althaea's brothers, took an immediate dislike to the girl, convinced that her presence could lead only to mischief. Thus the chase began under bad auspices; Artemis had seen to this.

The first blood shed was human: two Centaurs, Hylaeus and Rhaecus, who had joined the chase, decided to ravish Atalanta, each in turn assisting the other. But as soon as they ran towards her, she shot them both down.

Presently the boar came bounding out, killed two of the hunters, hamstrung another, and drove young Nestor up a tree. Jason and several others flung ill-aimed javelins, Iphicles alone contriving to graze its shoulder. Then Telamon and Peleus went in boldly with boar-spears; but Telamon tripped and, while Peleus was pulling him to his feet, the boar saw them and charged. Atalanta let fly a timely arrow, which sank in behind the ear, and set it scurrying off. Ancaeus swung his battle-axe at the boar as it charged, but was not quick enough; the next instant he lay castrated and disembowelled. In his excitement, Peleus killed Eurytion with a javelin aimed at the boar, which Amphiaraus had succeeded in blinding. Next, it rushed at Theseus, whose javelin flew wide; but Meleager also flung and transfixed its right flank, and then, as the boar whirled around in pain, drove his hunting-spear deep to the heart.

The boar fell dead at last.

At once, Meleager flayed it, and presented the pelt to Atalanta, saying: 'You drew first blood, and had we left the beast alone, it would soon have succumbed to your arrow.'

His uncles were deeply offended. The eldest, Plexippus, argued that Meleager had won the pelt himself and that, on his refusal, it should have gone to the most honourable person present — namely himself, as Oeneus's brother-in-law. Plexippus's younger brother supported him with the contention that Iphicles, not Atalanta, had drawn first blood. Meleager, in a lover's range, killed them both.

Althaea, as she watched the dead bodies being carried home, set a curse upon Meleager; which prevented him from defending Calydon when his two surviving uncles declared war on the city. At last his wife Cleopatra persuaded him to take up arms, and he killed both these uncles, whereupon the Furies instructed Althaea to take the unburned brand from the chest and cast it on the fire. Meleager felt a sudden scorching of his innards, and the enemy overcame him with ease. Althaea and Cleopatra hanged themselves, and Artemis turned all but two of Meleager's shrieking sisters into guinea-hens.

Delighted by Atalanta's success, Iasus recognized her at last as his daughter; but when she arrived at the palace his first words were: 'My child, prepare to take a husband!' — a disagreeable announcement, since the Delphic Oracle had warned her against marriage. She answered: 'Father, I consent on one condition. Any suitor for my hand must either beat me in a foot race, or else let me kill him.' 'So be it,' said Iasus.

Many unfortunate princes lost their lives in consequence, because she was the swiftest mortal alive; but Melanion, a son of Amphidamas the Arcadian, invoked Aphrodite's assistance. She gave him three golden apples, saying: 'Delay Atlanta by letting these fall, one after the other, in the course of the race.' The stratagem was successful. Atalanta stooped to pick each apple in turn and reached the winning-post just behind Melanion.

The marriage took place, but the Oracle's warning was justified because, one day, as they passed by a precinct of Zeus, Melanion persuaded Atalanta to come inside and lie with him there. Vexed that his precinct had been defiled, Zeus changed them both into lions: for lions do not mate with lions, but only with leopards, and they were thus prevented from ever again enjoying each other. This was Aphrodite's punishment, first for Atalanta's obstinacy in remaining a virgin, and then for her lack of gratitude in the matter of the golden apples.

Midas

Midas, son of the Great Goddess of Ida by a satyr, was a pleasure-loving King of Macedonian Bromium, where he ruled over the Brigians and planted his celebrated rose gardens. In his infancy, a procession of ants was observed carrying grains of wheat up the side of his cradle and placing them between his lips as he slept — a prodigy

Perseus with Medusa's head.
Detail from a red-figured
water jug (British Museum)

which the soothsayers read as an omen of the great wealth that would accrue to him.

One day, the debauched old satyr Silenus, Dionysus's former pedagogue, happened to straggle from the main body of the riotous Dionysian army as it marched out of Thrace into Boeotia, and was found sleeping off his drunken fit in the gardens. The gardeners bound him with garlands of flowers and led him before Midas, to whom he told wonderful tales. Midas, enchanted by Silenus's fictions, entertained him for five days and nights, and then ordered a guide to escort him to Dionysus's headquarters.

Dionysus, who had been anxious on Silenus's account, sent to ask how Midas wished to be rewarded. He replied without hesitation: 'Pray grant that all I touch be turned to gold.' However, not only

opposite above: *The Dioscuri: Castor and Polydeuces. Amphora*
by Exekias (Vatican Museum)
opposite below: *Pegasus (British Museum)*

stones, flowers, and the furnishing of his house turned to gold, but the food he ate and the water he drank. Midas soon begged to be released from his wish, because he was fast dying of hunger and thirst; whereupon Dionysus told him to visit the source of the river Pactolus, near Mount Tmolus, and there wash himself. He obeyed, and was at once freed from the golden touch, but the sands of the river Pactolus are bright with gold to this day.

Midas, having thus entered Asia, was adopted by the childless Phrygian King Gordius. While only a poor peasant, Gordius had been surprised one day to see a royal eagle perch on the pole of his ox-cart. He drove the team towards Phrygian Telmissus, where there was a reliable oracle; but at the gate of the city he met a young prophetess who, when she saw the eagle still perched on the pole, insisted on his offering immediate sacrifices to Zeus the King. 'Let me come with you, peasant,' she said, 'to make sure that you choose the correct victims.' 'By all means,' replied Gordius. 'You appear to be a wise and considerate young woman. Are you prepared to marry me?' 'As soon as the sacrifices have been offered,' she answered.

Meanwhile, the King of Phrygia had died suddenly, without issue, and an oracle announced: 'Phrygians, your new king is approaching with his bride, seated in an ox-cart!'

When the ox-cart entered the market place of Telmissus, Gordius was unanimously acclaimed king. In gratitude, he dedicated the cart to Zeus, together with its yoke, which he had knotted to the pole in a peculiar manner. An oracle then declared that whoever discovered how to untie the knot would become the lord of all Asia. Yoke and pole were consequently laid up in the Acropolis at Gordium where the priests of Zeus guarded them jealously for centuries — until Alexander the Macedonian cut the knot with his sword. After Gordius's death, Midas succeeded to the throne, promoted the worship of Dionysus, and founded the city of Ancyra.

Midas attended the famous musical contest between Apollo and Marsyas, umpired by the River-god Tmolus. Tmolus awarded the prize to Apollo who, when Midas dissented from the verdict, punished him with a pair of ass's ears. For a long time, Midas managed to conceal these under a Phrygian cap; but his barber, made aware of the deformity, found it impossible to keep the shameful secret close, as Midas had enjoined him to do on pain of death. He therefore dug a hole in the river-bank and, first making sure that nobody was about, whispered into it: 'King Midas has ass's ears!' Then he filled up the hole, and went away, at peace with himself until a reed sprouted from the bank and whispered the secret to all who passed. When Midas learned that his disgrace had become public knowledge, he condemned the barber to death, drank bull's blood, and perished miserably.

Narcissus

Narcissus was a Thespian, the son of the blue Nymph Leiriope, whom the River-god Cephisus had once ravished. The seer Teiresias told Leiriope, the first person ever to consult him: 'Narcissus will live to a ripe old age, provided that he never knows himself.' Anyone might excusably have fallen in love with Narcissus, even as a child, and when he reached the age of sixteen, his path was strewn with heartlessly rejected lovers of both sexes; for he had a stubborn pride in his own beauty.

Among these was the nymph Echo, who could no longer use her voice, except in foolish repetition of another's: a punishment for having kept Hera entertained with long stories while Zeus's concubines made good their escape. One day when Narcissus went out to net stags, Echo stealthily followed him, longing to address him, but unable to speak first. At last Narcissus, finding that he had strayed from his companions, shouted: 'Is anyone here?'

'Here!' Echo answered, which surprised Narcissus, since no one was in sight.

'Come!'

'Come!'

'Why do you avoid me?'

'Why do you avoid me?'

'Let us come together here!'

'Let us come together here!' repeated Echo, and joyfully rushed from her hiding place to embrace Narcissus. Yet he shook her off roughly, and ran away. 'I will die before you ever lie with me!' he cried.

'Lie with me!' Echo pleaded.

But Narcissus had gone, and she spent the rest of her life pining away for love and mortification, until only her voice remained.

One day, Narcissus sent a sword to Ameinius, his most insistent suitor. Ameinius killed himself on Narcissus's threshold, calling on the gods to avenge his death. Artemis heard the plea. At Donacon in Thespia, Narcissus came upon a spring, clear as silver, and as he cast himself down, exhausted, on the grassy verge to slake his thirst, he fell in love with his reflection, gazing enraptured into the pool. How could he endure both to possess and yet not to possess?

Echo, although she had not forgiven Narcissus, grieved with him; she sympathetically echoed 'Alas! Alas!' as he plunged a dagger in his breast, and also the final 'Ah, youth, beloved in vain, farewell!' as he expired. His blood soaked the earth, and up sprang the white narcissus flower with its red corolla.

Arion

Arion of Lesbos, a son of Poseidon and the Nymph Oneaea, was a master of the lyre. One day his patron Periander, tyrant of Corinth, reluctantly gave him permission to visit Taenarus in Sicily to compete in a musical festival. Arion won the prize, and so many rich gifts that these excited the greed of the sailors engaged to bring him back to Corinth.

Pegasus and Bellerophon
with the Chimaera (British Museum)

'We much regret, Arion, that you will have to die,' remarked the captain of the ship.

'What crime have I committed?' asked Arion.

'You are too rich,' replied the captain.

'Spare my life, and I will give you all my prizes,' Arion pleaded.

'You would only retract your promise on reaching Corinth,' said the captain, 'and so would I, in your place. A forced gift is no gift.'

'Very well,' cried Arion resignedly. 'But pray allow me to sing a last song.'

When the captain gave his permission, Arion, dressed in his finest robe, mounted on the prow, where he invoked the gods with impassioned strains, and then leaped overboard. The ship sailed on.

However, his song had attracted a school of music-loving dolphins, one of which took Arion on his back, and that evening he overtook the ship and reached the port of Corinth several days before it cast anchor there. Periander was overjoyed at his miraculous escape, and when the ship docked, sent for the captain and crew, whom he asked with pretended anxiety for news of Arion.

'He has been delayed at Taenarus,' the captain answered, 'by the lavish hospitality of the inhabitants.'

Periander made them all swear that this was the truth, and then suddenly confronted them with Arion. Unable to deny their guilt, they were executed on the spot. Apollo later set the images of Arion and his lyre among the stars.

4

MINOS AND THESEUS

Minos and His Brothers
WHEN ZEUS LEFT EUROPE, after having fathered Minos, Rhadamanthys, and Sarpedon on her in Crete, she married Asterius, the reigning king. This marriage proving childless, Asterius adopted Minos, Rhadamanthys, and Sarpedon, and made them his heirs. But when the brothers grew to manhood, they quarrelled for the love of a beautiful boy named Miletus, begotten by Apollo on the Nymph Areia. Miletus having decided that he like Sarpedon best, was driven from Crete by Minos, and sailed with a large fleet to Caria in Asia Minor, where he founded the city and kingdom of Miletus.

After Asterius's death, Minos claimed the Cretan throne and, in proof of his right to reign, boasted that the gods would answer whatever prayer he offered. First dedicating an altar to Poseidon, and making all preparations for a sacrifice, he then prayed that a bull might emerge from the sea. At once, a dazzlingly-white bull swam ashore, but Minos was so struck by its beauty that he sent it to join his own herds, and slaughtered another instead. Mino's claim to the throne was accepted by every Cretan, except Sarpedon who, still grieving for Miletus, declared that it had been Asterius's intention to divide the kingdom equally between his three heirs; and, indeed, Minos himself had already divided the island into three parts, and chosen a capital for each.

Expelled from Crete by Minos, Sarpedon fled to Cilicia in Asia Minor, where he allied himself with Cilix against the Milyans, conquered them, and became their king. Zeus granted him the privilege of living for three generations; and when he finally died, the Milyan kingdom was called Lycia, after his successor Lycus.

Meanwhile, Minos had married Pasiphaë, a daughter of Helius and the nymph Crete, but Poseidon, to avenge the affront offered him by Minos, made Pasiphaë fall in love with the white bull which had been withheld from sacrifice. She confided her unnatural passion to Daedalus, the famous Athenian craftsman, who now lived in exile at Cnossus. Daedalus promised to help her, and built a hollow wooden cow, which he set on wheels concealed in its hooves, and pushed into the meadow near Gortys, where Poseidon's bull was grazing. Then, having shown Pasiphaë how to open the folding doors in the cow's back, and slip inside with her legs thrust down into its hindquarters, he discreetly retired. Soon the white bull ambled up and mounted the cow, so that Pasiphaë had all her desire, and later gave birth to the Minotaur, a monster with a bull's head and a human body.

Minos consulted an oracle to know how he might best avoid scandal and conceal Pasiphaë's disgrace. The response was: 'Instruct Daedalus to build you a retreat at Cnossus!' This Daedalus did, and Minos spent the remainder of his life in the inextricable maze called the Labyrinth, at the very heart of which he concealed Pasiphaë and the Minotaur.

Rhadamanthys, wiser than Sarpedon, remained in Crete; he lived at peace with Minos, and was awarded a third part of Asterius's dominions. Renowned as a just and upright law-giver, inexorable in his punishment of evildoers, he legislated both for the Cretans and for the islanders of Asia Minor. Every ninth year, he would visit Zeus's cave and bring back a new set of laws, a custom afterwards followed by his brother Minos. He bequeathed land in Crete to his son Gortys, after whom the Cretan city was named. Rhadamanthys also bequeathed land in Asia Minor to his son Erythrus; and the island of Chios to Oenopion, the son of Ariadne, whom Dionysus first taught how to make wine; and Lemnos to Thoas, another of Ariadne's sons.

Rhadamanthys eventually fled to Boeotia because he had killed a kinsman, and lived there in exile at Ocaleae, where he married Alcmene, Heracles's mother, after the death of Amphitryon. But some say that Alcmene was married to Rhadamanthys in the Elysian Fields, after her death. For Zeus had appointed him one of the three Judges of the Dead; his colleagues were Minos and Aeacus, and he resided in the Elysian Fields.

Scylla and Nisus

Minos was the first king to control the Mediterranean Sea, which he cleared of pirates, and in Crete ruled over ninety cities. When

97

the Athenians had murdered his son Androgeus, he decided to take vengeance on them, and sailed around the Aegean collecting ships and armed levies. Some islanders agreed to help him, some refused. Meanwhile, Minos was harrying the Isthmus of Corinth. He laid siege to Nisa, afterwards called Megara, ruled by Nisus the Egyptian, who had a daughter named Scylla. A tower stood in the city, and Scylla used to spend much time at its top. Here she climbed daily when the war began, to watch the fighting.

The siege of Nisa was protracted, and Scylla soon came to know the name of every Cretan warrior. Struck by the beauty of Minos, she fell perversely in love with him.

One night Scylla crept into her father's chamber, and cut off the famous bright lock on which his life and throne depended; then, taking from him the keys of the city gate, she opened it, and stole out. She made straight for Minos's tent, and offered him the lock of hair in exchange for his love. That same night, having entered the city and sacked it, he duly lay with Scylla; but would not take her to Crete, because he loathed the crime of parricide. Scylla, however, swam after his ship, and clung to the stern until her father Nisus's soul in the form of a sea-eagle swooped down upon her with talons and hooked beak. The terrified Scylla let go and was drowned; her soul flew off as a ciris-bird.

This war dragged on until Minos, finding that he could not subdue Athens, prayed Zeus to avenge Androgeus's death; and the whole of Greece was consequently afflicted with earthquakes and famine. The kings of the various city states assembled at Delphi to consult the Oracle, and were instructed to make Aeacus offer up prayers on their behalf. When this had been done, the earthquakes everywhere ceased, except in Attica.

The Athenians thereupon sought to redeem themselves from the curse by sacrificing to Persephone the daughters of Hyacinthus on the grave of the Cyclops Geraestus. These girls, had come to Athens from Sparta. Yet the earthquakes continued and, when the Athenians again consulted the Delphic Oracle, they were told to give Minos whatever satisfaction he might ask; which proved to be a tribute of seven youths and seven maidens, sent every nine years to Crete as a prey for the Minotaur.

Daedalus and Talos

The parentage of Daedalus is disputed. His mother is named Alcippe by some; by others, Merope; by still others, Iphinoë, and all give him a different father, though it is generally agreed that he belonged to the royal house of Athens. He was a wonderful smith, having been instructed in his art by Athene herself.

One of his apprentices, Talos the son of his sister Polycaste, had already surpassed him in craftsmanship while only twelve years old. Talos happened one day to pick up the jawbone of a serpent and, finding that he could use it to cut a stick in half, copied it in iron and thereby invented the saw. This, and other inventions of his secured him a great reputation at Athens, and Daedalus, who himself claimed to have forged the first saw, soon grew unbearably jealous. Leading Talos up to the roof of Athene's temple on the Acropolis, he suddenly toppled him over the edge. Yet, for all his jealousy, he would have done Talos no harm had he not suspected him of incestuous relations with his mother Polycaste. Daedalus then hurried down to the foot of the Acropolis, and thrust Talos's corpse into a bag, proposing to bury it secretly. But his crime did not escape detection, whereupon the Areiopagus banished him for murder.

Now, Talos was also the name of Minos's bull-headed bronze servant, given him by Zeus to guard Crete. He was forged by Hephaestus in Sardinia, and had a single vein which ran from his neck down to his ankles, where it was stoppered by a bronze pin. It was his task to run thrice daily around the island of Crete and throw rocks at any foreign ship; and also to go thrice yearly, at a more leisurely pace, through the villages of Crete, displaying Minos's laws inscribed on brazen tablets. In the end, Medea killed Talos by pulling out the pin and letting his life-blood escape.

Daedalus took refuge in one of the Attic demes, whose people are named Daedalids after him; and then in Cretan Cnossus, where King Minos delighted to welcome so skilled a craftsman. He lived there for some time, at peace and in high favour, until Minos, learning that he had helped Pasiphaë to couple with Poseidon's white bull, locked him up for a while in the Labyrinth, together with his son Icarus, but Pasiphaë freed them both.

It was not easy, however to escape from Crete, since Minos kept all his ships under military guard, and now offered a large reward for his apprehension. But Daedalus made a pair of wings for himself, and another for Icarus, the quill feathers of which were threaded together, but the smaller ones held in place by wax. Having tied on Icarus's pair for him, he said with tears in his eyes 'My son, be warned! Neither soar too high, lest the sun melt the wax; nor swoop too low, lest the feathers be wetted by the sea.' Then he slipped his arms into his own pair of wings and they flew off. 'Follow me closely,' he cried, 'do not set your own course!'

As the sped away from the island in a north-easterly direction, flapping their wings, the fishermen, shepherds, and ploughmen who gazed upward mistook them for gods.

They had left Naxos, Delos, and Paros behind them on the left hand, and were leaving Lebynthos and Calymne behind on the right, when Icarus disobeyed his father's instructions and began soaring towards the sun, rejoiced by the lift of his great sweeping wings. Presently, when Daedalus looked over his shoulder, he could no longer see Icarus; but scattered feathers floated on the waves below. The heat of the sun had melted the wax, and Icarus had fallen into the sea and drowned. Daedalus circled around, until the corpse rose to the surface, and then carried it to the near-by island now called Icaria, where he buried it. This island has now given its name to the surrounding sea.

Daedalus flew westward until, alighting at Cumae near Naples, he dedicated his wings to Apollo there, and built him a golden-roofed temple. Afterwards, he visited Camicus in Sicily, where he was hospitably received by King Cocalus, and lived among the Sicilians, enjoying great fame and erecting many fine buildings.

Meanwhile, Minos had raised a fleet, and set out in search of Daedalus. He brought with him a Triton shell, and wherever he went promised to reward anyone who could pass a linen thread through it: a problem which, he knew, Daedalus alone would be able to solve. Arrived at Camicus, he offered the shell to Cocalus, who undertook to have it threaded; and, sure enough, Daedalus found out how to do this. Fastening gossamer thread to an ant, he bored a hole at the point of the shell and lured the ant up the spirals by smearing honey on the edges of the hole. Then he tied the linen thread to the other end of the gossamer and drew that through as well. Cocalus returned the threaded shell, claiming the reward, and Minos, assured that he had at last found Daedalus's hiding place, demanded his surrender. But Cocalus's daughters were loth to lose Daedalus, who made them such beautiful toys, and with his help they concocted a plot. Daedalus led a pipe through the roof of the bathroom, down which they poured boiling water upon Minos, while he luxuriated in a warm bath. Cocalus returned the corpse to the Cretans, saying that Minos had stumbled over a rug and fallen into a cauldron of boiling water.

Minos's followers buried him with great pomp, and Zeus made him a judge of the dead in Tartarus, with his brother Rhadamanthys and his enemy Aeacus as colleagues. But Daedalus left Sicily to join Iolaus, the nephew and charioteer of Tirynthian Heracles, who led a body of Athenians and Thespians to Sardinia. Many of his works survived in Sardinia; they were called Daedaleia.

The Birth of Theseus

Aegeus's first wife was Melite, daughter of Hoples; and his second, Chalciope, daughter of Rhexenor; but neither bore him any children. Ascribing this, and the misfortunes of his sisters Procne and Philomela, to Aphrodite's anger, he introduced her worship into Athens, and then went to consult the Delphic Oracle. The Oracle warned him not to untie the mouth of his bulging wine-skin until he reached the highest point of Athens, lest he die one day of grief, a response which Aegeus could not interpret.

On his way home he called at Corinth; and here Medea made him swear a solemn oath that he would shelter her from all enemies if she ever sought refuge at Athens, and undertook in return to procure him a son by magic. Next, he visited Troezen, where his old comrades Pittheus and Troezen, sons of Pelops, had recently come from Pisa to share a kingdom with King Aetius.

Now, while Pittheus was still living at Pisa, Bellerophon had asked to marry his daughter Aethra, but had been sent away to Caria in disgrace before the marriage could be celebrated; though still contracted to Bellerophon, she had little hope of his return. Pittheus, therefore, grieving at her enforced virginity, and influenced by the spell which Medea was casting on all of them from afar, made Aegeus drunk, and sent him to bed with Aethra. Later in the same night, Poseidon also enjoyed her. Poseidon, however, generously conceded to Aegeus the paternity of any child born to Aethra in the course of the next four months.

Aegeus, when he awoke and found himself in Aethra's bed, told her that if a son were born to them he must not be exposed or sent away, but secretly reared in Troezen. Then he sailed back to Athens, to celebrate the All-Athenian Festival, after hiding his sword and his sandals under a hollow rock, known as the Altar of Strong Zeus, which stood on the road from Troezen to Hermium. If, when the boy grew up, he could move this rock and recover the tokens, he was to be sent with them to Athens. Meanwhile, Aethra

101

Fresco showing a contemporary view of the Palace of Cnossus
(The Minoan Royal Palace, Knossos, Crete)

*Coin showing Scylla
(Pennisi Collection,
Acireale, Sicily)*

*Relief of a bull's head (The
Minoan Royal Palace,
Knossos, Crete)*

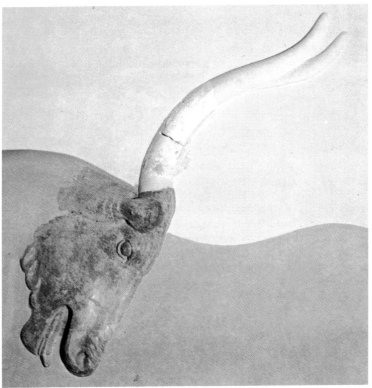

must keep silence, lest Aegeus's nephews, the fifty children of Pallas, plotted against her life. The sword was an heirloom from Cecrops.

At a place called Genethlium, on the way from the city to the harbour of Troezen, Aethra gave birth to a boy. He was brought up in Troezen, where his guardian Pittheus discreetly spread the rumour that Poseidon had been his father; and one Connidas acted as his pedagogue.

One day Heracles, dining at Troezen with Pittheus, removed his lion-skin and threw it over a stool. When the palace children came in, they screamed and fled, all except seven-year-old Theseus, who ran to snatch an axe from the woodpile, and returned boldly, prepared to attack a real lion.

At the age of 16 years he visited Delphi, and offered his first manly hair-clippings to Apollo. He shaved, however, only the forepart of his head, like the Arabians and Mysians, or like the war-like Abantes of Euboea, who thereby deny their enemies any advantage in close combat. This kind of tonsure, and the precinct where he performed the ceremony, were both later called Thesean. He was now a strong, intelligent and prudent youth; and Aethra, leading him to the rock underneath which Aegeus had hidden the sword and sandals, told him the story of his birth. He had no difficulty in moving the rock, and recovered the tokens. Yet, despite Pittheus's warnings and his mother's entreaties, he would not visit Athens by the safe sea route, but insisted on travelling overland; impelled by a desire to emulate the feats of his cousin-german Heracles, whom he greatly admired.

The Labours of Theseus

Theseus set out to free the bandit-ridden coast road which led from Troezen to Athens. He would pick no quarrels but take vengeance on all who dared molest him, making the punishment fit the crime, as was Heracles's way. At Epidaurus, Periphetes the cripple waylaid him. Periphetes, whom some call Poseidon's son, and others the son of Hephaestus and Anticleia, owned a huge brazen club, with which he used to kill wayfarers; hence his nickname Corunetes, or 'cudgel-man'. Theseus wrenched the club from his hands and battered him to death. Delighted with its size and weight, he proudly carried it about ever afterwards; and though he himself had been able to parry its murderous swing, in his hands it never failed to kill.

At the narrowest point of the Isthmus, where both the Corinthian and Saronic Gulfs are visible, lived Sinis, the son of Polypemon. He had been nicknamed Pityocamptes, or 'pine-bender', because he was strong enough to bend down the tops of pine-trees until they touched the earth, and would often ask innocent passers-by to help him with this task, but suddenly release his hold. As the tree sprang upright again, they were hurled high into the air, and killed by the fall. Or he would bend down the tops of two neighbouring trees until they met, and tie one of his victim's arms to each, so that he was torn asunder when the trees were released.

Theseus wrestled with Sinis, overpowered him, and served him as he had served others. At this, a beautiful girl ran to hide herself in a thicket of rushes and wild asparagus. He followed her and, after a long search, found her invoking the plants, promising never to burn or destroy them if they hid her safely. When Theseus swore not to do her any violence, she consented to emerge, and proved to be Sinis's daughter Perigune. Perigune fell in love with Theseus at sight, forgiving the murder of her hateful father and, in due course, bore him a son, Melanippus.

Next, at Crommyum, he hunted and destroyed a fierce and monstrous wild sow, which had killed so many Crommyonians that they no longer dared plough their fields. Then, following the coast road, Theseus came to the precipitous cliffs rising sheer from the sea, which had become a stronghold of the bandit Sciron. Sciron used to seat himself upon a rock and force passing travellers to wash his feet: when they stooped to the task he would kick them over the cliff into the sea, where a giant turtle swam about, waiting to devour them. Theseus, refusing to wash Sciron's feet, lifted him from the rock and flung him into the sea.

Continuing his journey to Athens, Theseus met Cercyon the Arcadian. He would challenge passers-by to wrestle with him and then crush them to death in his powerful embrace; but Theseus lifted him up by the knees and, to the delight of Demeter, who witnessed the struggle, dashed him headlong to the ground. Cercyon's death was instantaneous. Theseus did not trust to strength so much as skill, for he had invented the art of wrestling, the principles of which were not hitherto understood.

On reaching Attic Corydallus, Theseus slew Sinis's father Polypemon, surnamed Procrustes, who lived beside the road and had two beds in his house, one small, the other large. Offering a night's lodging to travellers, he would lay the short men on the large bed, and rack them out to fit it; but the tall men on the small bed, sawing off as much of their legs as projected beyond it. Some say, however, that he used only one bed, and lengthened or shortened his lodgers according to its measure. In either case, Theseus served him as he had served others.

Theseus and Medea

Arrived in Attica, Theseus was met beside the river Cephissus by the sons of Phytalus, who purified him from the blood he had spilled, but especially from that of Sinis, a maternal kinsman of his.

Theseus moving the rock to reveal the sword of Aegeus
(British Museum)

opposite: *A bronze miniature of Icarus about to fly (British Museum)*

Afterwards, the Phytalids welcomed Theseus as their guest, which was the first true hospitality he had received since leaving Troezen. Dressed in a long garment that reached to his feet and with his hair neatly plaited, he entered Athens. As he passed the nearly-completed temple of Apollo the Dolphin, a group of masons working on the roof mistook him for a girl, and impertinently asked why he was allowed to wander about unescorted. Disdaining to reply, Theseus unyoked the oxen from the masons' cart and tossed one of them into the air, high above the temple roof.

Now, while Theseus was growing up in Troezen, Aegeus had kept his promise to Medea. He gave her shelter in Athens when she fled from Corinth in the celebrated chariot drawn by winged serpents, and married her, rightly confident that her spells would enable him to beget an heir; for he did not yet know that Aethra had borne him Theseus. Medea, however, recognized Theseus as soon as he arrived in the city, and grew jealous on behalf of Medus, her son by Aegeus. She therefore persuaded Aegeus that Theseus came as a spy or an assassin, and had him invited to a feast at the Dolphin Temple; Aegeus, who used the temple as his residence, was then to offer him a cup of wine already prepared by her. This cup contained wolfsbane, a poison which she had brought from Bithynian Acherusia. Some say that when the roast beef was served Theseus drew his sword, as if to carve, and thus attracted his father's attention. Others that he had unsuspectingly raised the cup to his lips before Aegeus noticed the Erechtheid serpents carved on the ivory sword-hilt and dashed the poison to the floor.

Then followed the greatest rejoicing that Athens had ever known. Aegeus embraced Theseus, summoned a public assembly, and acknowledged him as his son. He lighted fires on every altar and heaped the gods' images with gifts; hecatombs of garlanded oxen were sacrificed and, throughout the palace and the city, nobles and commoners feasted together, and sang of Theseus's glorious deeds that already outnumbered the years of his life.

Theseus then went in vengeful pursuit of Medea, who eluded him by casting a magic cloud about herself; and presumably left Athens with Medus, and an escort which Aegeus generously provided.

Pallas and his fifty sons, who even before this had declared that Aegeus was not a true Erechtheid and thus had no right to the throne, broke into open revolt when this footloose stranger threatened to balk their hopes of ever ruling Athens. They divided their forces: Pallas with twenty-five of his sons and numerous retainers marched against the city from the direction of Sphettus, while the other twenty-five lay in ambush at Gargettus. But Theseus, informed of their plans by a herald named Leos, sprang the ambush and destroyed the entire force. Pallas thereupon sued for peace.

Theseus in Crete

It is a matter of dispute whether Medea persuaded Aegeus to send Theseus against Poseidon's ferocious white bull, or whether it was after her expulsion from Athens that he undertook the destruction of this fire-breathing monster, hoping thereby to ingratiate himself further with the Athenians. Brought by Heracles from Crete, let loose on the plain of Argos, and driven thence across the Isthmus to Marathon, the bull had killed men by the hundred between the cities of Probalinthus and Tricorynthus. Yet Theseus boldy seized those murderous horns and dragged the bull in triumph through the streets of Athens, and up the steep slope of the Acropolis, where he sacrificed it to Athene, or to Apollo.

In requital for the murder of Androgeus, Minos had given orders that the Athenians should send seven youths and seven maidens every ninth year to the Cretan Labyrinth, where the Minotaur waited to devour them. This Minotaur, whose name was Asterius, was the bull-headed monster which Pasiphaë had borne to the white bull. Soon after Theseus's arrival at Athens the tribute fell due for the third time, and he so deeply pitied those parents whose children were liable to be chosen by lot, that he offered himself as one of the victims, despite Aegeus's earnest attempts at dissuasion.

On the two previous occasions, the ship which conveyed the fourteen victims had carried black sails, but Theseus was confident that the gods were on his side, and Aegeus therefore gave him a white sail to hoist on return, in signal of success.

Theseus with the bandit Sciron, whose feet he refused to wash. Red-figured drinking vessel (Antikenabteilung, Charlottenburg, Berlin)

When the lots had been cast at the Law Courts, Theseus led his companions to the Dolphin Temple where, on their behalf, he offered Apollo a branch of consecrated olive, bound with white wool. The fourteen mothers brought provisions for the voyage, and told their children fables and heroic tales to hearten them. Theseus, however, replaced two of the maiden victims with a pair of effeminate youths, possessed of unusual courage and presence of mind. These he commanded to take warm baths, avoid the rays of the sun, perfume their hair and bodies with unguent oils, and practise how to talk, gesture, and walk like women. He was thus able to deceive Minos by passing them off as maidens.

The Delphic Oracle had advised Theseus to take Aphrodite for his guide and companion on the voyage. He therefore sacrificed to her on the strand; and lo! the victim, a she-goat, became a he-goat in its death-throes. This prodigy won Aphrodite her title of Epitragia.

Theseus sailed on the sixth day of Munychion [April]. Every year on this date the Athenians would send virgins to the Dolphin Temple in propitiation of Apollo, because Theseus had omitted to do so before taking his leave. The god's displeasure was shown in a storm, which forced him to take shelter at Delphi and there offer belated sacrifices.

When the ship reached Crete some days afterwards, Minos rode down to the harbour to count the victims. Falling in love with one of the Athenian maidens, he would have ravished her then and there, had Theseus not protested that it was his duty as Poseidon's son to defend virgins against outrage by tyrants. Minos, laughing lewdly, replied that Poseidon had never been known to show delicate respect for any virgins who took his fancy.

'Ha!' he cried, 'prove yourself a son of Poseidon, by retrieving this bauble for me!' So saying, he flung his golden signet ring into the sea.

'First prove that you are a son of Zeus!' retorted Theseus.

This Minos did. His prayer: 'Father Zeus, hear me!' was at once answered by lightning and a clap of thunder. Without more ado, Theseus dived into the sea, where a large school of dolphins escorted him honourably down to the palace of the Nereids. Some say that Thetis the Nereid then gave him the jewelled crown, her wedding gift from Aphrodite, which Ariadne afterwards wore; others, that Amphitrite the Sea-goddess did so herself, and that she sent the Nereids swimming in every direction to find the golden ring. At all

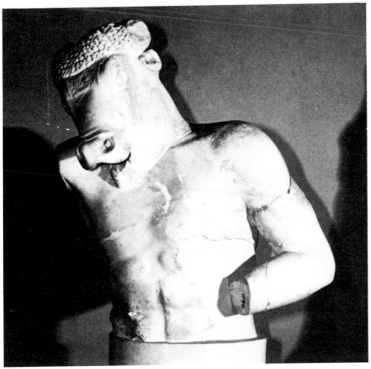

The Minotaur
(National Archaeological Museum, Athens)

events, when Theseus emerged from the sea, he was carrying both the ring and the crown.

Aphrodite had indeed accompanied Theseus: for not only did two of the Athenian maidens invite the chivalrous Theseus to their couches, and were not spurned, but Minos's own daughter Ariadne fell in love with him at first sight. 'I will help you to kill my half-brother, the Minotaur,' she secretly promised him, 'if I may return to Athens with you as your wife.' This offer Theseus gladly accepted, and swore to marry her. Now, before Daedalus left Crete, he had given Ariadne a magic ball of thread, and instructed her how to enter and leave the labyrinth. She must open the entrace door and tie the loose end of the thread to the lintel; the ball would then roll along, diminishing as it went and making, with devious turns and twists, for the innermost recess where the Minotaur was lodged. This ball Ariadne gave to Theseus, and instructed him to follow it until he reached the sleeping monster, whom he must seize by the hair and sacrifice to Poseidon. He could then find his way back by rolling up the thread into a ball again.

That same night Theseus did as he was told; but whether he killed the Minotaur with a sword given him by Ariadne, or with his bare hands, or with his celebrated club, is much disputed. A sculptured frieze at Amyclae shows the Minotaur bound and led in triumph by Theseus to Athens; but this is not the generally accepted story.

When Theseus emerged from the Labyrinth, spotted with blood, Ariadne embraced him passionately, and guided the whole Athenian party to the harbour. For, in the meantime, the two effeminate-looking youths had killed the guards of the women's quarters, and released the maiden victims. They all stole aboard their ship, and rowed hastily away. But although Theseus had first stove in the hulls of several Cretan ships, to prevent pursuit, the alarm sounded and he was forced to fight a sea-battle in the harbour, before escaping, fortunately without loss, under cover of darkness.

Some days later, after disembarking on the island then named Dia, but later known as Naxos, Theseus left Ariadne asleep on the shore, and sailed away. Why he did so must remain a mystery. Some say that he deserted her in favour of a new mistress, Aegle, daughter of Panopeus; others that, while wind-bound on Dia, he reflected on the scandal which Ariadne's arrival at Athens would cause. Others again, that Dionysus, appearing to Theseus in a dream, threateningly demanded Ariadne for himself, and that, when Theseus awoke to see Dionysius's fleet bearing down on Dia, he weighed anchor in sudden terror; Dionysus having cast a spell which made him forget his promise to Ariadne and even her very existence.

Whatever the truth of the matter may be, Dionysus's priests at Athens affirm that when Ariadne found herself alone on the deserted shore, she broke into bitter laments, remembering how she had trembled while Theseus set out to kill her monstrous half-brother; how she had offered silent vows for his success; and how, through love of him, she had deserted her parents and motherland. She now invoked the whole universe for vengeance, and Father Zeus nodded assent. Then, gently and sweetly, Dionysus with his merry train of satyrs and maenads came to Ariadne's rescue. He married her without delay, setting Thetis's crown upon her head, and she bore him many children. Of these only Thoas and Oenopion are sometimes called Theseus's sons. The crown, which Dionysus later set among the stars as the Corona Borealis, was made by Hephaestus of fiery gold and red Indian gems, set in the shape of roses.

To resume the history of Theseus: from Naxos he sailed to Delos, and there sacrificed to Apollo, celebrating athletic games in his honour. It was then that he introduced the novel custom of crowning the victor with palm-leaves, and placing a palm-stem in his right hand. He also prudently dedicated to the god a small wooden image of Aphrodite, the work of Daedalus, which Ariadne had brought from Crete and left aboard his ship — it might have been the subject of cynical comment by the Athenians.

Ariadne was soon revenged on Theseus. Whether in grief for her loss, or in joy at the sight of the Attic coast, from which he had been kept by prolonged winds, he forgot his promise to hoist the white sail. Aegeus, who stood watching for him on the Acropolis, where the Temple of the Wingless Victory was to stand, sighted the black sail, swooned, and fell headlong to his death into the valley below. But some say that he deliberately cast himself into the sea, which was thenceforth named the Aegean.

Theseus was not informed of this sorrowful accident until he had completed the sacrifices vowed to the gods for his safe return; he then buried Aegeus, and honoured him with a hero-shrine.

The Federalization of Attica

When Thesues succeeded his father Aegeus on the throne of Athens, he reinforced his sovereignty by executing nearly all his opponents, except Pallas and the remainder of his fifty sons. Some years later he killed these too as a precautionary measure and was purified of their blood at Troezen, where his son Hippolytus now reigned as king, and spent a whole year there. On his return, he suspected a half-brother, also named Pallas, of disaffection, and banished him at once; Pallas then founded Pallantium in Arcadia.

Theseus proved to be a law-abiding ruler, and initiated the policy of federalization, which was the basis of Athens' later well-being. Hitherto, Attica had been divided into twelve communities, each managing its own affairs without consulting the Athenian king, except in time of emergency. The Eleusinians had even declared war on Erechtheus, and other internecine quarrels abounded. If these communities were to relinquish their independence, Theseus must approach each clan and family in turn; which he did. He found the

Theseus and Antiope (Archaeological Museum, Chalcis)

A Centaur biting a Lapith (Archaeological Museum, Olympia)

yeomen and serfs ready to obey him, and persuaded most of the large landowners to agree with his scheme by promising to abolish the monarchy and substitute democracy for it, though remaining commander-in-chief and supreme judge. Those who remained unconvinced by the arguments he used respected his strength at least.

Theseus was thus empowered to dissolve all local governments, after summoning their delegates to Athens, where he provided these with a common Council Hall and Law Court. But he forbore to interfere with the laws of private property. Next, he united the suburbs with the city proper which, until then, had consisted of the

115

Acropolis and its immediate Southern dependencies, including the ancient Temples of Olympian Zeus, Pythian Apollo, Mother Earth, Dionysus of the Marshes, and the Aqueduct of Nine Springs.

He named the sixteenth day of Hecatomboeon [July] 'Federation Day', and made it a public festival in honour of Athene, when a bloodless sacrifice was also offered to Peace. By renaming the Athenian Games celebrated on this day 'All-Athenian', he opened it to the whole of Attica; and also introduced the worship of Federal Aphrodite and Persuasion. Then, resigning the throne, as he had promised, he gave Attica its new constitution, and under the best of auspices: for the Delphic Oracle prophesied that Athens would now ride the stormy seas as safely as a pig's bladder.

To enlarge the city still further, Theseus invited all worthy strangers to become his fellow-citizens. His heralds, who went throughout Greece, used a formula, namely: 'Come hither, all ye people!' Great crowds thereupon flocked into Athens, and he divided the population of Attica into three classes: the Eupatrids, or 'those who deserve well of their fatherland'; the Georges, or 'farmers'; and the Demiurges, or 'artificers'. The Eupatrids took charge of religious affairs, supplied magistrates, interpreted the laws, embodying the highest dignity of all; the Georges tilled the soil and were the backbone of the state; the Demiurges, by far the most numerous class, furnished such various artificers as soothsayers, surgeons, heralds, carpenters, sculptors, and confectioners. Thus Theseus became the first king to found a commonwealth, which is why Homer, in the *Catalogue of Ships*, styles only the Athenians a sovereign people.

Theseus, the first Athenian king to mint money, stamped his coins with the image of a bull. His coinage caused the standard of value to be quoted in terms of 'ten oxen', or 'one hundred oxen', for a considerable time. In emulation of Heracles, who had appointed his father Zeus patron of the Olympic Games, Theseus now appointed his father Poseidon patron of the Isthmian Games. Next, Theseus made good the Athenian claim to the sovereignty of Megara and then, having summoned Peloponnesian delegates to the Isthmus, prevailed upon them to settle a long-standing frontier dispute with their Ionian neighbours. At a place agreed by both parties, he raised the celebrated column marked on its eastern side: 'This is not the Peloponnese!' He also won Corinthian assent to the Athenians' taking the place of honour at the Isthmian Games.

Theseus and the Amazons

Some say that Theseus took part in Heracles's successful expedition against the Amazons, and received as his share of the booty their queen Antiope, also called Melanippe; but that this was not so unhappy a fate for her as many thought, because she had betrayed the city of Themiscyra on the river Thermodon to him, in proof of the passion he had already kindled in her heart.

Others say that Theseus visited their country some years later, in the company of Peirithous and his comrades; and that the Amazons, delighted at the arrival of so many handsome warriors, offered them no violence. Antiope came to greet Theseus with gifts, but she had hardly climbed aboard his ship, before he weighed anchor and abducted her.

Antiope's sister Oreithyia, mistaken by some for Hippolyte whose girdle Heracles won, swore vengeance on Theseus. She concluded an alliance with the Scythians, and led a large force of Amazons across the ice of the Cimmerian Bosphorous, then crossed the Danube and passed through Thrace, Thessaly, and Boeotia. At Athens she encamped on the Areiopagus and there sacrificed to Ares; an event from which, some say, the hill won its name; but first she ordered a detachment to invade Laconia and discourage the Peloponnese from

Bull-leaping (The Minoan Royal Palace, Knossos, Crete)

reinforcing Theseus by way of the Isthmus.

The Athenian forces were already marshalled, but neither side cared to begin hostilities. At last, on the advice of an oracle, Theseus sacrificed to Phobus, son of Ares, and offered battle on the seventh day of Boedromion, th date on which the Boedromia was celebrated at Athens; though some say the festival had already been founded in honour of the victory which Xuthus won over Eumolpus in the reign of Erechtheus. The Amazons' battle-front stretched between what was later called the Amazonium and the Pnyx Hill near Chrysa. Theseus's right wing moved down from the Museum and fell upon their left wing, but was routed and forced to retire as far as the Temple of Furies. The Athenian left wing, however, charged from the Palladium, Mount Ardrettus and the Lyceum, and drove the Amazon right wing back to their camp, inflicting heavy casualties.

Some say that the Amazons offered peace terms only after four months of hard fighting; the armistice, sworn near the sanctuary of Theseus, was later commemorated in the Amazonian sacrifice on the eve of his festival. But others say that Oreithyia with a few followers escaped to Megara, where she died of grief and despair; and that the remaining Amazons, driven from Attica by the victorious Theseus, settled in Scythia.

This, at any rate, was the first time that the Athenians repulsed foreign invaders. Some of the Amazons left wounded on the field of battle were sent to Chalcis to be cured, and Molpadia is buried near the temple of Mother Earth. Others lie in Amazonium.

The truth about Antiope seems to be that she survived the battle, and that Theseus was eventually compelled to kill her, as the Delphic Oracle had foretold, when he entered into an alliance with King Deucalion the Cretan, and married his sister Phaedra. The jealous Antiope, who was not his legal wife, interrupted the wedding festivities by bursting in, fully armed, and threatening to massacre the guests. Theseus and his companions hastily closed the doors, and despatched her in a grim combat, though she had borne him Hippolytus, and never lain with another man.

Phaedra and Hippolytus

After marrying Phaedra, Theseus sent his bastard son Hippolytus to Pittheus, who adopted him as heir to the throne of Troezen. Thus Hippolytus had no cause to dispute the right of his legimate brothers Acamas and Demophoön, Phaedra's sons, to reign over Athens.

Hippolytus, who had inherited his mother Antiope's exclusive devotion to chaste Artemis, raised a new temple to the goddess at Troezen, not far from the theatre. Thereupon Aphrodite, determined to punish him for what she took as an insult to herself, saw to it that when he attended the Eleusinian Mysteries, Phaedra should fall passionately in love with him.

Since at that time Theseus was away in Thessaly with Peirithous, Phaedra followed Hippolytus to Troezen. There she built the Temple of Peeping Aphrodite to overlook the gymnasium, and would daily watch unobserved while he kept himself fit by running, leaping, and wrestling, stark naked. An ancient myrtle-tree stood in the Temple enclosure; Phaedra would jab at its leaves, in frustrated passion, with a jewelled hair-pin. When, later, Hippolytus attended the All-Athenian Festival and lodged in Theseus's palace, she used the Temple of Aphrodite on the Acropolis for the same purpose.

Phaedra disclosed her incestuous desire to no one, but ate little, slept badly, and grew so weak that her old nurse guessed the truth at last, and officiously implored her to send Hippolytus a letter. This Phaedra did: confessing her love, and saying that she was now converted by it to the cult of Artemis, whose two wooden images, brought from Crete, she had just rededicated to the goddess. Would he not come hunting one day? 'We women of the Cretan Royal House,' she wrote, 'are doubtless fated to be dishonoured in love: witness my grandmother Europe, my mother Pasiphaë, and lastly my own sister Ariadne! Ah, wretched Ariadne, deserted by your father, the faithless Theseus, who has since murdered your own royal mother — why have the Furies not punished you for showing such unfilial indifference to her fate? — and must one day murder me! I count on you to revenge yourself on him by paying homage to Aphrodite in my company. Could we not go away and live together, for a while at least, and make a hunting expedition the excuse? Meanwhile, none can suspect our true feelings for each other. Already we are lodged under the same roof, and our affection will be regarded as innocent, and even praiseworthy.'

Hippolytus burned this letter in horror, and came to Phaedra's chamber, loud with reproaches; but she tore her clothes, threw open the chamber doors, and cried out: 'Help, help! I am ravished!' Then she hanged herself from the lintel, and left a note accusing him of monstrous crimes.

Theseus, on receiving the note, cursed Hippolytus, and gave orders that he must quit Athens at once, never to return. Later he remembered the three wishes granted him by his father Poseidon, and prayed earnestly that Hippolytus might die that very day. 'Father,' he pleaded, 'send a beast across Hippolytus's path, as he makes for Troezen!'

Hippolytus had set out from Athens at full speed. As he drove along the narrow part of the Isthmus a huge wave, which overtopped even the Molurian Rock, rolled roaring shoreward; and from its crest sprang a great dog-seal bellowing and spouting water. Hippolytus's four horses swerved towards the cliff, mad with terror, but being an expert charioteer he restrained them from plunging over the edge. The beast then galloped menacingly behind the chariot, and he failed to keep his team on a straight course. Not far from the sanctuary of Saronian Artemis stood a wild olive, and it was on a branch of this tree that a loop of Hippolytus's rein caught. His chariot was flung sideways against a pile of rocks and broken into pieces. Hippolytus, entangled in the reins, and thrown first against the tree-trunk, and then agains the rocks, was dragged to death by his horses, while the pursuer vanished.

The Athenians raised a barrow in Hippolytus's memory close to the Temple of Themis, because his death had been brought about by curses. Some say that Theseus, accused of his murder, was found guilty, ostracized, and banished to Scyros, where he ended his life in

A red-figured Attic case depicting Theseus carrying off Helen (Antikensammlung, Munich)

shame and grief. But his downfall is more generally believed to have been caused by an attempted rape of Persephone.

Hippolytus's ghost descended to Tartarus, and Artemis, in high indignation, begged Asclepius to revive his corpse. Asclepius opened the doors of his ivory medicine cabinet and took out the herb with which Cretan Glaucus had been revived. With it he thrice touched Hippolytus's breast, repeating certain charms, and at the third touch the dead man raised his head from the ground. But Hades and the Three Fates, scandalized by this breach of privilege, persuaded Zeus to kill Asclepius with a thunderbolt.

Lapiths and Centaurs

Some say that Peirithous the Lapith was the son of Ixion and Dia, daughter of Elioneus; others, that he was the son of Zeus who, disguised as a stallion, coursed around Dia before seducing her.

Almost incredible reports of Theseus's strength and valour had reached Peirithous, who ruled over the Magnetes, at the mouth of the river Peneus; and one day he resolved to test them by raiding Attica and driving away a herd of cattle that were grazing at Marathon. When Theseus at once went in pursuit, Peirithous boldly turned about to face him; but each was filled with such admiration for the other's nobility of appearance that the cattle were forgotten, and they swore an oath of everlasting friendship.

Peirithous married Hippodameia, daughter of Butes, and invited all the Olympians to his wedding, except Ares and Eris; he remembered the mischief which Eris had caused at the marriage of Peleus and Thetis. Since more feasters came to Peirithous's palace than it could contain, his cousins the Centaurs, together with Nestor, Caeneus, and other Thessalian princes, were seated at tables in a vast, tree-shaded cave near by.

The Centaurs, however, were unused to wine and, when they smelled its fragrance, pushed away the sour milk which was set before them, and ran to fill their silver horns from the wine-skins. In their ignorance they swilled the strong liquor unmixed with water, becoming so drunk that when the bride was escorted into the cavern to greet them, Eurytion leaped from his stool, overturned the table, and dragged her away by the hair. At once the other Centaurs followed his disgraceful example, lecherously straddling the nearest women and boys.

Peirithous and his paranymph Theseus sprang to Hippodameia's rescue, cut off Eurytion's ears and nose and, with the help of the

left: *The deeds of Theseus,
Vase (British Museum)*

opposite: *Amazons on
horseback. Silver panel with
gold sections (British
Museum)*

below: *Theseus and the
Minotaur. Detail from a
black-figured vase (British
Museum)*

123

Lapiths, threw him out of the cavern. The ensuing fight, in the course of which Caeneus the Lapith was killed, lasted until nightfall; and thus began the long feud between the Centaurs and their Lapith neighbours, engineered by Ares and Eris in revenge for the slight offered them.

On this occasion the Centaurs suffered a serious reverse, and Theseus drove them from their ancient hunting grounds on Mount Pelion to the land of the Aethices near Mount Pindus. But it was not an easy task to subdue the Centaurs, who now, rallying their forces, invaded Lapith territory. They supervised and slaughtered the main Lapith army, and when the survivors fled to Pholoë in Elis, the vengeful Centaurs expelled them and converted Pholoë into a bandit stronghold of their own. Finally the Lapiths settled in Malea.

Theseus in Tartarus

After Hippodameia's death Peirithous persuaded Theseus, whose wife Phaedra had recently hanged herself, to visit Sparta in his company and carry away Helen, a sister of Castor and Polydeuces, the Dioscuri, with whom they were both ambitious to be connected by marriage. They swore to stand by each other in this perilous enterprise; to draw lots for Helen when they had won her; and then to carry off another of Zeus's daughters for the loser, whatever the danger might be.

This decided, they led an army into Lacedaemon; then, riding ahead of the main body, seized Helen while she was offering a sacrifice in the Temple of Upright Artemis at Sparta, and galloped away with her. They soon outdistanced their pursuers, shaking them off at Tegea where, as had been agreed, lots were drawn for Helen; and Theseus proved the winner. He foresaw, however, that the Athenians would by no means approve his having thus picked a quarrel with the redoubtable Dioscuri, and therefore sent Helen, who was not yet nubile, to the Attic village of Aphidnae, where he charged his friend Aphidnus to guard her with the greatest attention and secrecy. Aethra, Theseus's mother, accompanied Helen and cared well for her.

Some years passed and, when Helen was old enough for Theseus to marry her, Peirithous reminded him of their pact. Together they consulted an oracle of Zeus, and his ironical response was: 'Why not visit Tartarus and demand Persephone, the wife of Hades, as a bride for Peirithous? She is the noblest of my daughters.' Theseus was outraged when Peirithous, who took this suggestion seriously, held him to his oath; but he dared not refuse to go, and presently they descended, sword in hand, to Tartarus, and were soon knocking at the gates of Hades's palace. Hades listened calmly to their impudent request and, feigning hospitality, invited them to be seated. Unsuspectingly they took the settee he offered, which proved to be the Chair of Forgetfulness and at once became part of their flesh, so that they could not rise again without self-mutilation. Coiled serpents hissed all about them, and they were well lashed by the Furies and mauled by Cerberus's teeth, while Hades looked on, smiling grimly.

Thus they remained in torment for four full years, until Heracles, coming at Eurystheus's command to fetch up Cerberus, recognized them as they mutely stretched out their hands, pleading for his help. Persephone received Heracles like a brother, graciously permitting him to release the evil-doers and take them back to the upper air, if he could. Heracles thereupon grasped Theseus by both hands and heaved with gigantic strength until, with a rending noise, he was torn free; but a great part of his flesh remained sticking to the rock, which is why Theseus's Athenian descendants were all so absurdly small-buttocked. Next, he seized hold of Peirithous's hands, but the earth quaked warningly, and he desisted; Peirithous had, after all, been the leading spirit in this blasphemous enterprise.

The Death of Theseus

During Theseus's absence in Tartarus the Dioscuri assembled an army of Laconians and Arcadians, marched against Athens, and demanded the return of Helen. When the Athenians denied that they were sheltering her, or had the least notion where she might be, the Dioscuri proceeded to ravage Attica, until the inhabitants of Deceleia, who disapproved of Theseus's conduct, guided them to Aphidnae, where they found and rescued their sister. The Dioscuri then razed Aphidnae to the ground; but the Deceleians became immune from all Spartan taxes and entitled to seats of honour at Spartan festivals—their lands alone were spared in the Peloponnesian War, when the invading Spartans laid Attica waste.

Now, Peteos son of Orneus and grandson of Erechtheus had been banished by Aegeus, and the Dioscuri, to spite Theseus, brought back his son Menestheus from exile, and made him regent of Athens. This Menestheus was the first demagogue. During Theseus's absence in Tartarus he ingratiated himself with the people by reminding the nobles of the power which they had forfeited through Federalization, and by telling the poor that they were being robbed of country and

Battle of the Centaurs and the Lapiths (British Museum)

religion, and had become subject to an adventurer of obscure origin — who, however, had now vacated the throne and was rumoured dead.

When Aphidnae fell, and Athens was in danger, Menestheus persuaded the people to welcome the Dioscuri into the city as their benefactors and deliverers. They did indeed behave most correctly, and asked only to be admitted to the Eleusinian Mysteries, as Heracles had been. This request was granted, and the Dioscuri became honorary citizens of Athens. Aphidnus was their adoptive father, as Pylius had been Heracles's on a similar occasion. Divine honours were thereafter paid them at the rising of their constellation, in gratitude for the clemency which they had shown to the common people; and they cheerfully brought Helen back to Sparta, with Theseus's mother Aethra and a sister of Peirithous as her bondwoman. Some say that they found Helen still a virgin; others, that Theseus had got her with child and that at Argos, on the way home, she gave birth to a girl, Iphigeneia, and dedicated a sanctuary to

Artemis in gratitude for her safe delivery.

Theseus, who returned from Tartarus soon afterwards, at once raised an altar to Heracles the Saviour, and reconsecrated to him all but four of his temples and groves. However, he had been greatly weakened by his tortures, and found Athens so sadly corrupted by faction and sedition, that he was no longer able to maintain order. First smuggling his children out of the city to Euboea, where Elpenor son of Chalcodon sheltered them and then, solemnly cursing the people of Athens from Mount Gargettus, he sailed for Crete, where Deucalion had promised to shelter him.

A storm blew the ship off her course, and his first landfall was the island of Scyros, near Euboea, where King Lycomedes, though a close friend of Menestheus, received him with all the splendour due to his fame and lineage. Theseus, who had inherited an estate on Scyros, asked permission to settle there. But Lycomedes had long regarded this estate as his own and, under the pretence of showing Theseus its boundaries, inveigled him to the top of a high cliff, pushed him over, and then gave out that he had fallen accidentally while taking a drunken, post-prandial stroll.

Menestheus, now left in undisturbed possession of the throne, was among Helen's suitors, and led the Athenian forces to Troy, where he won great fame as a strategist but was killed in battle. The sons of Theseus succeeded him.

Theseus was a skilled lyre-player and has now become joint-patron with Heracles and Hermes of every gymnasium and wrestling school in Greece. His resemblance to Heracles is proverbial. He took part in the Calydonian Hunt; avenged the champions who fell at Thebes; and only failed to be one of the Argonauts through being detained in Tartarus when they sailed for Colchis.

Ill-treated slaves and labourers, whose ancestors looked to him for protection against ther oppressors, used to seek refuge in his sanctuary, where sacrifices were offered to him on the eighth day of every month. This day may have been chosen because he first arrived at Athens from Troezen on the eighth of Hecatomboeon, and returned from Crete on the eighth day of Pyanepsion. Or perhaps because he was a son of Poseidon: for Poseidon's feasts are also observed on that day of the month, since eight, being the first cube of an even number, represents Poseidon's unshakable power.

5

THEBES AND MYCENAE

Oedipus

LAIUS, SON OF LABDACUS, married Iocaste, and ruled over Thebes. Grieved by his prolonged childlessness, he secretly consulted the Delphic Oracle, which informed him that this was a blessing, because any child born to Iocaste would become his murderer. He therefore put Iocaste away, without offering any reason for his decision, which caused her such vexation that, having made him drunk, she inveigled him into her arms again as soon as night fell. When, nine months later, Iocaste was brought to bed of a son, Laius snatched him from the nurse's arms, pierced his feet with a nail and, binding them together, exposed him on Mount Cithaeron.

Yet the Fates had ruled that this boy should reach a green old age. A Corinthian shepherd found him, named him Oedipus because his feet were deformed by the nail-wound, and brought him to Corinth. Here King Polybus was reigning at the time, and being childless, was pleased to rear Oedipus as his own son.

One day, taunted by a Corinthian youth with not in the least resembling his supposed parents, Oedipus went to ask the Delphic Oracle what future lay in store for him. 'Away, wretch!' the Pythoness cried in disgust. 'You will kill your father and marry your mother!'

Since Oedipus loved Polybus and Periboa, his queen, he at once decided against returning to Corinth. But in the narrow defile between Delphi and Daulis he happened to meet Laius, who ordered him roughly to step off the road and make way for his betters. Laius was in a chariot and Oedipus on foot. Oedipus retorted that he acknowledged no betters except the gods and his own parents.

'So much the worse for you!' cried Laius, and ordered his charioteer Polyphontes to drive on. One of the wheels bruised Oedipus's foot and, transported by rage, he killed Polyphontes with his spear. Then, flinging Laius on the road entangled in the reins, and whipping up the team, he made them drag him to death. It was left to the king of Plataeae to bury both corpses.

Laius had been on his way to ask the Oracle how he might rid Thebes of the Sphynx. This monster, with her woman's head, lion's body, serpent's tail, and eagle's wings, had flown to Thebes from the uttermost part of Ethiopia. Hera had recently sent her to punish

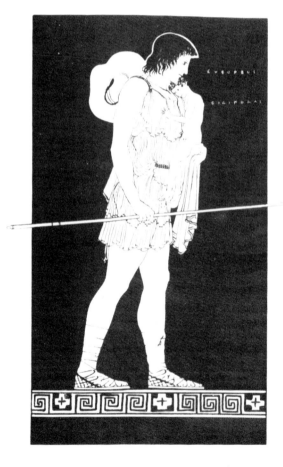

Oedipus as an infant

Oedipus and the Sphinx (National Archaeological Museum, Athens)

Oedipus being questioned by the Sphinx. An Attic vase (Vatican Museum)

opposite: *The Sphinx (Archaeological Museum, Delphi)*

Thebes for Laius's abduction of the boy Chrysippus. Settling close to the city, the Sphinx now asked every Theban wayfarer a riddle taught her by the Three Muses: 'What being, with only one voice, has sometimes two feet, sometimes three, sometimes four, and is weakest when it has the most?' Those who could not solve the riddle she throttled and devoured on the spot.

Oedipus, approaching Thebes, guessed the answer. 'Man,' he replied, 'because he crawls on all fours as an infant, stands firmly on his two feet in his youth, and leans upon a staff in his old age.' The mortified Sphinx leaped from Mount Phicium and dashed herself to pieces in the valley below. At this the grateful Thebans acclaimed Oedipus king, and he married Iocaste, unaware that she was his mother.

Plague then descended upon Thebes, and the Delphic Oracle, when consulted once more, replied: 'Expel the murderer of Laius!' Oedipus, not knowing whom he had met in the defile, pronounced a curse on Laius's murderer and sentenced him to exile.

Blind Teiresias, the most renowned seer in Greece at this time, now demanded an audience with Oedipus. Some say that once, on Mount Cyllene, Teiresias had seen two serpents in the act of coupling. When both attacked him, he struck at them with his staff, killing the female. Immediately he was turned into a woman, and became a celebrated harlot; but seven years later he happened to see the same sight again at the same spot, and this time regained his manhood by killing the male serpent.

Once Hera began reproaching Zeus for his numerous infidelities. He defended them by arguing that, at any rate, when he did share her couch, she had the more enjoyable time by far, deriving infinitely greater pleasure from the sexual act than he.

'What nonsense!' cried Hera.

Teirsias, summoned to settle the dispute from his personal experience, answered:

> 'If the parts of love-pleasure be counted as ten,
> Thrice three go to women, one only to men.'

Hera was so exasperated by Zeus's triumphant grin that she blinded Teiresias; but Zeus compensated him with inward sight, and a life extended to seven generations.

Teiresias now appeared at Oedipus's court, and revealed to Oedipus the will of the gods: that plague would cease only if a Sown Man died for the sake of the city. Iocaste's father Menoeceus, one of those who had risen out of the earth when Cadmus sowed the serpent's teeth, at once leaped from the walls.

Teiresias then announced further: 'The plague will now cease. Yet the gods had another in mind, for he has killed his father and married his mother. Know, Queen Iocaste, that it is your husband Oedipus!'

At first, none would believe Teiresias, but his words were soon confirmed by a letter from Periboea at Corinth. She wrote that the sudden death of King Polybus now allowed her to reveal the circumstances of Oedipus's adoption. Iocaste then hanged herself for shame and grief, while Oedipus blinded himself with a pin taken from her garments.

Some say that Iocaste's brother Creon expelled Oedipus, who, after wandering for many years through country after country, guided by his faithful daughter Antigone, finally came to Colonus in Attica. Here the Erinnyes, who have a grove there, hounded him to death, and Theseus buried his body in the precinct of the Solemn Ones at Athens, lamenting by Antigone's side.

The Seven Against Thebes

So many princes visited Argos in the hope of marrying either Aegeia, or Deiplya, the daughters of King Adrastus, that, fearing to make powerful enemies if he singled out any two of them as his sons-in-law, he consulted the Delphic Oracle. Apollo's response was: 'Yoke to a two-wheeled chariot the boar and lion which fight in your palace.'

Among the less fortunate of these suitors were Polyneices and Tydeus. Polyneices and his twin Eteocles had been elected co-kings of Thebes after the banishment of Oedipus, their father. They agreed to reign for alternate years, but Eteocles, to whom the first term fell, would not relinquish the throne at the end of the year, pleading the evil disposition shown by Polyneices, and banished him from the city. Tydeus, son of Oeneus of Calydon, had killed his brother Melanippus when out hunting; though he claimed that this was an accident, it had been prophesied that Melanippus would kill him, and the Calydonians therefore suspected him of having tried to forestall his fate, and he was also banished.

Now, the emblem of Thebes is a lion, and the emblem of Calydon, a boar; and the two fugitive suitors displayed these devices on their shields. Adrastus, mindful of the prophecy, therefore married Aegia to Polyneices, and Deipyla to Tydeus, with a promise to restore both princes to their kingdoms; but said that he would first march against Thebes, which lay nearer.

Adrastus mustered his Argive chieftains, bidding them arm themselves and set out eastward. Of these champions, Amphiaraus, foreseeing that all except Adrastus would die fighting against Thebes, at first refused to go.

Now Adrastus's sister Eriphyle was married to Amphiaraus. Tydeus therefore called Polyneices and said: 'Eriphyle fears that she is losing her looks; if you were to offer her the magic necklace which was Aphrodite's wedding gift to your ancestress Harmonia, Cadmus's wife, she would soon compel Amphiaraus to come with us.'

This was discreetly done, and the expedition set out, their march taking them through Nemea, where Lycurgus was king. When they asked leave to water their troops in his country, Lycurgus consented, and his bond-woman Hypsipyle guided them to the nearest spring. Hypsipyle was acting as nursemaid to Lycurgus's son Opheltes. She set the boy down for a moment while she guided the Argive army to the drinking pool, whereupon a serpent writhed around his limbs and bit him to death. Adrastus and his men returned from the spring too late to do more than kill the serpent and bury the boy. When Amphiaraus warned them that this was an ominous sign, they instituted the Nemean Games in the boy's honour.

Arrived at Cithaeron, Adrastus sent Tydeus as his herald to the Thebans, with a demand that Eteocles should resign the throne in favour of Polyneices. When this was refused, Tydeus challenged their chieftains to single combat, one after another, and emerged victorious from every encounter; soon, no more Thebans dared come forward. The Argives then approached the city walls, and each of the champions took up his station facing one of the seven gates.

Teiresias the seer, whom Eteocles consulted, prophesied that the Thebans would be victorious only if a prince of the royal house freely offered himself as a sacrifice to Ares; whereupon Menoeceus, the son of Creon, killed himself before the gates. Teiresias's prophecy was fulfilled: the Thebans were, indeed, defeated in a skirmish and withdrew into the city; but no sooner had Capaneus set a scaling-ladder against the wall and begun to mount it, than Zeus struck him dead with a thunderbolt. At this, the Thebans took courage, and made a furious sally, killing three more of the seven champions.

Polyneices, to save further slaughter, offered to decide the succession of the throne by single combat with Eteocles. Eteocles accepted the challenge and each mortally wounded the other. Creon, their uncle, then took command and routed the dismayed Argives. Amphiaraus fled in his chariot along the banks of the river Ismenus,

The Seven against Thebes. Part of the Thracian Panagyurishté Treasure (Plovdiv Museum, Bulgaria)

Apollo in his temple at Delphi. Detail of vase (Allard Pierson Museum, Amsterdam)

135

and was on the point of being thrust between the shoulders by a Theban pursuer, when Zeus cleft the earth with a thunderbolt and he vanished from sight, chariot and all, and now reigns alive among the dead.

Seing that the day was lost, Adrastus escaped; but when, later he heard that Creon would not permit his dead enemies to be buried, visited Athens as a suppliant and persuaded Theseus to march against Thebes and punish Creon's impiety. Theseus took the city in a surprise attack, imprisoned Creon, and gave the dead champions' corpses to their kinsfolk.

Now, before Theseus's arrival at Thebes, Antigone, sister of Eteocles and Polyneices, had disobeyed Creon's orders by secretly building a pyre and laying Polyneices's corpse upon it. Creon noticed and, going to investigate, surpised Antigone in her act of disobedience. He summoned his son Haemon, to whom Antigone had been affianced, and ordered him to bury her alive in Polyneices's tomb. Haemon feigned readiness to do as he was told but, instead, married Antigone secretly, and sent her away to live among his shepherds. She bore him a son who, many years later, came to Thebes, and took part in certain funeral games; but Creon, who was still King of Thebes, guessed his identity by the serpent mark on his body, borne by all descendants of Cadmus, and sentenced him to death. Heracles interceded for his life, but Creon proved obdurate; whereupon Haemon killed both Antigone and himself.

The Epigoni

The sons of the seven champions who had fallen at Thebes swore to avenge their fathers. They are known as the Epigoni. The Delphic Oracle promised them victory if Alcmaeon, son of Amphiaraus, took command. But he felt no desire to attack Thebes, and hotly disputed the propriety of the campaign with his brother Amphilochus. When they could not agree whether to make war or no, the decision was referred to their mother Eriphyle. Recognizing the situation as a familiar one, Thersander, the son of Polyneices, followed his father's example: he bribed Eriphyle with the magic robe which Athene had given his ancestress Harmonia at the same time as Aphrodite had given her the magic necklace. Eriphyle decided for war, and Alcmaeon reluctantly assumed command.

In a battle fought before the walls of Thebes, the Epigoni lost Aegialeus, son of Adastrus, and Teiresias the seer then warned the Thebans that their city would be sacked. The walls, he announced, were fated to stand only so long as one of the original seven champions remained alive, and Adrastus, now the sole survivor, would die of grief when he heard of Aegialieus's death. Consequently, the Thebans' wisest course was to flee that very night. Teiresias added that whether they took his advice or no made no odds to him; he was destined to die as soon as Thebes fell into Argive hands. Under cover of darkness, therefore, the Thebans escaped northward with their wives, children, weapons, and a few belongings, and when they had travelled far enough, called a halt and founded the city of Hestiaea. At dawn, Teiresias, who went with them, paused to drink at the spring of Tilphussa, and suddenly expired.

That same day, which was the very day on which Adrastus heard of Aegialeus's death and died of grief, the Argives, finding Thebes evacuated, broke in, razed the walls, and collected the booty. They sent the best of it to Apollo at Delphi, including Teiresias's daughter Manto, who had stayed behind; and she became his Pythoness.

Nor was this the end of the matter. Thersander happened to boast in Alcmaeon's hearing that most of the credit for the Argive victory was due to himself: he bribed Eriphyle, just as his father Polyneices did before him, to give the order to march. Alcmaeon thus learned for the first time that Eriphyle's vanity had caused his father's death, and might well have caused his own. He consulted the Delphic Oracle, and Apollo replied that she deserved death. Alcmaeon mistook this for a dispensation to matricide and, on his return, he duly killed Eriphyle, but, as she lay dying, Eriphyle cursed Alcmaeon: 'Lands of all the world: deny shelter to my murderer!' The avenging Erinnyes thereupon pursued him and drove him mad.

Alcmaeon fled first to Thesprotia and then to Psophis, where King Phegeus purified him for Apollo's sake. Phegeus married him to his daughter Arsinoë, to whom Alcmaeon gave the necklace and the robe, which he had brought in his baggage. But the Erinnyes, disregarding this purification, continued to plague him, and the land of Psophis grew barren on his account. The Delphic Oracle then advised Alcmaeon to approach the River-god Achelous, by whom he was once more purified; he married Achelous's daughter Callirrhoë, and settled on land recently formed by the silt of the river, which had not been included in Eriphyle's ban. There he lived at peace for a while.

A year later, Callirrhoë, fearing that she might lose her beauty, refused Alcmaeon admittance to her couch unless he gave her the celebrated robe and necklace. For love of Callirrhoë, he dared revisit

Psophis, where he deceived Phegeus: making no mention of his marriage to Callirrhoë, he invented a prediction of the Delphic Oracle, to the effect that he would never be rid of the Erinnyes until he had dedicated both robe and necklace to Apollo's shrine. Phegeus thereupon made Arsinoë surrender them, which she was glad to do, believing that Alcmaeon would return to her as soon as the Erinnyes left him. But one of Alcmaeon's servants blabbed the truth and Phegeus grew so angry that he ordered his sons to kill Alcmaeon when he left the palace. Arsinoë witnessed the murder and, unaware of Alcmaeon's double-dealing, loudly upbraided her father and brothers. Phegeus begged her to be silent and listen; but Arsinoë stopped her ears and wished violent death upon him and her brothers before the next new moon. In retaliation, Phegeus locked her in a chest and presented her as a slave to the King of Nemea; at the same time telling his sons: 'Take this robe and this necklace to Delphic Apollo. He will see to it that they cause no further mischief.'

Meanwhile, Callirrhoë, informed of what had happened at Psophis, prayed that her infant sons by Alcmaeon might become full-grown men in a day, and avenge his murder. Zeus heard her plea, and her sons went to Nemea, where, they knew, the sons of Phegeus had broken their return journey from Delphi in the hope of persuading Arsinoë to retract her curse. But she would not listen to them either; and Callirrhoë's sons not only surprised and killed them but, hastening towards Psophis, killed Phegeus too, before the next moon appeared in the sky. Since no king or river-god in Greece would consent to purify them of their crimes, they travelled westward to Epirus, and colonized Acarnania, which was named after the elder of the two, Acarnan.

Tantalus

The parentage and origin of Tantalus are disputed. His mother was Pluto, a daughter of Cronus and Rhea or, some say, of Oceanus and Tethys; and his father either Zeus, or Tmolus, the oak-chapleted deity of Mount Tmolus, who, with his wife Omphale, ruled over the kingdom of Lydia and had judged the contest between Pan and Apollo.

By his wife Euryanassa, daughter of the River-god Pactolus, Tantalus became the father of Pelops, Niobe, and Broteas. Yet some call Pelops a bastard, or the son of Atlas and the nymph Linos.

Tantalus was the intimate friend of Zeus, who admitted him to Olympian banquets of nectar and ambrosia until, good fortune turning his head, he betrayed Zeus's secrets and stole the divine food to share among his mortal friends. Before this crime could be discovered, he committed a worse. Having called the Olympians to a banquet on Mount Sipylus, Tantalus found that the food in his larder was insufficient for the company and, either to test Zeus's omniscience, or merely to demonstrate his good will, cut up his son Pelops, and added the pieces to the stew prepared for them, as the sons of Lycaon had done with their brother Nyctimus when they entertained Zeus in Arcadia. None of the gods failed to notice what was on their trenchers, or to recoil in horror, except Demeter who, being dazed by her loss of Persephone, ate the flesh from the left shoulder.

For these two crimes Tantalus was punished with the ruin of his kingdom and, after his death by Zeus's own hand, with eternal torment in the company of Ixion, Sisyphus, Tityus, the Danaids, and others. Now he hangs, perennially consumed by thirst and hunger, from the bough of a fruit-tree which leans over a marshy lake. Its waves lap against his waist, and sometimes reach his chin, yet whenever he bends down to drink, they slip away, and nothing remains but the black mud at his feet; or, if he ever succeeds in scooping up a handful of water, it slips through his fingers before he can do more than wet his cracked lips, leaving him thirstier than ever. The tree is laden with pears, shining apples, sweet figs, ripe olives and pomegranates, which dangle against his shoulders; but whenever he reaches for the luscious fruit, a gust of wind whirls them out of his reach.

Moreover, an enormous stone, a crag from Mount Sipylus, overhangs the tree and eternally threatens to crush Tantalus's skull. This is his punishment for a third crime: namely theft, aggravated by perjury. One day, while Zeus was still an infant in Crete, being suckled by the she-goat Amaltheia, Hephaestus had made Rhea a golden mastiff to watch over him; which subsequently became the guardian of his temple at Dicte. But Pandareus, son of Merops, a native of Miletus, dared to steal the mastiff, and brought it to Tantalus for safe keeping on Mount Sipylus. After the hue and cry had died down, Pandareus asked Tantalus to return it to him, but Tantalus swore by Zeus that he had neither seen nor heard of a golden dog. This oath coming to Zeus's ears, Hermes was given orders to investigate the matter; and although Tantalus continued to perjure himself, Hermes recovered the dog by force or by stratagem, and Zeus crushed Tantalus under a crag of Mount Sipylus.

After punishing Tantalus, Zeus was pleased to revive Pelops; and therefore ordered Hermes to collect his limbs and boil them again in the same cauldron, on which he laid a spell. The Fate Clotho then rearticulated them; Demeter gave him a solid ivory shoulder in place of the one she had picked clean; and Rhea breathed life into him; while Goat-Pan danced for joy.

Pelops emerged from the magic cauldron clothed in such radiant beauty that Poseidon fell in love with him on the spot, and carried him off to Olympus in a chariot drawn by golden horses. There he appointed him his cup-bearer and bed-fellow as Zeus later appointed Ganymedes, and fed him on ambrosia. Pelops first noticed that his left shoulder was of ivory when he bared his breast in mourning for his sister Niobe. All true descendants of Pelops are marked in this way and, after his death, the ivory shoulder-blade was laid up at Pisa.

Tantalus's ugly son Broteas carved the oldest image of the Mother of the Gods, which still stands on the Coddinian Crag, to the north of Mount Sipylus. He was a famous hunter, but refused to honour Artemis, who drove him mad; crying aloud that no flame could burn him, he threw himself upon a lighted pyre and let the flames consume him.

Pelops and Oenomaus

Pelops inherited the Paphlagonian throne from his father Tantalus, and for a while resided at Enete, on the shores of the Black Sea, whence he also ruled over the Lydians and Phrygians. But he was expelled from Paphlagonia by the barbarians, and retired to Lydian Mount Sipylus, his ancestral seat. When Ilus, King of Troy, would not let him live in peace even there, but ordered him to move on, Pelops brought his fabulous treasures across the Aegean Sea. He was resolved to make a new home for himself and his great horde of followers, but first to sue for the hand of Hippodameia, daughter of King Oenomaus, the Arcadian, who ruled over Pisa and Elis.

Whether he had been warned by an oracle that his son-in-law would kill him, or whether he had himself fallen in love with Hippodameia, is disputed; but Oenomaus devised a new way to prevent her from ever getting married. He challenged each of Hipodameia's suitors in turn to a chariot race, and laid out a long course from Pisa, which lies beside the river Alpheius, opposite Olympia, to Poseidon's altar on the Isthmus of Corinth. Oenomaus insisted that Hippodameia must ride beside each suitor, thus distracting his attention from the team — but allowed him a start of half an hour or so, while he himself sacrificed a ram on the altar of Warlike Zeus at Olympia. Both chariots would then race towards the Isthmus and the suitor, if overtaken, must die; but should he win the race, Hippodameia would be his, and Oenomaus must die. Since, however, the wind-begotten mares, Psylla and Harpinna, which Ares had given him, were immeasurably the best in Greece, being swifter even than the North Wind; and since his chariot, skilfully driven by Myrtilus, was especially designed for racing, he had never yet failed to overtake his rival and transfix him with his spear, another gift from Ares.

Myrtilus, Oenomaus's charioteer, was the son of Hermes by Theobule. He too had fallen in love with Hippodameia, but dared not enter the contest. Meanwhile, the Olympians had decided to intervene and put an end to the slaughter, because Oenomaus was boasting that he would one day build a temple of skulls, as Evenus, Diomedes, and Antaeus had done. When therefore Pelops, landing in Elis, begged his lover Poseidon, whom he invoked with a sacrifice on the seashore, either to give him the swiftest chariot in the world for his

Bronze statue of a charioteer
(Archaeological Museum, Delphi)

141

courtship of Hippodameia, or to stay the rush of Oenomaus's brazen spear, Poseidon was delighted to be of assistance. Pelops soon found himself the owner of a winged golden chariot, which could race over the sea without wetting the axles, and was drawn by a team of tireless, winged, immortal horses.

Having visited Mount Sipylus and dedicated to Temnian Aphrodite an image made of green myrtle-wood, Pelops tested his chariot by driving it across the Aegean Sea. Almost before he had time to glance about him, he had reched Lesbos, where his charioteer Cillus died because of the swiftness of the flight. Pelops spent the night in Lesbos and, in a dream, saw Cillus's ghost lamenting his fate, and pleading for heroic honours. At dawn, he burned his body, heaped a barrow over the ashes, and founded the sanctuary of Cillaean Apollo close by. Then he set out again, driving the chariot himself.

On coming to Pisa, Pelops was alarmed to see the row of heads nailed above the palace gates, and began to regret his ambition. He therefore promised Myrtilus, if he betrayed his master, half the kingdom and the privilege of spending the bridal night with Hippodameia when she had been won.

Before entering the race Pelops sacrificed to Cydonian Athene. Some say that Cillus's ghost appeared and undertook to help him; others, that Sphaerus was his charioteer; but it is more generally believed that he drove his own team, Hippodameia standing beside him.

Meanwhile, Hippodameia had fallen in love with Pelops and, far from hindering his progress, had herself offered to reward Myrtilus generously, if her father's course could by some means be checked. Myrtilus therefore removed the lynch-pins from the axles of Oenomaus's chariot, and replaced them with others made of wax. As the chariots reached the neck of the Isthmus and Oenomaus, in hot pursuit, was poising his spear, about to transfix Pelops's back, the wheels of his chariot flew off, he fell entangled in the wreckage and was dragged to death. His ghost later haunted the Horse-scarer at Olympia. But Oenomaus, before he died, laid a curse on Myrtilus, praying that he might perish at the hands of Pelops.

Pelops, Hippodameia, and Myrtilus then set out for an evening drive across the sea. 'Alas!' cried Hippodameia, 'I have drunk nothing all day; thirst parches me.' The sun was setting and Pelops called a halt at the desert island of Helene, which lies not far from the island of Euboea, and went up the strand in search of water. When he returned with his helmet filled, Hippodameia ran weeping towards him and complained that Myrtilus had tried to ravish her. Pelops sternly rebuked Myrtilus, and struck him in the face, but he protested indignantly: 'This is the bridal night, on which you swore that I should enjoy Hippodameia. Will you break your oath?' Pelops made no reply, but took the reins from Myrtilus and drove on. As they approached Cape Geraestus Pelops dealt Myrtilus a sudden kick, which sent him flying head-long into the sea; and Myrtilus, as he sank, laid a curse on Pelops and all his house.

Hermes set Myrtilus's image among the stars as the constellation of the Charioteer; but his corpse was washed ashore on the coast of Euboea and buried in Arcadian Pheneus, behind the temple of Hermes.

Pelops drove on, until he reached the western stream of Oceanus, where he was cleansed of blood guilt by Hephaestus; afterwards he came back to Pisa, and succeeded to the throne of Oceanus. He soon subjugated nearly the whole of what was then known as Apia, or Pelasgiotis, and renamed it the Peloponnese, meaning 'the island of Pelops', after himself. His courage, wisdom, wealth, and numerous children, earned him the envy and veneration of all Greece.

To atone for the murder of Myrtilus, who was Hermes's son, Pelops built the first temple of Hermes in the Peloponnese; he also tried to appease Myrtilus's ghost by building a cenotaph for him in the hippodrome at Olympia, and paying him heroic honours. Some say that Oenomaus was not the true Horse-scarer: it was the ghost of Myrtilus.

Over the tomb of Hippodameia's unsuccessful suitors, on the farther side of the river Alpheius, Pelops raised a tall barrow, paying them heroic honours too; and about a furlong away stood the sanctuary of Artemis Cordax, so called because Pelops's followers there celebrated his victories by dancing the Rope Dance, which they had brought from Lydia.

Atreus and Thyestes

Eurystheus's father, Sthenelus, having banished Amphitryon, and seized the throne of Mycenae, sent for Atreus and Thyestes, his brothers-in-law, and installed them at near-by Midea. A few years later, when Sthenelus and Eurystheus were both dead, an oracle advised the Mycenaeans to choose a prince of the Pelopid house to rule over them. They thereupon summoned Atreus and Thyestes from Midea and debated which of these two (who were fated to be always at odds) should be crowned king.

Now, Atreus had once vowed to sacrifice the finest of his flocks to Artemis; and Hermes, anxious to avenge the death of Myrtilus on the Pelopids, consulted his old friend Goat-Pan, who made a horned lamb with a golden fleece appear among the Acarnanian flock which Pelops had left to his sons Atreus and Thyestes. He foresaw that Atreus would claim it as his own and, from his reluctance to give Artemis the honours due to her, would become involved in fratricidal war with Thyestes. Atreus kept his vow, in part at least, by sacrificing the lamb's flesh; but he stuffed and mounted the fleece and locked it in a chest. He grew so proud of his life-like treasure that he could not refrain from boasting about it in the market place, and the jealous Thyestes, for whom Atreus's newly married wife Aerope had conceived a passion, agreed to be her lover if she gave him the lamb. For Artemis had laid a curse upon it, and this was her doing.

In the debate Atreus claimed the throne of Mycenae by right of primogeniture, and also as possessor of the lamb. Thyestes asked him: 'Do you then publicly declare that its owner should be king?' 'I do,' Atreus replied. 'And I concur,' said Thyestes, smiling grimly. A herald then summoned the people of Mycenae to acclaim their new king, but Thyestes unexpectedly rose to upbraid Atreus as a vainglorious boaster, and led the magistrates to his home, where he displayed the lamb, justified his claim to its ownership, and was pronounced the rightful king of Mycenae.

Zeus, however favoured Atreus, and sent Hermes to him, saying: 'Call Thyestes, and ask him whether, if the sun goes backward on the dial, he will resign his claim to the throne in your favour?' Atreus did as he was told, and Thyestes agreed to abdicate should such a portent occur. Thereupon Zeus reversed the laws of Nature. Helius, already in mid-career, wrested his chariot about and turned his horses' heads towards the dawn. The seven Pleiades, and all the other stars, retraced their courses; and that evening, fo the first and last time, the sun set in the east. Thyestes's deceit and greed being thus plainly attested, Atreus succeeded to the throne of Mycenae, and banished him.

When, later, Atreus discovered that Thyestes had committed adultery with Aerope, he could hardly contain his rage. Nevertheless, for a while he feigned forgiveness.

Atreus now sent a herald to lure Thyestes back to Mycenae, with the offer of an amnesty and a half-share in the kingdom; but, as soon as Thyestes accepted this, slaughtered Aglaus, Orchomenus, and Callileon, Thyestes's three sons by one of the Naiads, on the very

Helius (National Archaeological Museum, Athens)

altar of Zeus where they had taken refuge; and then sought out and killed the infant Pleisthenes the Second, and Tantalus the Second, his twin. He hacked them all limb from limb, and set chosen morsels of their flesh, boiled in a cauldron, before Thyestes, to welcome him on his return. When Thyestes had eaten heartily, Atreus sent in their bloody heads and feet and hands, laid out on another dish, to show him what was now inside his belly. Thyestes fell back, vomiting, and laid an ineluctable curse upon the seed of Atreus.

Exiled once more, Thyestes fled first to King Thesprotus at Sicyon, where his own daughter Pelopia was a priestess. For, desiring revenge at whatever cost, he had consulted the Delphic Oracle and been advised to beget a son on his own daughter. Thyestes found Pelopia sacrificing by night to Athene Colocasia and, being loth to profane the rites, concealed himself in a near-by grove. Presently Pelopia, who was leading the solemn dance, slipped in a pool of blood that had flowed from the throat of a back ewe, the victim, and stained her tunic. She ran at once to the temple fish-pond, removed her tunic and was washing out the stain, when Thyestes sprang from the grove and ravished her. Pelopia did not recognize him, because he was wearing a mask, but contrived to steal his sword; and Thyestes, finding the scabbard empty and fearing detection, escaped to Lydia, the land of his fathers.

Meanwhile, fearing the consequences of his crime, Atreus consulted the Delphic Oracle, and was told: 'Recall Thyestes from Sicyon!' He reached Sicyon too late to meet Thyestes and, falling in love with Pelopia, whom he assumed to be King Thesprotus's daughter, asked leave to make her his third wife; having by this time executed Aerope. Thesprotus did not undeceive Atreus, and the wedding took place at once. In due course she bore the son begotten on her by Thyestes, whom she exposed on a mountain; but goatherds rescued him and gave him to a she-goat for suckling — hence his

145

name, Aegisthus, or 'goat-strength'. Atreus believed that Thyestes had fled from Sicyon at news of his approach; that the child was his own; and that Pelopia had been affected by the temporary madness which sometimes overtakes women after childbirth. He therefore recovered Aegisthus from the goatherds and reared him as his heir.

A succession of bad harvests then plagued Mycenae, and Atreus sent his sons, Agamemnon and Menelaus, to Delphi for news of Thyestes, whom they met by chance on his return from a further visit to the Oracle. They haled him back to Mycenae, where Atreus, having thrown him into prison, ordered Aegisthus, then seven years of age, to kill him as he slept.

Thyestes awoke suddenly to find Aegisthus standing over him, sword in hand; he quickly rolled sideways and escaped death. Then he rose, disarmed the boy with a shrewd kick at his wrist, and sprang to recover the sword. But it was his own, lost years before in Sicyon!

Menelaus (Museo delle Terme, Rome)

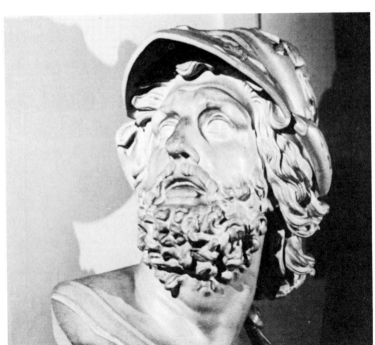

Agamemnon. Detail of vase (British Museum)

He seized Aegisthus by the shoulder and cried: 'Tell me instantly how this came into your possession?' Aegisthus stammered: 'Alas, my mother Pelopia gave it me.' 'I will spare your life, boy,' said Thyestes, 'if you carry out the three orders I now give you.' 'I am your servant in all things,' wept Aegisthus, who had expected no mercy. 'My first order is to bring your mother here,' Thyestes told him.

Aegisthus thereupon brought Pelopia to the dungeon and, recognizing Thyestes, she wept on his neck, called him her dearest father, and commiserated with his sufferings. 'How did you come by this sword, daughter?' Thyestes asked. 'I took it from the scabbard of an unknown stranger who ravished me one night at Sicyon,' she replied. 'It is mine,' said Thyestes. Pelopia, stricken with horror, seized the sword, and plunged it into her breast. Aegisthus stood aghast, not understanding what had been said. 'Now take this sword to Atreus,' was Thyestes's second order, 'and tell him that you have carried out your commission. Then return!' Dumbly Aegisthus took the bloody thing to Atreus, who went joyfully down to the seashore, where he offered a sacrifice of thanksgiving to Zeus, convinced that he was rid of Thyestes at last.

When Aegisthus returned to the dungeon, Thyestes revealed himself as his father, and issued his third order: 'Kill Atreus, my son Aegisthus, and this time do not falter!' Aegisthus did as he was told, and Thyestes reigned once more in Mycenae.

Another golden-fleeced horned lamb then appeared among Thyestes's flock and grew to be a ram and, afterwards, every new Pelopid king was thus divinely confirmed in possession of his golden sceptre; these rams grazed at ease in a paddock enclosed by unscalable walls.

Agamemnon and Clytaemnestra

When Aegisthus killed Atreus, his sons, Agammenon and Menelaus, were still infants. Snatching them up, one under each arm, their nurse fled with them to Polypheides, king of Sicyon, at whose instance they were subsequently entrusted to Oeneus the Aetolian. After they had spent some years at Oeneus's court, King Tyndareus of Sparta restored their fortunes. Marching against Mycenae, he exacted an oath from Thyestes that he would bequeath the sceptre to Agamemnon, as Atreus's heir, and go into exile, never to return. Thyestes thereupon departed to Cythera, while Aegisthus, fearing Agamemnon's vengeance, fled to King Cylarabes, son of King Sthenelus the Argive.

Agamemnon first made war against Tantalus, King of Pisa, killed him in battle and forcibly married his widow Clytaemnestra, whom Leda had borne to King Tyndareus of Sparta. The Dioscuri, Clytaemnestra's brothers, thereupon marched on Mycenae; but Agamemnon had already gone to his benefactor Tyndareus, who forgave him and let him keep Clytaemnestra. After the death of the Dioscuri, Menelaus married their sister Helen, and Tyndareus abdicated in his favour. Clytaemnestra bore Agamemnon one son, Orestes, and three daughters: Electra, Iphigeneia, and Chrysothemis.

When Paris, the son of King Priam of Troy, abducted Helen and thus provoked the Trojan War, both Agamemnon and Menelaus were absent from home for ten years; but Aegisthus did not join their expedition, preferring to stay behind at Argos and seek revenge on the House of Atreus.

Now, Nauplius, the husband of Clymene, having failed to obtain requital from Agamemnon and the other Greek leaders for the stoning of his son Palamedes, had sailed away from Troy and coasted around Attica and the Peloponnese, inciting the lonely wives of his enemies to adultery. Aegisthus, therefore, when he heard that Clytaemnestra was among those most eager to be convinced by Nauplius, planned not only to become her lover, but to kill Agamemnon, with her assistance, as soon as the Trojan War ended.

Hermes, sent to Aegisthus by Omniscient Zeus, warned him to abandon this project, on the ground that when Orestes had grown to manhood, he would be bound to avenge his father. However, Hermes failed to deter Aegisthus. At first, Clytaemnestra rejected his advances, because Agamemnon, apprised of Nauplius's visit to Mycenae, had instructed his court bard to keep close watch on her and report to him, in writing, the least sign of infidelity. But Aegisthus seized the old minstrel and marooned him without food on a lonely island, where birds of prey were soon picking his bones. Clytaemnestra then yielded to Aegisthus's embraces, and he celebrated his unhoped-for success with burnt offerings to Aphrodite, and gifts of tapestries and gold to Artemis, who was nursing a grudge against the House of Atreus.

Clytaemnestra had small cause to love Agamemnon: after killing her former husband Tantalus, and the new-born child at her breast, he had married her by force, and then gone away to a war which promised never to end; he had also sanctioned the sacrifice of Iphigeneia at Aulis, and was said to be bringing back Priam's daughter Cassandra, the prophetess, as his wife in all but name. It is true that Cassandra had borne Agamemnon twin sons: Teledamus and Pelops, but he does not seem to have intended any insult to Clytaemnestra. Her informant had been Nauplius's surviving son Oeax who, in vengeance for his brother's death, was maliciously provoking her to do murder.

Clytaemnestra therefore conspired with Aegisthus to kill both Agamemnon and Cassandra. Fearing, however, that they might arrive unexpectedly, she wrote Agamemnon a letter asking him to light a beacon on Mount Ida when Troy fell; and herself arranged for a chain of fires to relay his signal to Argolis. A watchman was also stationed on the roof of the palace at Mycenae, gazing towards Mount Arachne. At last, one dark night, he saw the distant beacon blaze and ran to wake Clytaemnestra. Aegisthus thereupon posted one of his own men in a watch-tower near the sea, promising him two gold talents for the first news of Agamemnon's landing.

No sooner had Agamemnon disembarked, than he bent down to kiss the soil, weeping for joy. Meanwhile the watchman hurried to Mycenae to collect his fee, and Aegisthus chose twenty of the boldest warriors, posted them in ambush inside the palace, ordered a great banquet and then, mounting his chariot, rode down to welcome Agamemnon.

Clytaemnestra greeted her travel-worn husband with every appearance of delight, unrolled a purple carpet for him, and led him to the bath-house; but Cassandra remained outside the palace, caught in a prophetic trance, refusing to enter, and crying that she smelt blood, and that the curse of Thyestes was heavy upon the dining-hall. When Agamemnon had washed himself and set one foot out of the bath, Clytaemnestra came forward, as if to wrap a towel about him, but instead threw over his head a garment of net. Entangled in this, like a fish, Agamemnon perished at the hands of Aegisthus, who struck him twice with a two-edged sword. He fell back, into the silver-sided bath, where Clytaemnestra avenged her wrongs by beheading him with an axe. She then ran out to kill Cassandra with the same weapon, not troubling first to close her husband's eyelids or mouth; but wiped off on his hair the blood which had splashed her, to signify that he had brought about his own death.

A fierce battle was now raging in the palace, between Agamemnon's bodyguard and Aegisthus's supporters, but Aegisthus won the day. Outside, Cassandra's head rolled to the ground, and Aegisthus also had the satisfaction of killing her twin sons by Agamemnon; yet he failed to do away with another of Agamemnon's bastards, by name Halesus, who contrived to make his escape and, after long wandering in exile, founded the Italian city of Falerii.

The Vengeance of Orestes

Orestes was reared by his loving grand-parents Tyndareus and Leda and, as a boy, accompanied Clytaemnestra and Iphigeneia to Aulis. On the evening of the murder, Orestes, then ten years of age, was rescued by his sister Electra who, aided by her father's ancient tutor, wrapped him in a robe embroidered with wild beasts, which she herself had woven, and smuggled him out of the city.

After hiding for a while among the shepherds of the river Tanus, which divides Argolis from Laconia, the tutor made his way with Orestes to the court of Strophius, a firm ally of the House of Atreus, who ruled over Crisa, at the foot of Mount Parnassus. At Crisa, Orestes found an adventurous playmate, namely Strophius's son

Pylades, who was somewhat younger than himself, and their friend-ship was destined to become proverbial. From the old tutor he learned with grief that Agamemnon's body had been flung out of the house and hastily buried by Clytaemnestra, without either libations or myrtle-boughs; and that the people of Mycenae had been forbidden to attend the funeral.

Aegisthus reigned at Mycenae for seven years, yet he was little more than a slave to Clytaemnestra, the true ruler of Mycenae, and he lived in abject fear of vengeance. Even while surrounded by a trusty foreign bodyguard, he never passed a single night in sound sleep, and had offered a handsome reward for Orestes's assasination.

Electra had been betrothed to her cousin Castor of Sparta, before his death and demi-deification. Though the leading princes of Greece now contended for her hand, Aegisthus feared that she might bear a son to avenge Agamemnon, and therefore announced that no suitor could be accepted. He would gladly have destroyed Electra, who showed him implacable hatred, lest she lay secretly with one of the Palace officers and bore him a bastard; but Clytaemnestra, feeling no qualms about her part in Agamemnon's murder, and scrupulous not to incur the displeasure of the gods, forbade him to do so. She allowed him, however, to marry Electra to a Mycenaean peasant who, being afraid of Orestes and also chaste by nature, never consummated their unequal union.

Thus, negelected by Clytaemnestra, who had now borne Aegisthus

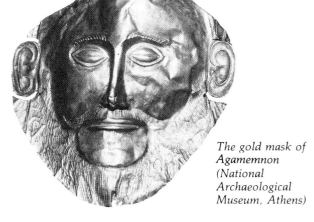

The gold mask of Agamemnon (National Archaeological Museum, Athens)

three children, by name Erigone, Aletes, and the second Helen, Electra lived in disgraceful poverty, and was kept under constant close supervision. In the end it was decided that, unless she would accept her fate, as her sister Chrysothemis had done, and refrain from publicly calling Aegisthus and Clytaemnestra 'murderous adulterers', she would be banished to some distant city and there confined in a dungeon where the light of the sun never penetrated. Yet Electra despised Chrysothemis for her subservience and disloyalty to their dead father, and secretly sent frequent reminders to Orestes of the vengeance required from him.

Orestes, now grown to manhood, visited the Delphic Oracle, to enquire whether or not he should destroy his father's murderers. Apollo's answer, authorized by Zeus, was that if he neglected to avenge Agamemnon he would become an outcast from society, debarred from entering any shrine or temple, and afflicted with a leprosy that ate into his flesh, making it sprout white mould. He was recommended to pour libations beside Agamemnon's tomb, lay a ringlet of his hair upon it and, unaided by any company of spearmen, craftily exact the due punishment from the murderers. At the same time the Pythoness observed that the Erinnyes would not readily forgive a matricide, and therefore, on behalf of Apollo, she gave Orestes a bow of horn, with which to repel their attacks, should they become insupportable. After fulfilling his orders, he must come again to Delphi, where Apollo would protect him.

In the eighth year Orestes secretly returned to Mycenae, by way of Athens, determined to destroy both Aegisthus and his own mother.

One morning, with Pylades at his side, he visited Agamemnon's tomb and there, cutting off a lock of his hair, he invoked Infernal Hermes, patron of fatherhood. When a group of slave-women approached, dirty and dishevelled for the purposes of mourning, he took shelter in a near-by thicket to watch them. Now, on the previous night, Clytaemnestra had dreamed that she gave birth to a serpent, which she wrapped in swaddling clothes and suckled. Suddenly she screamed in her sleep, and alarmed the whole Palace by crying that the serpent had drawn blood from her breast, as well as milk. The opinion of the sooth-sayers whom she consulted was that she had incurred the anger of the dead; and those mourning slave-women consequently came on her behalf to pour libations upon Agamemnon's tomb, in the hope of appeasing his ghost. Electra, who was one of the party, poured the libations in her own name, not her mother's; offered prayers to Agamemnon for vengeance, instead of pardon; and bade Hermes summon Mother Earth and the gods of the Underworld to hear her plea. Noticing a ringlet of fair hair upon the tomb, she decided that it could belong only to Orestes: both because it closely resembled her own in colour and texture, and because no one else would have dared to make such an offering.

Torn between hope and doubt, she was measuring her feet against Orestes's foot-prints in the clay beside the tomb, and finding a family resemblance, when he emerged from his hiding-place, showed her the ringlet was his own, and produced the robe in which he had escaped from Mycenae.

Electra welcomed him with delight, and together they invoked their ancestor, Father Zeus, whom they reminded that Agamemnon had always paid him great honour and that, were the House of Atreus to die out, no one would be left in Mycenae to offer him the customary hecatombs: for Aegisthus worshipped other deities.

When the slave-women told Orestes of Clytaemnestra's dream he recognized the serpent as himself, and declared that he would indeed play the cunning serpent and draw blood from her false body. Then he instructed Electra to enter the Palace and tell Clytaemnestra nothing about their meetng; he and Pylades would follow, after an interval, and beg hospitality at the gate, as strangers and suppliants, pretending to be Phocians and using the Parnassian dialect. If the porter refused them admittance, Aegisthus's inhospitality would outrage the city; if he granted it, they would not fail to take vengeance.

Presently Orestes knocked at the Palace gate, and asked for the master or mistress of the house. Clytaemnestra herself came out, but did not recognize Orestes. He pretended to be an Aeolian from Daulis, bearing sad news from one Strophius, whom he had met by chance on the road to Argos: namely, that her son Orestes was dead, and that his ashes were being kept in a brazen urn. Strophius wished to know whether he should send these back to Mycenae, or bury them at Crisa.

Clytaemnestra at once welcomed Orestes inside and, concealing her joy from the servants, sent his old nurse, Geilissa to fetch Aegisthus from a near-by temple. But Geilissa saw through Orestes's disguise and, altering the message, told Aegisthus to rejoice because he could now safely come alone and weaponless to greet the bearers of glad tidings: his enemy was dead.

Unsuspectingly, Aegisthus entered the Palace where, to create a further distraction, Pylades had just arrived, carrying a brazen urn.

He told Clytaemnestra that it held Orestes's ashes, which Strophius had now decided to send to Mycenae. This seeming confirmation of the first message put Aegisthus completely off his guard; thus Orestes had no difficulty in drawing his sword and cutting him down. Clytaemnestra then recognized her son, and tried to soften his heart by baring her breast, and appealing to his filial duty; Orestes, however, beheaded her with a single stroke of the same sword, and she fell beside the body of her paramour. Standing over the corpses, he addressed the Palace servants, holding aloft the still blood-stained net in which Agamemnon had died, eloquently exculpating himself for the murder of Clytaemnestra by this reminder of her treachery, and adding that Aegisthus had suffered the sentence prescribed by law for adulterers.

Not content with killing Aegisthus and Clytaemnestra, Orestes next disposed of the second Helen, their daughter; and Pylades beat off the sons of Nauplius, who had come to Aegisthus's rescue.

The Trial of Orestes
The Mycenaeans who had supported Orestes in his unheard-of action would not allow the bodies of Clytaemnestra and Aegisthus to lie within their city, but buried them at some distance beyond the walls. That night, Orestes and Pylades stood guard at Clytaemnestra's tomb, lest anyone should dare to rob it; but, during their vigil, the serpent-haired, dog-headed, bat-winged Erinnyes appeared, swinging their scourges. Driven to distraction by these fierce attacks, against which Apollo's bow of horn was of little avail, Orestes fell prostrate on a couch, where he lay for six days, his head wrapped in a cloak — refusing either to eat or to wash.

Old Tyndareus now arrived from Sparta, and brought a charge of matricide against Orestes, summoning the Mycenaean chieftains to judge his case. He decreed that, pending the trial, none should speak either to Orestes or Electra, and that both should be denied shelter, fire, and water. Thus Orestes was prevented even from washing his blood-stained hands.

Meanwhile, Menelaus, laden with treasure, landed at Nauplia, where a fisherman told him that Aegisthus and Clytaemnestra had been murdered. He sent Helen ahead to confirm the news at Mycenae; but by night, lest the kinsmen of those who had perished at Troy should stone her. Helen, feeling ashamed to mourn in public for her sister Clytaemnestra, since she herself had caused even more bloodshed by her infidelities, asked Electra, who was now nursing the

*Orestes and Electra (National
Museum, Naples)*

afflicted Orestes: 'Pray, niece, take offerings of my hair and lay them
on Clytaemnestra's tomb, after pouring libations to her ghost.'
Electra, when she saw that Helen had been prevented by vanity from
cutting off more than the very tips of her hair, refused to do so. 'Send
your daughter Hermione instead,' was her curt advice. Helen
thereupon summoned Hermione from the palace.

Menelaus then entered the palace, where he was greeted by his
foster-father Tyndareus, clad in deep mourning, and warned not to
set foot on Spartan soil until he had punished his criminal nephew and
niece. Tyndareus held that Orestes should have contented himself
with allowing his fellow-citizens to banish Clytaemnestra. If they had
demanded her death he should have interceded on her behalf. As
matters now stood, they must be persuaded, willy-nilly, that not only

155

Orestes, but Electra who had spurred him on, should be stoned to death as matricides.

Fearing to offend Tyndareus, Menelaus secured the desired verdict. But at the eloquent plea of Orestes himself, who was present in court and had the support of Pylades, the judges commuted the sentence to one of suicide. Pylades then led Orestes away, nobly refusing to desert either him or Electra, to whom he was betrothed; and proposed that, since all three must die, they should first punish Menelaus's cowardice and disloyalty by killing Helen, the originator of every misfortune that had befallen them. While, therefore, Electra waited outside the walls to intercept Hermione on her return from Clytaemnestra's tomb and hold her as a hostage for Menelaus's good behaviour, Orestes and Pylades entered the palace, with swords hidden beneath their cloaks, and took refuge at the central altar, as though they were suppliants. Helen, who sat near by, was deceived by their lamentations, and approached to welcome them. Whereupon both drew their swords and, while Pylades chased away Helen's Phrygian slaves, Orestes attempted to murder her. But Apollo, at Zeus's command, rapt her in a cloud to Olympus, where she became an immortal; joining her brothers, the Dioscuri, as a guardian of sailors in distress.

Meanwhile, Electra had secured Hermione, led her into the palace, and barred the gates. Menelaus, seeing his daughter threatened, ordered an immediate rescue. His men burst open the gates, and Orestes was just about to set the palace alight, kill Hermione, and die himself either by sword or fire, when Apollo providentially appeared, wrenched the torch from his hand, and drove back Menelaus's warriors. Apollo commanded Menelaus to take another wife, betroth Hermione to Orestes, and return to rule over Sparta; Clytaemnestra's murder need no longer concern him, now that the gods had intervened.

Orestes then set out for Delphi, still pursued by the Erinnyes. The Pythian Priestess was terrified to see him crouched as a suppliant on the marble navel-stone — stained by the blood from his unwashed hands — and the hideous troop of black Erinnyes sleeping beside him. Apollo, however, reassured her by promising to act as an advocate for Orestes, whom he ordered to face his ordeal with courage. After a period of exile, he must make his way to Athens, and there embrace the ancient image of Athene who, as the Dioscuri had already prophesied, would shield him with her Gorgon-faced aegis, and annul the curse. While the Erinnyes were still fast asleep, Orestes escaped under the guidance of Hermes.

Orestes's exile lasted for one year: he wandered far, over land and sea, pursued by the tireless Erinnyes and constantly purified both with the blood of pigs and with running water; yet these rites never served to keep his tormentors at bay for more than an hour or two, and he soon lost his wits.

When a year had passed, Orestes visited Athens, which was then governed by his kinsman Pandion. He went at once to Athene's temple on the Acropolis, sat down, and embraced her image. The Black Erinnyes soon arrived, out of breath, having lost track of him while he crossed the Isthmus. Though at his first arrival none wished to receive him, as being hated by the gods, presently some were emboldened to invite him into their houses, where he sat at a separate table and drank from a separate wine cup.

The Erinnyes, who had already begun to accuse him to the Athenians, were soon joined by Tyndareus with his grand-daughter Erigone, daughter of Aegisthus and Clytaemnestra. But Athene hurried to Athens and, swearing-in the noblest citizens as judges, summoned the Areopagus to try what was then only the second case of homicide to come before it.

In due course the trial took place, Apollo appearing as counsel for the defence, and the eldest of the Erinnyes as public prosecutrix. In an elaborate speech, Apollo denied the importance of motherhood, asserting that a woman was no more than the inert furrow in which the husbandman cast his seed; and that Orestes had been abundantly justified in his act, the father being the one parent worthy of the name. When the voting proved equal, Athene confessed herself wholly on the father's side, and gave her casting vote in favour of Orestes. Thus

A silver plate of Athene (Antikenabteilung, Charlottenburg, Berlin)

157

honourably acquitted, he returned in joy to Argolis, swearing to be a faithful ally to Athens so long as he lived. The Erinnyes, however, loudly lamented this subversal of the ancient law by upstart gods; and Erigone hanged herself for mortification.

The Pacification of the Erinnyes
In gratitude for his acquittal, Orestes dedicated an altar to Warlike Athene; but the Erinnyes threatened, if the judgement were not reversed, to let fall a drop of their own hearts' blood which would bring barrennes upon the soil, blight the crops, and destroy all the offspring of Athens. Athene nevertheless soothed their anger by flattery: acknowledging them to be far wiser than herself, she suggested that they should take up residence in a grotto at Athens, where they would gather such throngs of worshippers as they could never hope to find elsewhere. If they accepted this invitation she would decree that no house where worship was withheld from them might prosper; but they, in return, must undertake to invoke fair winds for her ships, fertility for her land, and fruitful marriages for her people — also rooting out the impious, so that she might see fit to grant Athens victory in war. The Erinnyes, after a short deliberation, graciously agreed to these proposals.

With expressions of gratitude, good wishes, and charms against withering winds, drought, blight, and sedition, the Erinnyes — henceforth addressed as the Solemn Ones — bade farewell to Athene, and were conducted by her people in a torchlight procession to the entrance of a deep grotto at the south-eastern angle of the Areopagus. Appropriate sacrifices were there offered to them, and they descended into the grotto, which now became both an oracular shrine and, like the Sanctuary of Theseus, a place of refuge for suppliants.

Yet only three of the Erinnyes had accepted Athene's generous offer; the remainder continued to pursue Orestes; and some people go so far as to deny that the Solemn Ones were ever Erinnyes. The name 'Eumenides' was first given to the Erinnyes by Orestes, in the following year, after his daring adventure in the Tauric Chersonese, when he finally succeeded in appeasing their fury at Carneia with the holocaust of a black sheep.

Iphigeneia among the Taurians
Still pursued by such of the Erinnyes as had turned deaf ears to Athene's eloquent speeches, Orestes went in despair to Delphi, where he threw himself on the temple floor and threatened to take his own

life unless Apollo saved him from their scourgings. In reply, the Pythian priestess ordered him to sail up the Bosphorus and northward across the Black Sea; his woes would end only when he had seized an ancient wooden image of Artemis from her temple in the Tauric Chersonese, and brought it to Athens.

Now, the king of the Taurians was the fleet-footed Thoas, a son of Dionysus and Ariadne, and father of Hypsipyle; and his people, so called because Osiris once yoked bulls (*tauroi*) and ploughed their land, came of Scythian stock. They lived by rapine, and whenever one of their warriors took a prisoner he beheaded him, carried the head home, and there impaled it on a tall stake above the chimney, so that his household might live under the dead man's protection. Moreover, every sailor who had been shipwrecked, or driven into their port by rough weather, was publicly sacrificed to Taurian Artemis. When they had performed certain preparatory rites, they felled him with a club and nailed his severed head to a cross; after which the body was either buried, or tossed into the sea from the precipice crowned by Artemis's temple. But any princely stranger who fell into their hands was killed with a sword by the goddess's virgin-priestess; and she threw his corpse into the sacred fire, welling up from Tartarus, which burns in the divine precinct. The ancient image of the goddess, which Orestes was ordered to seize, had fallen here from Heaven. This temple was supported by vast columns, and approached by forty steps, its altar of white marble permanently stained with blood.

Now, Iphigeneia had been rescued from sacrifice at Aulis by Artemis, wrapped in a cloud, and wafted to the Tauric Chersonese, where she was at once appointed Chief Priestess and granted the sole right of handling the sacred image. The Taurians thereafter addressed her as Artemis. Iphigeneia loathed human sacrifice, but piously obeyed the goddess.

Orestes and Pylades knew nothing of all this; they still believed that Iphigeneia had died under the sacrificial knife at Aulis. Nevertheless, they hastened to the land of the Taurians in a fifty-oared ship which, on arrival, they left at anchor, guarded by their oarsmen, while they hid in a sea-cave. It was their intention to approach the temple at nightfall, but they were surprised beforehand by some credulous herdsmen who, assuming them to be the Dioscuri, or some other pair of immortals, fell down and adored them. At this juncture Orestes went mad once more, bellowing like a calf and howling like a dog; he mistook a herd of calves for Erinnyes, and rushed from the cave, sword in hand, to slaughter them. The disillusioned herdsmen thereupon overpowered the two friends who, at Thoas's orders, were marched off to the temple for immediate sacrifice.

During the preliminary rites Orestes conversed in Greek with Iphigeneia; soon they joyfully discovered each other's identity, and on learning the nature of his mission, she began to lift down the image for him to carry away. Thoas, however, suddenly appeared, impatient at the slow progress of the sacrifice, and the resourceful Iphigeneia pretended to be soothing the image. She explained to Thoas that the goddess had avertd her gaze from the victims whom he had sent, because one was a matricide, and the other was abetting him: both were quite unfit for sacrifice. She must take them, together with the image, which their presence had polluted, to be cleansed in the sea, and offer the goddess a torchlight sacrifice of young lambs. Meanwhile, Thoas was to purify the temple with a torch, cover his head when the strangers emerged, and order everyone to remain at home and thus avoid pollution.

Thoas, wholly deceived, began to purify the temple. Presently Iphigeneia, Orestes, and Pylades conveyed the image down to the shore by torchlight but, instead of bathing it in the sea, hastily carried it aboard their ship. The Taurian temple-servants, who had come with them, now suspected treachery and showed fight. They were subdued in a hard struggle, after which Orestes's oarsmen rowed the ship away. A sudden gale, however, sprang up, driving her back towards the rocky shore, and all would have perished, had not Poseidon calmed the sea at Athene's request; with a favouring breeze, they made the Island of Sminthos.

This was the home of Chryses, the priest of Apollo, and his grandson of the same name, whose mother Chryseis now proposed to surrender the fugitives to Thoas. For, although some hold that Athene had visited Thoas, who was manning a fleet to sail in pursuit, and cajoled him so successfully that he even consented to repatriate Iphigeneia's Greek slave-women, it is certain that he came to Sminthos with murderous intentions. Then Chryses the Elder, learning the identity of his guests, revealed to Chryses the Younger that he was not, as Chryseis had always pretended, Apollo's son, but Agamemnon's, and therefore half-brother to Orestes and Iphigeneia. At this, Chryses and Orestes rushed shoulder to shoulder against Thoas, whom they succeeded in killing; and Orestes, taking up the image, sailed safely home to Mycenae, where the Erinnyes at last abandoned their chase.

The Reign of Orestes

Aegisthus's son Aletes now usurped the kingdom of Mycenae, believing that Orestes and Pylades had been sacrificed on the altar of Tauric Artemis. But Electra, doubting its truth, went to consult the Delphic Oracle. Iphigeneia had just arrived at Delphi, and was pointed out to Electra as Orestes's murderess. Revengefully she seized a firebrand from the altar and, not recognizing Iphigeneia after the lapse of years, was about to blind her with it, when Orestes himself entered and explained all. The reunited children of Agamemnon then went joyfully back to Mycenae, where Orestes ended the feud between the House of Atreus and House of Thyestes, by killing Aletes; whose sister Erigone, it is said, would also have perished by his hand, had not Artemis snatched her away to Attica.

Some say that Iphigeneia died either at Brauron, or at Megara, where she now has a sanctuary; others, that Artemis immortalized her as the Younger Hecate. Electra, married to Pylades, bore him Medon and Strophius the Second; she lies buried at Mycenae. Orestes married his cousen Hermione: by her he fathered Tisamenus, his heir and successor; and by Erigone his second wife, Penthilus.

When Menelaus died, the Spartans invited Orestes to become their king, preferring him, as a grandson of Tyndareus, to Nicostratus and Megapenthes, begotten by Menelaus on a slave-girl. Orestes who, with the help of troops furnished by his Phocian allies, had already added a large part of Arcadia to his Mycenaean domains, now made himself master of Argos as well; for King Cylarabes, grandson of Capaneus, left no issue. He also subdued Achaea but, in obedience to the Delphic Oracle, finally emigrated from Mycenae to Arcadia where, at the age of seventy, he died of a snake bite at Oresteium, or Orestia, the town which he had founded during his exile.

Orestes was buried at Tegea, but in the reign of Anaxandrides, co-king with Aristo, and the only Laconian who ever had two wives and occupied two houses at the same time, the Spartans, in despair because they had hitherto lost every battle fought with the Tegeans, sent to Delphi for advice, and were instructed to possess themselves of Orestes's bones. Since the whereabouts of these were unknown, they sent Lichas, one of Sparta's benefactors, to ask for further enlightenment. He was given the following response in hexameters:

> Level and smooth the plain of Arcadian Tegea. Go thou
> Where two winds are ever, by strong necessity, blowing;
> Where stroke rings upon stroke, where evil lies upon evil;

top: *Orestes slaying Aegisthus (National Archaeological Museum, Athens).* above: *Orestes and Clytaemnestra. Amphora (British Museum)*

162

There all-teeming earth doth enclose the prince whom
thou seekest.
Bring thou him to thy house, and thus be Tegea's master!

Because of a temporary truce between the two states, Lichas had no difficulty in visiting Tegea; where he came upon a smith forging a sword of iron, instead of bronze, and gazed open-mouthed at the novel sight. 'Does this work surprise you?' cried the jovial smith. 'Well, I have something here to surprise you even more! It is a coffin, seven cubits long, containing a corpse of the same length, which I found beneath the smithy floor while I was digging yonder well.'

Lichas guessed that the winds mentioned in the verses must be those raised by the smith's bellows; the strokes those of his hammer; and the evil lying upon the evil, his hammer-head beating out the iron sword — for the Iron Age brought in cruel days. He at once returned with the news to Sparta, where the judges, at his own suggestion, pretended to condemn him for a crime of violence; then, fleeing to Tegea as if from execution, he persuaded the smith to hide him in the smithy. At midnight, he stole the bones out of the coffin and hurried back to Sparta, where he re-interred them near the sanctuary of the Fates. Spartan armies ever after were victorious over the Tegeans.

Tisamenus succeeded to his father's dominions, but was driven from the capital cities of Sparta, Mycenae, and Argos by the sons of Heracles, and took refuge with his army in Achaea. His son Cometes emigrated to Asia.

6

HERACLES

The Birth of Heracles

ELECTRYON, SON OF PERSEUS, High King of Mycenae and husband of Anazo, marched vengefully against the Taphians and Teleboans. They had joined in a successful raid on his cattle, which had resulted in the death of Electryon's eight sons. While he was away, his nephew King Amphitryon of Troezen acted as regent. 'Rule well, and when I return victorious, you shall marry my daughter Alcmene,' Electryon cried in farewell. Amphitryon, informed by the King of Elis that the stolen cattle were now in his possession, paid the large ransom demanded, and recalled Electryon to identify them. Electryon, by no means pleased to learn that Amphitryon expected him to repay this ransom, asked harshly what right had the Eleans to sell stolen property, and why did Amphitryon condone in a fraud? Disdaining to reply, Amphitryon vented his annoyance by throwing a club at one of the cows which had strayed from the herd; it struck her horns, rebounded, and killed Electryon. Thereupon Amphitryon was banished from Argolis by his uncle Sthenelus.

Amphitryon, accompanied by Alcmene, fled to Thebes, where King Creon purified him and gave his sister Perimede in marriage to Electryon's only surviving son, Licymnius, a bastard borne by a Phrygian woman named Midea. But the pious Alcmene would not lie with Amphitryon until he had avenged the death of her eight brothers. Creon therefore gave him permission to raise a Boeotian army for this purpose. Then, aided by Athenian, Phocian, Argive, and Locrian contingents, Amphitryon overcame the Teleboans and Taphians, and bestowed their islands on his allies.

Meanwhile, Zeus, taking advantage of Amphitryon's absence, impersonated him and, assuring Alcmene that her brothers were now avenged — since Amphitryon had indeed gained the required victory that very morning — lay with her all one night, to which he gave the

A cameo of Heracles (National Archaeological Museum, Athens)

length of three. For Hermes, at Zeus's command, had ordered Helius to quench the solar fires, have the Hours unyoke his team, and spend the following day at home; because the procreation of so great a champion as Zeus had in mind could not be accomplished in haste. Hermes next ordered the Moon to go slowly, and Sleep to make mankind so drowsy that no one would notice what was happening. Alcmene, wholly deceived, listened delightedly to Zeus's account of the crushing defeat inflicted on Pterelaus at Oechalia, and sported innocently with her supposed husband for the whole thirty-six hours. On the next day, when Amphitryon returned, eloquent of victory and of his passion for her, Alcmene did not welcome him to the marriage couch so rapturously as he had hoped. 'We never slept a wink last night,' she complained. 'And surely you do not expect me to listen twice to the story of your exploits?' Amphitryon, unable to understand these remarks, consulted the seer Teiresias, who told him that he had been cuckolded by Zeus; and thereafter he never dared sleep with Alcmene again, for fear of incurring divine jealousy.

Nine months later, on Olympus, Zeus happened to boast that he had fathered a son, now at the point of birth, who would be called Heracles, which means 'Glory of Hera', and rule the noble House of Perseus. Hera thereupon made him promise that any prince born before nightfall to the House of Perseus should be High King. When Zeus swore an unbreakable oath to this effect, Hera went at once to Mycenae, where she hastened the pangs of Nicippe, wife of King Sthenelus. She then hurried to Thebes, and squatted cross-legged at Alcmene's door, with her clothing tied into knots, and her fingers locked together; by which means she delayed the birth of Heracles, until Eurystheus, son of Sthenelus, a seven-months' child, already lay in his cradle. When Heracles appeared, one hour too late, he was found to have a twin, Iphicles, Amphitryon's son, younger by a night. At first, Heracles was called Alcaeus, or Palaemon.

When Hera returned to Olympus, and calmly boasted of her success in keeping Eileithyia, goddess of childbirth, from Alcmene's door, Zeus fell into a towering rage; seizing his eldest daughter Ate, who had blinded him to Hera's deceit, he took a might oath that she should never visit Olympus again. Whirled around his head by her golden hair, Ate was sent hurtling down to earth. Though Zeus could not go back on his word and allow Heracles to rule the House of Perseus, he persuaded Hera to agree that, after performing whatever twelve labours Eurystheus set him, his son should become a god.

Now, unlike Zeus's former human loves, from Niobe onwards,

Alcmene had been selected not so much for his pleasure as with a view to begetting a son powerful enough to protect both gods and men against destruction. Alcmene was the last mortal woman with whom Zeus lay, and he honoured her so highly that, instead of roughly violating her, he disguised himself as Amphitryon and wooed her with affectionate words and caresses. He knew Alcmene to be incorruptible and when he presented her with a Carchesian goblet, she accepted it without question as spoil won in the victory.

The Youth of Heracles

Alcmene, fearing Hera's jealousy, exposed her newly-born child in a field outside the walls of Thebes; and here, at Zeus's instigation, Athene took Hera for a casual stroll. 'Look, my dear! What a wonderfully robust child!' said Athene, pretending surprise as she stopped to pick him up. 'His mother must have been out of her mind to abandon him in a stony field! Come, you have milk. Give the poor little creature suck!' Thoughtlessly Hera took him and bared her breast, at which Heracles drew with such force that she flung him down in pain, and a spurt of milk flew across the sky and became the Milky Way. 'The young monster!' Hera cried. But Heracles was now immortal, and Athene returned him to Alcmene with a smile, telling her to guard and rear him well. Hera was thus Heracles's foster-mother, if only for a short while; and the Thebans therefore style him her son, and say that he had been Alcaeus before she gave him suck, but was renamed in her honour.

One evening, when Heracles had reached the age of eight or ten months and was still unweaned, Alcmene having washed and suckled her twins, laid them to rest under a lamb-fleece coverlet, on the broad brazen shield which Amphtryon had won from Pterelaus. At midnight, Hera sent two prodigious azure-scaled serpents to Amphitryon's house, with strict orders to destroy Heracles. The gates opened as they approached; they glided through, and over the marble floors to the nursery — their eyes shooting flames, and poison dripping from their fangs.

The twins awoke, to see the serpents writhed above them, with darting, forked tongues; for Zeus again divinely illumined the chamber. Iphicles screamed, kicked off the coverlet and, in an attempt to escape, rolled from the shield to the floor. His frightened cries, and the strange light shining under the nursery door, roused Alcmene. 'Up with you, Amphitryon!' she cried. Without waiting to put on his sandals, Amphitryon leaped from the cedar-wood bed, and seized his sword. At that moment the light in the nursery went out. Shouting to his drowsy slaves for lamps and torches, Amphitryon rushed in; and Heracles, who had not uttered so much as a whimper, proudly displayed the serpents, which he was in the act of strangling, one in either hand.

While Alcmene comforted the terror-stricken Iphicles, Amphitryon spread the coverlet over Heracles again, and returned to bed. At dawn, when the cock had crowed three times, Alcmene summoned the aged Teiresias and told him of the prodigy. Teiresias, after foretelling Heracles's future glories, advised her to strew a broad hearth with dry faggots of gorse, thorn and brambles, and burn the serpents upon them at midnight. In the morning, a maid-servant must collect their ashes, take them to the rock where the Sphynx had perched, scatter them to the winds, and run away without looking back. On her return, the palace must be purged with fumes of sulphur and salted spring water; and its roof crowned with wild olive. Finally, a boar must be sacrificed at Zeus's high altar. All this Alcmene did.

When Heracles ceased to be a child, Amphitryon taught him how to drive a chariot, and how to turn corners without grazing the goal. Castor gave him fencing lessons, instructed him in weapon drill, in cavalry and infantry tactics, and in the rudiments of strategy. One of Hermes's sons became his boxing teacher, and Eurytus taught him archery. But Heracles surpassed all archers ever born, even his companion Alcon, father of Phalerus the Argonaut, who could shoot through a succession of rings set on the helmets of soldiers standing in file, and could cleave arrows held up on the points of swords or lances.

Eumolpus taught Heracles how to sing and play the lyre; while Linus, son of the River-god Ismenius, introduced him to the study of literature. Once, when Eumolpus was absent, Linus gave the lyre lessons as well; but Heracles, refusing to change the principles in which he had been grounded by Eumolpus, and being beaten for his stubbornness, killed Linus with a blow of the lyre. At his trial for murder, Heracles quoted a law of Rhadamanthys, which justified forcible resistance to an aggressor, and thus secured his own acquittal. Nevertheless Amphitryon, fearing that the boy might commit further crimes of violence, sent him away to a cattle ranch, where he remained until his eighteenth year, outstripping his contemporaries in height, strength and courage. It is not known who taught Heracles astronomy, and philosophy, yet he was learned in both.

Heracles's eyes flashed fire, and he had an unerring aim, both with javelin and arrow. He ate sparingly at noon; for supper his favourite food was roast meat and Doric barley-cakes. His tunic was short-skirted and neat; and he preferred a night under the stars to one spent indoors. A profound knowledge of augury led him especially to welcome the appearance of vultures, whenever he was about to undertake a new labour. 'Vultures', he would say, 'are the most righteous of birds; they do not attack even the smallest living creature'.

Heracles claimed never to have picked a quarrel, but always to have given aggressors the same treatment as they intended for him. One Termerus used to kill travellers by challenging them to a butting match; Heracles's skull prove the stronger, and he crushed Termerus's head as though it had been an egg. Heracles was, however, naturally courteous, and the first mortal who freely yielded the enemy their dead for burial.

The Daughters of Thespius

In his eighteenth year, Heracles left the cattle ranch and set out to destroy the lion of Cithaeron, which was havocking the herds of Amphitryon and his neighbour, King Thespius, the Athenian Erectheid. The lion hd another lair on Mount Helicon, at the foot of which stands the city of Thespiae.

King Thespius had fifty daughters by his wife Megamede, daughter of Arneus. Fearing that they might make unsuitable matches, he determined that every one of them should have a child by Heracles, for Heracles lodged at Thespiae for fifty nights running. 'You may have my eldest daughter Procris as your bed-fellow,' Thespius told him hospitably. But each night another of his daughters visited Heracles, until he had lain with every one. Some say, however, that he enjoyed them all in a single night, except one, serving as his priestess in the shrine at Thespiae. But he had begotten fifty-one sons on her sisters: Procris, the eldest, bearing him the twins Antileon and Hippeus; and the youngest sister, another pair.

Having at last racked down the lion, and despatched it with an untrimmed club cut from a wild-olive tree which he uprooted on Helicon, Heracles dressed himself in its pelt and wore the gaping jaws for a helmet.

Erginus

Some years before these events, during Poseidon's festival at

Heracles and Hera. Amphora (British Museum)

Heracles (National Museum, Naples)

171

Onchestus, a trifling incident vexed the Thebans, whereupon Menoeceus's charioteer flung a stone which mortally wounded the Minyan King Clymenus. Clymenus was carried back, dying, to Orchomenus where, with his last breath, he charged his sons to avenge him. The eldest of these, Erginus, whose mother was the Boeotian princess Budeia, mustered an army, marched against the Thebans, and utterly defeated them. By the terms of a treaty the Thebans would pay Erginus an annual tribute of one hundred cattle for twenty years in requital for Clymenus's death.

Heracles, on his return from Helicon, fell in with the Minyan heralds as they went to collect the Theban tribute. When he enquired their business, they replied scornfully that they had come once more to remind the Thebans of Erginus's clemency in not lopping off the ears, nose and hands of every man in the city. 'Does Erginus indeed hanker for such tribute?' Heracles asked angrily. Then he maimed the heralds in the very manner that they had described, and sent them back to Orchomenus.

When Erginus instructed King Creon at Thebes to surrender the author of this outrage, he was willing enough to obey, because the Minyans had disarmed Thebes; nor could he hope for the friendly intervention of any neighbour, in so bad a cause. Yet Heracles persuaded his youthful comrades to strike a blow for freedom. Making a round of city temples, he tore down all the shields, helmets, breastplates, greaves, swords, and spears, which had been dedicated there as spoils. Thus Heracles armed every Theban of fighting age, taught them the use of their weapons, and himself assumed command. An oracle promised him victory if the noblest-born person in Thebes would take his own life. All eyes turned expectantly towards Antipoenus, a descendant of the Sown Men; but, when he grudged dying for the common good, his daughters Androcleia and Alcis gladly did so in his stead.

Presently, the Minyans marched against Thebes, but Heracles ambushed them in a narrow pass, killing Erginus and the greater number of his captains. This victory, won almost single-handed, he exploited by making a sudden descent on Orchomenus, where he battered down the gates, sacked the palace, and compelled the Minyans to pay a double tribute to Thebes. Unfortunately, Amphitryon, his foster-father, was killed in the fighting.

The Madness of Heracles

Heracles's defeat of the Minyans made him the most famous of heroes; and his reward was to marry King Creon's eldest daughter Megara, and be appointed protector of the city; while Iphicles married the youngest daughter. Some say that Heracles had two sons by Megara; others that he had three, four, or even eight. They are known as Alcaids.

Heracles next vanquished Pyraechmus, King of the Euboeans, an ally of the Minyans, when he marched against Thebes; and created terror throughout Greece by ordering his body to be torn in two by colts and exposed unburied beside the river Heracleius.

Hera, vexed by Heracles's excess, drove him mad. He first attacked his beloved nephew Iolaus, Iphicles's eldest son, who managed to escape his wild lunges; and then, mistaking six of his own children for enemies, shot them down, and flung their bodies into a fire, together with two other sons of Iphicles, by whose side they were performing martial exercises.

When Heracles recovered his sanity, he shut himself up in a dark chamber for some days, avoiding all human intercourse and then, after purification by King Thespius, went to Delphi, to enquire what he should do. The Pythoness, addressing him for the first time as Heracles, rather than Palaemon, advised him to reside at Tiryns; to serve Eurystheus for twelve years; and to perform whatever Labours might be set him, in payment for which he would be rewarded with immortality. At this, Heracles fell into deep despair, loathing to serve a man whom he knew to be far inferior to himself, yet afraid to oppose his father Zeus. Many friends came to solace him in his distress; and finally, when the passage of time had somewhat alleviated his pain, he placed himself at Eurystheus's disposal.

It has been said that when Heracles set forth on his Labours, Hermes gave him a sword, Apollo a bow and smooth-shafted arrows, feathered with eagle feathers; Hephaestus a golden breastplate; and Athene a robe. Athene and Hephaestus, it is added, vied with one another throughout in benefiting Heracles: she gave him enjoyment of peaceful pleasures; he, protection from the dangers of war. The gift of Poseidon was a team of horses; that of Zeus, a magnificent and unbreakable shield. Many were the stories worked on this shield in enamel, ivory, electrum, gold, and lapis lazuli; moreover, twelve serpents' heads carved about the boss clashed their jaws whenever Heracles went into battle, and terrified his opponents. The truth, however, is that Heracles scorned armour and, after his first Labour,

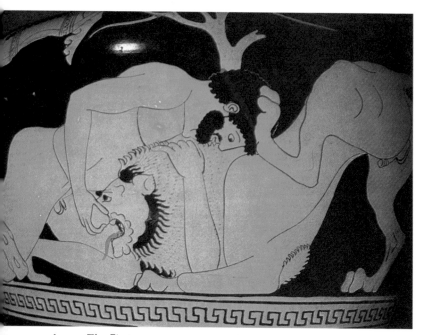

above: *The First Labour: Heracles battling with the Nemean Lion (University of Pennsylvania Museum)*

right: *The Second Labour: Hercules and the Lernaean Hydra. Red-figured vase (British Museum)*

174

The Third Labour: Heracles pursuing the Ceryneian Hind. Detail of Attic vase (British Museum)

175

seldom carried even a spear, relying rather on his club, bow and arrows. He had little use for the bronze-tipped club which Hephaestus gave him, preferring to cut his own from wild-olive: first on Helicon, next at Nemea. This second club he later replaced with a third, also cut from wild-olive, by the shores of the Saronic Sea: the club which, on his visit to Troezen, he leaned against the image of Hermes. It struck root, sprouted, and became a stately tree.

His nephew Iolaus shared in the Labours as his charioteer, or shield-bearer.

The First Labour: The Nemean Lion

The First Labour which Eurystheus imposed on Heracles, when he came to reside at Tiryns, was to kill and flay the Nemean, or Cleonaen lion, an enormous beast with a pelt proof against iron, bronze, and stone.

Arriving at Cleonae, between Corinth and Argos, Heracles lodged in the house of a day-labourer, or shepherd, named Molorchus, whose son the lion had killed. When Molorchus was about to offer a ram in propitiation of Hera, Heracles restrained him. 'Wait thirty days,' he said. 'If I return safely, sacrifice to Saviour Zeus; if I do not, sacrifice to me as a hero!'

Heracles reached Nemea at midday, but since the lion had depopulated the neighbourhood, he found no one to direct him; nor were any tracks to be seen. Having first searched Mount Apesas — so called after Apesantus, a shepherd whom the lion had killed — Heracles visited Mount Tretus, and presently descried the lion coming back to its lair, bespattered with blood from the day's slaughter. He shot a flight of arrows at it, but they rebounded harmlessly from the thick pelt, and the lion licked its chops, yawning. Next, he used his sword, which bent as though made of lead; finally he heaved up his club and dealt the lion such a blow on the muzzle that it entered its double-mouthed cave, shaking its head — not for pain, however, but because of the singing in its ears. Heracles, with a rueful glance at his shattered club, then netted one entrance of the cave, and went in by the other. Aware now that the monster was proof against all weapons, he began to wrestle with it. The lion bit off one of his fingers; but, holding its head in chancery, Heracles squeezed hard until it choked to death.

Carrying the carcass on his shoulders, Heracles returned to Cleonae, where he arrived on the thirtieth day, and found Molorchus on the point of offering him a heroic sacrifice; instead, they sacrificed together to Saviour Zeus. When this had been done, Heracles cut himself a new club and, after making several alterations in the Nemean Games hitherto celebrated in honour of Opheltes, and rededicating them to Zeus, took the lion's carcass to Mycenae. Eurystheus, amazed and terrifed, forbade him ever again to enter the city; in future he was to display the fruits of his Labours outside the gates.

For a while, Heracles was at a loss how to flay the lion, until by divine inspiration, he thought of employing its own razor-sharp claws, and soon could wear the invulnerable pelt as armour, and the head as a helmet. Meanwhile, Eurystheus ordered his smiths to forge him a bronze jar, which he buried beneath the earth. Henceforth, whenever the approach of Heracles was signalled, he took refuge in it and sent his orders by a herald — a son of Pelops, named Copreus, whom he had purified for murder.

The Second Labour: The Lernaean Hydra

The Second Labour ordered by Eurystheus was the destruction of the Lernaean Hydra, a monster born to Typhon and Echidne, and reared by Hera as a menace to Heracles.

Lerna stands beside the sea, some five miles from the city of Argos. To the west rises Mount Pontinus, with its sacred grove of plane-trees.

From the Fourth Labour: a miniature showing Eurystheus hiding in the bronze jar (Archaeological Museum, Delphi)

177

*The Fourth Labour: Heracles and the Erymanthian Boar.
Detail of vase (British Museum)*

Every year, secret nocturnal rites were held at Lerna in honour of
Dionysus, who descended to Tartarus at this point when he went to
fetch Semele; and, not far off, the Mysteries of Lernaean Demeter
were celebrated in an enclosure which marks the place where Hades
and Persephone also descended into Tartarus.

This fertile and holy district was once terrorized by the Hydra, which had its lair beneath a plane-tree at the sevenfold source of the river Amymone and haunted the unfathomable Lernaean swamp nearby, the grave of many an incautious traveller. The Hydra had a prodigious dog-like body, and eight or nine snaky heads, one of them immortal; but some credit it with fifty, or one hundred, or even ten thousand heads. At all events, it was so venomous that its very breath, or the smell of its tracks, could destroy life.

Athene had pondered how Heracles might best kill this monster and, when he reached Lerna, driven there in his chariot by Iolaus, she pointed out the Hydra's lair to him. On her advice, he forced the Hydra to emerge by pelting it with burning arrows, and then held his breath while he caught hold of it. But the monster twined around his feet, in an endeavour to trip him up. In vain did he batter at its heads with his club: no sooner was one crushed, than two or three more grew in its place.

An enormous crab scuttered from the swamp to aid the Hydra, and nipped Heracles's foot; furiously crushing its shell, he shouted to Iolaus for assistance. Iolaus set one corner of the grove alight and then, to prevent the Hydra from sprouting new heads, seared their roots with blazing branches; thus the flow of blood was checked. Now using a sword, or a golden falchion, Heracles severed the immortal head, part of which was of gold, and buried it, still hissing, under a heavy rock beside the road to Elaeus. The carcass he desembowelled, and dipped his arrows in the gall. Henceforth, the least wound from one of them was invariably fatal.

In reward for the crab's services, Hera set its image among the twelve signs of the Zodiac; and Eurystheus would not count this Labour as duly accomplished, because Iolaus had supplied the fire-brands.

The Third Labour: The Ceryneian Hind
Heracles's Third Labour was to capture the Ceryneian Hind, and bring her alive from Oenoe to Mycenae. This swift, dappled creature had brazen hooves and golden horns like a stag, so that some call her a stag. She was sacred to Artemis who, when only a child, saw five hinds, larger than bulls, grazing on the banks of the dark-pebbled Thessalian river Anaurus at the foot of the Parrhasian Mountains; the sun twinkled on their horns. Running in pursuit, she caught four of them, one after the other, with her own hands, and harnessed them to her chariot; the fifth fled across the river Celadon to the Ceryneian Hill — as Hera intended, already having Heracles's Labours in mind.

Loth either to kill or wound the hind, Heracles performed this Labour without exerting the least force. He hunted her tirelessly for one whole year, his chase taking him as far as Istria and the Land of the Hyperboreans. When, exhausted at last, she took refuge on Mount Artemisium, and thence descended to the river Ladon, Heracles let fly and pinned her forelegs together with an arrow, which passed between bone and sinew, drawing no blood. He then caught her, laid her across his shoulders, and hastened through Arcadia to Mycenae. Artemis came to meet Heracles, rebuking him for having ill-used her holy beast, but he pleaded necessity, and put the blame on Eurystheus. Her anger was thus appeased, and she let him carry the hind alive to Mycenae.

The Fourth Labour: The Erymanthian Boar

The Fourth Labour imposed on Heracles was to capture alive the Erymanthian Boar: a fierce, enormous beast which haunted the cypress-covered slopes of Mount Erymanthus, and the thickets of Arcadian Mount Lampeia; and ravaged the country around Psophis.

Heracles, passing through Pholoë on his way to Erymanthus — where he killed one Saurus, a cruel bandit — was entertained by the Centaur Pholus, whom one of the ash-nymphs bore to Silenus. Pholus set roast meat before Heracles, but himself preferred the raw, and dared not open the Centaur's communal wine jar until Heracles reminded him that it was the very jar which, four generations earlier, Dionysus had left in the cave against this very occasion. The Centaurs grew angry when they smelt the strong wine. Armed with great rocks, uprooted fir-trees, firebrands, and butchers' axes, they made a rush at Pholus's cave. While Pholus hid in terror, Heracles boldly repelled Ancius and Agrius, his first two assailants, with a volley of firebrands. Nephele, the Centaurs' cloudy grandmother, then poured down a smart shower of rain, which loosened Heracles's bow-string and made the ground slippery. However, he showed himself worthy of his former achievements, and killed several Centaurs, among them Oreus and Hylaeus. The rest fled as far as Malea, where they took refuge with Cheiron, their king, who had been driven from Mount Pelion by the Lapiths.

A parting arrow from Heracles's bow passed through Elatus's arm, and stuck quivering in Cheiron's knee. Distressed at the accident to his old friend, Heracles drew out the arrow and, though Cheiron himself supplied the vulneraries for dressing the wound, they were of no avail and he retired howling in agony to his cave; yet could not die, because he was immortal. Prometheus later offered to accept immortality in his stead, and Zeus approved the arrangement.

Pholus, in the meantime, while burying his dead kinsmen, drew out one of Heracles's arrows and examined it. 'How can so robust a creature have succumbed to a mere scratch?' he wondered. But the arrow slipped from his fingers and, piercing his foot, killed him there and then. Heracles broke off the pursuit and returned to Pholoë, where he buried Pholus with unusual honours at the foot of the mountain which has taken his name.

Heracles now set off to chase the boar by the river Erymanthus. To take so savage a beast alive was a task of unusual difficulty; but he dislodged it from a thicket with loud halloos, drove it into a deep snow drift, and sprang upon its back. He bound it in chains, and carried it alive on his shoulders to Mycenae; but when he heard that the Argonauts were gathering for their voyage to Colchis, dropped the boar outside the market place and, instead of waiting for further orders from Eurystheus, who was hiding in his bronze jar, went off with Hylas to join the expedition. It is not known who despatched the captured boar, but its tusks were preserved in the temple of Apollo at Cumae.

The Fifth Labour: The Stables of Augeias

Heracles's Fifth Labour was to cleanse King Augeias's filthy cattle yard in one day. Eurystheus gleefully pictured Heracles's disgust at having to load the dung into baskets and carry these away on his shoulders. Augeias, King of Elis, was the son of Helius, by Naupiadame, a daughter of Amphidamus. Others call him the son of Poseidon. In flocks and herds he was the wealthiest man on earth: for, by a divine dispensation, his were immune against disease and inimitably fertile, nor did they ever miscarry. Although in almost every case they produced female offspring, he nevertheless had three hundred white-legged black bulls and two hundred red stud-bulls; besides twelve outstanding silvery-white bulls, sacred to his father Helius. These twelve defended his herds against marauding wild beasts from the wooded hills.

Now, the dung in Augeias's cattle yard and sheepfolds had not been cleared away for many years, and though its noisome stench did not affect the beasts themselves, it spread a pestilence across the whole Peloponnese. Moreover, the valley pastures were so deep in dung that they could no longer be ploughed for grain.

Heracles hailed Augeias from afar, and undertook to cleanse the yard before nightfall in return for a tithe of the cattle. Augeias laughed incredulously, and called Phyleus, his eldest son, to witness Heracles's offer. 'Swear to accomplish the task before nightfall,' Phyleus demanded. The oath which Heracles now took by his father's name was the first and last one he ever swore. Augeias likewise took an oath to keep his side of the bargain.

On the advice of Menedemus the Elean, and aided by Iolaus, Heracles first breached the wall of the yard in two places, and next diverted the neighbouring rivers Alpheus and Peneius, so that their streams rushed through the yard, swept it clean and then went on to cleanse the sheepfolds and the valley pastures. Thus Heracles accomplished this Labour in one day, restoring the land to health, and not soiling so much as his little finger. But Augeias, on being informed by Copreus that Heracles had already been under orders from Eurystheus to cleanse the cattle yards, refused to pay the reward and even dared deny that he and Heracles had struck a bargain.

Heracles suggested that the case be submitted to arbitration; yet when the judges were seated, and Phyleus, subpoenaed by Heracles, testified to the truth, Augeias sprang up in a rage and banished them both from Elis, asserting that he had been tricked by Heracles, since the River-gods, not he, had done the work. To make matters even worse, Eurystheus refused to count this Labour as one of the ten, because Heracles had been in Augeias's hire.

The Sixth Labour: The Stymphalian Birds

Heracles's Sixth Labour was to remove the countless brazen-beaked, brazen-clawed, brazen-winged, man-eating birds, sacred to Ares, which, frightened by the wolves of Wolves' Ravine on the Orchomenan Road, had flocked to the Stymphalian Marsh. Here they bred and waded beside the river of the same name, occasionally taking to the air in great flocks, to kill men and beasts by discharging a shower of brazen feathers and at the same time muting a poisonous excrement, which blighted the crops.

On arrival at the marsh, which lay surrounded by dense woods, Heracles found himself unable to drive away the birds with his arrows; they were too numerous. Moreover, the marsh seemed neither solid enough to support a man walking, nor liquid enough for the use of a boat. As Heracles paused irresolutely on the bank, Athene gave him a pair of brazen castanets, made by Hephaestus; or it may have been a rattle. Standing on a spur of Mount Cyllene, which overlooks the marsh, Heracles clacked the castanets, or shook the rattle, raising such a din that the birds soared up in one great flock,

The Sixth Labour: Heracles and the Stymphalian Birds. Detail of vase
(British Museum)

183

*The Seventh Labour: Heracles capturing the Cretan
Bull. Detail of vase (British Museum)*

mad with terror. He shot down scores of them as they flew off to the
Isle of Ares in the Black Sea, where they were afterwards found by the
Argonauts.

The Seventh Labour: The Cretan Bull
Eurystheus ordered Heracles, as his Seventh Labour, to capture the
Cretan Bull withheld by Minos from sacrifice to Poseidon, which
sired the Minotaur on Pasiphaë. At this time it was ravaging Crete,
especially the region watered by the river Tethris, rooting up crops
and levelling orchard walls.

When Heracles sailed to Crete, Minos offered him every assistance
in his power, but he preferred to capture the bull single-handed,
though it belched scorching flames. After a long struggle, he brought

*The Eighth Labour: Heracles harnessing the Mares of
Diomedes*

the monster across to Mycenae, where Eurystheus, dedicating it to
Hera, set it free. Hera, however, loathing a gift which redounded to
Heracles's glory, drove the bull first to Sparta, and then back through
Arcadia and across the Isthmus to Attic Marathon, whence Theseus
later dragged it to Athens as a sacrifice to Athene.

The Eighth Labour: The Mares of Diomedes.
Eurystheus ordered Heracles, as his Eighth Labour, to capture the
four savage mares of Thracian King Diomedes — it is disputed
whether he was the son of Ares and Cyrene, or born of an incestuous
relationship between Asterië and her father Atlas — who ruled the
warlike Bistones, and whose stables, at the now vanished city of
Tirida, were the terror of Thrace. Diomedes kept the mares tethered

with iron chains to bronze mangers, and fed them on the flesh of his unsuspecting guests.

With a number of volunteers Heracles set sail for Thrace, visiting his friend King Admetus of Pherae on the way. Arrived at Tirida, he overpowered Diomedes's grooms and drove the mares down to the sea, where he left them on a knoll in charge of his minion Abderus, and then turned to repel the Bistones as they rushed in pursuit. His party being outnumbered, he overcame them by ingeniously cutting a channel which caused the sea to flood the low-lying plain; when they turned to run, he pursued them, stunned Diomedes with his club, dragged his body around the lake that had now formed, and set it before his own mares, which tore at the still living flesh. Their hunger being now fully assuaged — for, while Heracles was away, they had also devoured Abderus — he mastered them without much trouble.

The Ninth Labour: Hippolyte's Girdle

Heracles's Ninth Labour was to fetch for Eurystheus's daughter Admete the golden girdle of Ares worn by the Amazonian queen Hippolyte. Taking one ship and a company of volunteers, among whom were Iolaus, Telamon of Aegina, Peleus of Iolcus and, according to some accounts, Theseus of Athens, Heracles set sail for the river Thermodon

The Amazons were children of Ares by the Naiad Harmonia, born in the glens of Phrygian Acmonia; but some call their mother Aphrodite, or Otrere, daughter of Ares. At first they lived beside the river Amazon, now named after Tanais, a son of the Amazon Lysippe, who offended Aphrodite by his scorn of marriage and his devotion to war. In revenge, Aphrodite caused Tanais to fall in love with his mother; but, rather than yield to an incestuous passion, he flung himself into the river and drowned. To escape the reproaches of his ghost, Lysippe then led her daughters around the Black Sea coast, to a plain by the river Thermodon, which rises in the lofty Amazonian mountains. There they formed three tribes, each of which founded a city.

The Amazons reckoned descent only through the mother, and Lysippe had laid it down that the men must perform all household tasks, while the women fought and governed. The arms and legs of infant boys were therefore broken to incapacitate them for war or travel. These unnatural women, whom the Scythians call Oeorpata, showed no regard for justice or decency, but were famous warriors, being the first to employ cavalry. They carried brazen bows and short shields shaped like a half moon; their helmets, clothes, and girdles were made from the skins of wild beasts. Lysippe, before she fell in battle, built the great city of Themiscyra, and defeated every tribe as far as the river Tanais. With the spoils of her campaigns she raised temples to Ares, and others to Artemis Tauropolus whose worship she established. Her descendants extended the Amazonian empire westward across the river Tanais, to Thrace; and again, on the southern coast, westward across the Thermodon to Phrygia. Three famous Amazonian queens, Marpesia, Lampado, and Hippo, seized a great part of Asia Minor and Syria, and founded the cities of Ephesus, Smyrna, Cyrene, and Myrine. It was on this expedition that the Amazons captured Troy, Priam being then still a child. But while detachments of the Amazonian army went home laden with vast quantities of spoil, the rest, staying to consolidate their power in Asia Minor, were driven out by an alliance of barbarian tribes, and lost their queen Marpesia.

From the Ninth Labour: a bronze of an Amazon (British Museum)

By the time that Heracles came to visit the Amazons, they had all returned to the river Thermodon, and their three cities were ruled by Hippolyte, Antiope, and Melanippe. On his way, he put in at the island of Paros, famous for its marble, which King Rhadamanthys had bequeathed to one Alcaeus, a son of Androgeus; but four of Minos's sons, Eurymedon, Chryses, Nephalion, and Philolaus, had also settled there. When a couple of Heracles's crew, landing to fetch water, were murdered by Minos's sons, he indignantly killed all four of them, and pressed the Parians so hard that they sent envoys offering, in requital for the dead sailors, any two men whom he might choose to be his slaves. Satisfied by this proposal, Heracles raised the siege and chose King Alcaeus and his brother Sthenelus, whom he took aboard his ship. Next, he sailed through the Hellespont and Bosphorus to Mariandyne in Mysia, where he was entertained by King Lycus the Paphlagonian, son of Dascylus and grandson of Tantalus. In return, he supported Lycus in a war with the Bebrycans, killing many, including their king Mygdon, brother of Amycus, and recovered much Paphlagonian land from the Bebrycans; this he restored to Lycus, who renamed it Heracleia in his honour. Later, Heracleia was colonized by Megarians and Tanagrans on the advice of the Pythoness at Delphi, who told them to plant a colony beside the Black Sea, in a region dedicated to Heracles.

Arrived at the mouth of the river Thermodon, Heracles cast anchor in the harbour of Themiscyra, where Hippolyte paid him a visit and, attracted by his muscular body, offered him Ares's girdle as a love gift. But Hera had meanwhile gone about, disguised in Amazon dress spreading a rumour that these strangers planned to abduct Hippolyte; whereupon the incensed warrior-women mounted their horses and charged down on the ship. Heracles, suspecting treachery, killed Hippolyte offhand, removed her girdle, seized her axe and other weapons, and prepared to defend himself. He killed each of the Amazon leaders in turn, putting their army to flight after great slaughter.

On his return from Themiscyra, Heracles came again to Mariandyne, and competed in the funeral games of King Lycus's brother Priolas, who had been killed by the Mysians. Heracles boxed against the Mariandynian champion Titias, knocked out all his teeth and killed him with a blow to the temple. In proof of his regret for this accident, he subdued the Mysians and the Phrygians on Dascylus's behalf; but he also subdued the Bithynians, as far as the mouth of the river Rhebas and the summit of Mount Colone, and claimed their kingdom for himself. Pelops's Paphlagonians voluntarily surrendered to him. However, no sooner had Heracles departed, than the Bebrycans, under Amycus, son of Poseidon, once more robbed Lycus of his land, extending their frontier to the river Hypius.

Sailing thence to Troy, Heracles rescued Hesione from a sea-monster; and continued his voyage to Thracian Aenus, where he was entertained by Poltys; and, just as he was putting to sea again, shot and killed on the Aenian beach Poltys's insolent brother Sarpedon, a son of Poseidon. Next, he subjugated the Thracians who had settled in Thasos, and bestowed the island on the sons of Androgeus, whom he had carried off from Paros; and at Torone was challenged to a wrestling match by Polygonus and Telegonus, sons of Proteus, both of whom he killed.

Returning to Mycenae at last, Heracles handed the girdle to Eurystheus, who gave it to Admete. As for the other spoil taken from the Amazons: he presented their rich robes to the Temple of Apollo at Delphi, and Hippolyte's axe to Queen Omphale, who included it among the sacred regalia of the Lydian kings. Eventually it was taken to a Carian temple of Labradian Zeus, and placed in the hand of his divine image.

The Tenth Labour: The Cattle of Geryon
Heracles's Tenth Labour was to fetch the famous cattle of Geryon from Erytheia, an island near the Ocean stream, without either demand or payment. Geryon, a son of Chrysaor and Callirrhoë, a daughter of the Titan Oceanus, was the King of Tartessus in Spain, and reputedly the strongest man alive. He had been born with three heads, six hands, and three bodies joined together at the waist. Geryon's shambling red cattle, beasts of marvellous beauty, were guarded by the herdsman Eurythion, son of Ares, and by the two-headed watchdog Orthrus — formerly Atlas's property — born of Typhon and Echidne.

During his passage through Europe, Heracles destroyed many wild beasts and, when at last he reached Tartessus, erected a pair of pillars facing each other across the straits, one in Europe, one in Africa. (These Pillars of Heracles are usually identified with Mount Calpe in Europe, and Abyle, or Abilyx in Africa.) Some hold that the two continents were formerly joined together, and that he cut a channel between them, or thrust the cliffs apart; others say that, on the contrary, he narrowed the existing straits to discourage the entry of whales and other sea-monsters.

Helius beamed down upon Heracles who, finding it impossible to work in such heat, strung his bow and let fly an arrow at the god. 'Enough of that!' cried Helius angrily. Heracles apologized for his ill-temper, and unstrung his bow at once. Not to be outdone in courtesy, Helius lent Heracles his golden goblet, shaped like a water-lily, in which he sailed to Erytheia; but the Titan Oceanus, to try him, made the goblet pitch violently upon the waves. Heracles again drew his bow, which frightened Oceanus into calming the sea.

On his arrival, he ascended Mount Abas. The dog Orthrus rushed at him, barking, but Heracles's club struck him lifeless; and Eurytion, Geryon's herdsman, hurrying to Orthrus's aid, died in the same manner. Heracles then proceeded to drive away the cattle. Menoetes, who was pasturing the cattle of Hades near by, took the news to Geryon. Challenged to battle, Heracles ran to Geryon's flank and shot him sideways through all three bodies with a single arrow. As Hera hastened to Geryon's assistance, Heracles wounded her with an arrow in the right breast, and she fled. Thus he won the cattle, without either demand or payment, and embarked in the golden goblet, which he then sailed across to Tartessus and gratefully returned to Helius. From Geryon's blood sprang a tree which, at the time of the Pleiades' rising, bears stoneless cherry-like fruit.

How he then drove the cattle to Mycenae is much disputed, but according to a probable account he passed through the territory of Abdera, a Phoenician settlement, and then through Spain, leaving behind some of his followers as colonists. In the Pyrenees, he courted and buried the Bebrycan princess Pyrene, from whom this mountain range takes its name. He then visited Gaul, where he abolished a barbarous native custom of killing strangers, and won so many hearts by his generous deeds that he was able to found a large city, to which he gave the name Alesia, or 'Wandering', in commemoration of his travels. The Gauls honoured Alesia as the hearth and mother-city of their whole land and claimed descent from Heracles's union with a tall princess named Galata, who chose him as her lover and bred that warlike people.

When Heracles was driving Geryon's cattle through Liguria, two sons of Poseidon named Ialebion and Dercynus tried to steal them from him, and were both killed. At one stage of his battle with hostile Ligurian forces, Heracles ran out of arrows, and knelt down, in tears, wounded and exhausted. The ground being of soft mould, he could find no stones to throw at the enemy — Ligys, the brother of Ialebion, was their leader — until Zeus, pitying his tears, overshadowed the earth with a cloud, from which a shower of stones hailed down; and with these he put the Ligurians to flight. Zeus set among the stars an image of Heracles fighting the Ligurians, known as the constellation Engonasis. Another memorial of this battle survives on earth: namely the broad, circular plain lying between Marseilles and the mouths of the river Rhône, about fifteen miles from the sea, called 'The Stony Plain', because it is strewn with stones the size of a man's fist; brine springs are also found there.

In his passage over the Ligurian Alps, Heracles carved a road fit for his armies and baggage trains; he also broke up all robber bands that infested the pass, before Cis-alpine Gaul and Etruria. Only after wandering down the whole coast of Italy, and crossing into Sicily, did it occur to him: 'I have taken the wrong road!' The Romans say that, on reaching the Albula — afterwards called the Tiber — he was welcomed by King Evander, an exile from Arcadia. At evening, he swam across, driving the cattle before him, and lay down to rest on a grassy bed. In a deep cave near by, lived a vast hideous, three-headed shepherd named Cacus, a son of Hephaestus and Medusa, who was the dread and disgrace of the Aventine Forest, and puffed flames from each of his three mouths. Human skulls and arms hung nailed above the lintels of his cave, and the ground inside gleamed white with the bones of his victims. While Heracles slept, Cacus stole the two finest of his bulls; as well as four heifers, which he dragged backwards by their tails into his lair.

At the first streak of dawn, Heracles awoke, and at once noticed that the cattle were missing. After searching for them in vain, he was about to drive the remainder onward, when one of the stolen heifers lowed hungrily. Heracles traced the sound to the cave, but found the entrance barred by a rock which ten yoke of oxen could hardly have moved; nevertheless, he heaved it aside as though it had been a pebble and, undaunted by the smoky flames which Cacus was now belching, grappled with him and battered his face to pulp.

Aided by King Evander, Heracles then built an altar to Zeus, at which he sacrificed one of the recovered bulls, and afterwards made arrangements for his own worship. According to the Romans, Heracles freed King Evander from the tribute owed to the Etruscans; killed King Faunus, whose custom was to sacrifice strangers at the altar of his father Hermes; and begot Latinus, the ancestor of the Latins, on Faunus's widow, or daughter. Heracles is also believed to have founded Pompeii and Herculaneum; to have fought giants on the Phlegraean Plain of Cumae; and to have built a causeway one

top: *The Tenth Labour: Heracles fetching the Cattle of Geryon. Attic cup (Antikensammlung, Munich).* above: *The Tenth Labour: Heracles and Geryon. Attic cup (Louvre)*

mile long across the Lucrine Gulf, called the Heracleian Road, down which he drove Geryon's cattle.

It is further said that, as he lay down to rest near the frontier of Rhegium and Epizephyrian Locris, a bull broke away from the herd and, plunging into the sea, swam over to Sicily. Heracles, going in pursuit, found it concealed among the herds of Eryx, King of the Elymans, a son of Aphrodite by Butes. Eryx, who was a wrestler and boxer, challenged him to a fivefold contest. Heracles accepted the challenge, on condition that Eryx would stake his kingdom against the runaway bull, and won the first four events; finally, in the wrestling match, he lifted Eryx high into the air, dashed him to the ground and killed him — which taught the Sicilians that not everyone born of a goddess is necessarily immortal. In this manner, Heracles won Eryx's kingdom, which he left the inhabitants to enjoy until one of his own descendants should come to claim it.

Continuing on his way through Sicily, Heracles came to the site where now stands the city of Syracuse; there he offered sacrifices, and instituted the annual festival beside the sacred chasm of Cyane, down which Hades snatched Core to the Underworld. To those who honoured Heracles in the Plain of Leontini, he left undying memorials of his visit. Close to the city of Agyrium, the hoof marks of his cattle were found imprinted on a stony road, as though in wax; and, regarding this as an intimation of his own immortality, Heracles accepted from the inhabitants those divine honours which he had hitherto consistently refused. Then, in acknowledgement of their favours, he dug a lake four furlongs in circumference outside the city walls, and established local sanctuaries of Iolaus and Geryon.

Returning to Italy in search of another route to Greece, Heracles drove his cattle up the eastern coast, proposing to drive them through Istria into Epirus, and thence to the Pelopennese by way of the Isthmus. But at the head of the Adriatic Gulf Hera sent a gadfly, which stampeded the cows, driving them across Thrace and into the Scythian desert. There Heracles pursued them and, having recovered most of the strayed cattle, drove them back across the river Strymon, which he damned with stones for the purpose, and encountered no further adventures until the giant herdsman Alcyoneus, having taken possession of the Corinthian Isthmus, hurled a rock at the army which once more followed Heracles, crushing no less than twelve chariots and double that number of horsemen. This was the same Alcyoneus who twice stole Helius's sacred cattle: from Erytheia, and from the citadel of Corinth. He now ran forward, picked up the rock again, and this time hurled it at Heracles, who bandied it back with his club and so killed the giant.

The Eleventh Labour: The Apples of the Hesperides
Heracles had performed these Ten Labours in the space of eight years and one month; but Eurystheus, discounting the Second and the Fifth, set him two more. The Eleventh Labour was to fetch fruit from the golden apple-tree, Mother Earth's wedding gift to Hera, with which she had been so delighted that she planted it in her own divine garden. This garden lay on the slopes of Mount Atlas, where the panting chariot-horses of the Sun complete their journey, and where Atlas's sheep and cattle, one thousand herds of each, wander over their undisputed pastures. When Hera found, one day, that Atlas's daughters, the Hesperides, to whom she had entrusted the tree, were pilfering the apples, she set the ever-watchful dragon Ladon to coil around the tree as its guardian.

Though the apples were Hera's, Atlas took a gardener's pride in them and, when Themis warned him: 'One day long hence, Titan, your tree shall be stripped of its gold by a son of Zeus,' Atlas, who had not then been punished with his terrible task of supporting the celestial globe upon his shoulders, built solid walls around the orchard, and expelled all strangers from his land.

Heracles, not knowing in what direction the Garden of the Hesperides lay, marched through Illyria to the river Po, the home of the oracular sea-god Nereus. When Heracles came, the river-nymphs, daughters of Zeus and Themis, showed him Nereus asleep. He seized the hoary old sea-god and, clinging to him despite his many Protean changes, forced him to prophesy how the golden apples could be won.

Nereus had advised Heracles not to pluck the apples himself, but to employ Atlas as his agent, meanwhile relieving him of his fantastic burden; therefore on arriving at the Garden of the Hesperides, he asked Atlas to do him a favour. Atlas would have undertaken almost any task for the sake of an hour's respite, but he feared Ladon, whom Heracles thereupon killed with an arrow shot over the garden wall. Heracles now bent his back to receive the weight of the celestial globe, and Atlas walked away, returning presently with three apples plucked by his daughters. He found the sense of freedom delicious. 'I will take these apples to Eurystheus myself without fail,' he said, 'if you hold up the heavens for a few months longer.' Heracles pretended to agree but, having been warned by Nereus not to accept any such offer, begged Atlas to support the globe for one moment more, while he put a pad on his head. Atlas, easily deceived, laid the apples on the ground and resumed his burden; whereupon Heracles picked them up and went away with an ironical farewell.

After some months Heracles brought the apples to Eurystheus, who handed them back to him; he then gave them to Athene, and she returned them to the nymphs, since it was unlawful that Hera's property should pass from their hands. Feeling thirsty after this Labour, Heracles stamped his foot and made a stream of water gush out, which later saved the lives of the Argonauts when they were cast up high and dry on the Libyan desert. Meanwhile Hera, weeping for Ladon, set his image among the stars as the constellation of the Serpent.

Heracles did not return to Mycenae by a direct route. He first traversed Libya, whose King Antaeus, son of Poseidon and Mother Earth, was in the habit of forcing strangers to wrestle with him until they were exhausted, whereupon he killed them; for not only was he a strong and skilful athlete, but whenever he touched the earth, his strength revived. He saved the skulls of his victims to roof a temple of Poseidon. It is not known whether Heracles, who was determined to end this barbarous practice, challenged Antaeus, or was challenged by him. Antaeus, however, proved no easy victim, being a giant who lived in a cave beneath a towering cliff, where he feasted on the flesh of lions, and slept on the bare ground in order to conserve and increase his already colossal strength.

In preparation for the wrestling match, both combatants cast off their lion pelts, but while Heracles rubbed himself with oil in the Olympic fashion, Antaeus poured hot sand over his limbs lest contact with the earth through the soles of his feet alone should prove insufficient. Heracles planned to preserve his strength and wear Antaeus down, but after tossing him full length on the ground, he was amazed to see the giant's muscles swell and a healthy flush suffuse his limbs as Mother Earth revived him. The combatants grappled again, and presently Antaeus flung himself down of his own accord, not waiting to be thrown; upon which, Heracles, realizing what he was at, lifted him high into the air, then cracked his ribs and, despite the hollow groans of Mother Earth, held him aloft until he died.

Next, Heracles visited the Oracle at Ammon, and then struck south, and founded a hundred-gated city, named Thebes in honour of his birthplace; but some say that Osiris had already founded it. All this time, the King of Egypt was Antaeus's brother Busiris, a son of Poseidon by Lysianassa, the daughter of Epaphus. Now, Busiris's kingdom had once been visited with drought and famine for eight or nine years, and he had sent for Greek augurs to give him advice. His nephew, a learned Cyprian seer, named Phrasius, son of Pygmalion, announced that the famine would cease if every year one stranger were sacrificed in honour of Zeus. Busiris began with Phrasius himself, and afterwards sacrificed other chance guests, until the arrival of Heracles, who let the priests hale him off the altar. They bound his hair with a fillet, and Busiris, calling upon the gods, was about to raise the sacrificial axe when, Heracles burst his bonds and slew Busiris, Busiris's son Amphidamas, and all the priestly attendants.

Next, Heracles traversed Asia and finally reached the Caucasus Mountains, where Prometheus had been fettered while every day a griffon-vulture, born of Typhon and Echidne, tore at his liver. Zeus had long repented of his punishment, because Prometheus had since sent him a kindly warning not to marry Thetis, lest he might beget one greater than himself; and now, when Heracles pleaded for Prometheus's pardon, granted this without demur. having once, however, condemned him to everlasting punishment, Zeus stipulated that, in order still to appear a prisoner, he must wear a ring made from his chains and set with Caucasian stone — and this was the first ring ever to contain a setting. But Prometheus's sufferings were destined to last until some immortal should voluntarily go to Tartarus in his stead; so Heracles reminded Zeus of Cheiron, who was longing to resign the gift of immortality ever since he had suffered his incurable wound. Thus no further impediment remained, and Heracles, invoking Hunter Apollo, shot the griffon-vulture through the heart and set Prometheus free.

The Twelfth Labour: The Capture of Cerberus
Heracles's last, and most difficult, Labour was to bring the dog Cerberus up from Tartarus. As a preliminary, he went to Eleusis where he asked to partake of the Mysteries and wear the myrtle wreath. Since in Heracles's day Athenians alone were admitted, Theseus suggested that a certain Pylius should adopt him. This Pylius did, and when Heracles had been purified for his slaughter of the Centaurs, because no one with blood-stained hands could view the Mysteries, he was duly initiated by Orpheus's son Musaeus, Theseus acting as his sponsor.

The Eleventh Labour: Heracles holding up the world while Atlas brings him the Apples of the Hesperides. White-ground vase (National Archaeological Museum, Athens)

Thus cleansed and prepared, Heracles descended to Tartarus from Laconian Taenarum. He was guided by Athene and Hermes — for whenever, exhausted by his Labours, he cried out in despair to Zeus, Athene always came hastening down to comfort him. Terrified by Heracles's scowl, Charon ferried him across the river Styx without demur. As Heracles stepped ashore from the crazy boat, all the ghosts fled, except Meleager and the Gorgon Medusa. At the sight of Medusa he drew his sword, but Hermes reassured him that she was only a phantom; and when he aimed an arrow at Meleager, who was wearing bright armour, Meleager laughed. 'You have nothing to fear from the dead,' he said, and the chatted amicably for a while, Heracles offering in the end to marry Meleager's sister Deianeira.

Near the gates of Tartarus, Heracles found his friends Theseus and Peirithous fastened to cruel chairs, and wrenched Theseus free, but was obliged to leave Peirithous behind; next, he rolled away the stone under which Demeter had imprisoned Ascalaphus; and then, wishing to gratify the ghosts with a gift of warm blood, slaughtered one of Hades's cattle. Their herdsman, Menoetes, or Menoetius, the son of Ceuthonymus, challenged him to a wrestling match, but was seized around the middle and had his ribs crushed. At this, Persephone, who came out from her palace and greeted Heracles like a brother,

The Twelfth Labour: Heracles capturing Cerberus. Red-figured vase (Louvre)

Heracles with Apollo's tripod. Detail of red-figured vase (Wagner Museum, Würzburg)

opposite:
Heracles and the Cercopes twins. White-ground vase (Cinquantennaire, Brussels)

198

intervened and pleaded for Menoetes's life.

When Heracles demanded Cerberus, Hades, standing by his wife's side, replied grimly: 'He is yours, if you can master him without using your club or your arrows.' Heracles found the dog chained to the gates of Acheron, and resolutely gripped him by the throat — from which rose three heads, each maned with serpents. The barbed tail flew up to strike, but Heracles, protected by the lion pelt, did not relax his grip until Cerberus choked and yielded.

With Athene's assistance, Heracles recrossed the river Styx in safety, and then half-dragged, half-carried Cerberus up the chasm near Troezen, through which Dionysus had conducted his mother Semele. When Heracles brought him to Mycenae, Eurystheus, who was offering a sacrifice, handed him a slave's portion, reserving the best ˙ cuts for his own kinsmen; and Heracles showed his just resentment by killing three of Eurystheus's sons: Perimedes, Eurybius, and Erypilus.

The Murder of Iphitus
When Heracles returned to Thebes after his Labours, he gave Megara, his wife, now thirty-three years old, in marriage to his nephew and charioteer Iolaus, who was only sixteen, remarking that his own union with her had been inauspicious. He then looked about for a younger and more fortunate wife; and, hearing that his friend Eurytus, a son of Melanius, King of Oechalia, had offered to marry his daughter Iole to any archer who could outshoot him and his four sons, took the road there. Eurytus had been given a fine bow and taught its use by Apollo himself, whom he now claimed to surpass in marksmanship, yet Heracles found no difficulty in winning the contest. The result displeased Eurytus excessively and, when he learned that Heracles had discarded Megara after murdering her children, he refused to give him Iole. Having drunk a great deal of wine to gain confidence, 'You could never compare with me and my sons as an archer,' he told Heracles, 'were it not that you unfairly use magic arrows, which cannot miss their mark. This contest is void, and I would not, in any case, entrust my beloved daughter to such a ruffian as yourself! Moreover, you are Eurystheus's slave, and like a slave, deserve only blows from a free man.' So saying, he drove Heracles out of the Palace. Heracles did not retaliate at once, as he might well have done; but swore to take vengeance.

Three of Eurytus's sons, namely Didaeon. Clytius, and Toxeus, had supported their father in his dishonest pretensions. The eldest, however, whose name was Iphitus, declared that Iole should in all fairness have been given to Heracles; and when, soon afterwards, twelve strong-hooved brood-mares and twelve sturdy mule-foals disappeared from Euboea, he refused to believe that Heracles was the thief. As a matter of fact, they had been stolen by the well-known thief Autolycus, who magically changed their appearance and sold them to the unsuspecting Heracles as if they were his own. Iphitus followed the tracks of the mares and foals and found that they led towards Tiryns, which made him suspect Heracles was, after all, avenging the insult offered him by Eurytus. Coming suddenly face to face with Heracles, who had just returned from his rescue of Alcestis, he concealed his suspicions and merely asked for advice in the matter. Heracles did not recognize the beasts from Iphitus's description as those sold to him by Autolycus, and with his usual heartiness promised to search for them if Iphitus would consent to become his guest. Yet he now divined that he was suspected of theft, which galled his sensitive heart. After a grand banquet, he led Iphitus to the top of the highest tower in Tiryns. 'Look about you,' he demanded, 'and tell me whether your mares are grazing anywhere in sight.' 'I cannot see them,' Iphitus admitted. 'Then you have falsely accused me in your heart of being a thief!' Heracles roared, distraught with anger, and hurled him to his death.

Heracles presently went to Neleus, King of Pylus, and asked to be purified; but Neleus refused, because Eurytus was his ally. Nor would any of his sons, except the youngest, Nestor, consent to receive Heracles, who eventually persuaded Deiphobus, the son of Hippolytus, to purify him at Amyclae. However, he still suffered from evil dreams, and went to ask the Delphic Oracle how he might be rid of them. The Pythoness Xenoclea refused to answer this question. 'You murdered your guest,' she said. 'I have no oracles for such as you!' 'Then I shall be obliged to institute an oracle of my own!' cried Heracles. With that, he plundered the shrine of its votive offerings, and even pulled away the tripod on which Xenoclea sat. 'Heracles of Tiryns is a very different man from his Canopic namesake,' the Pythoness said severely as he carried the tripod from the shrine; she meant that the Egyptian Heracles had once come to Delphi and behaved with courtesy and reverence.

Up rose the indignant Apollo, and fought Heracles until Zeus parted the combatants with a thunderbolt, making them clasp hands in friendship. Heracles restored the sacred tripod, and together they founded the city of Gythium where images of Apollo, Heracles, and

top: *Two coins of Heracles (Pennisi Collection, Acireale, Sicily)*

bottom: *Heracles saves Hesione from the sea-monster. Black-figured vase (Archaeological Museum, Taranto)*

opposite: *Head of Pan (National Archaeological Museum, Rome)*

Dionysus stood side by side in the market place. Xenoclea then gave Heracles the following oracle: 'To be rid of your affliction you must be sold into slavery for one whole year and the price you fetch must be offered to Iphitus's children. Zeus is enraged that you have violated the laws of hospitality, whatever the provocation.' 'Whose slave am I to be?' asked Heracles humbly. 'Queen Omphale of Lydia will purchase you.' Xenoclea replied. 'I obey,' said Heracles, 'but one day I shall enslave the man who has brought this suffering upon me, and all his family too!'

Omphale

Heracles was taken to Asia and offered for sale as a nameless slave by Hermes, patron of all important financial transactions, who afterwards handed the purchase money of three silver talents to Iphitus's orphans. Nevertheless, Eurytus stubbornly forbade his grandchildren to accept any monetary compensation, saying that only blood would pay for blood; and what happened to the silver, Hermes alone knows. As the Pythoness had foretold, Heracles was bought again by Omphale, Queen of Lydia, a woman with a good eye for a bargain; and he served her faithfully either for one year, or for three, ridding Asia Minor of the bandits who infested it.

Among the many bye-works which Heracles performed during this servitude was his capture of the two Ephesian Cercopes, who had constantly robbed him of his sleep. They were twin brothers named Passalus and Acmon, sons of Oceanus by Theia, and the most accomplished cheats and liars known to mankind, who roamed the world, continually practising new deceptions. They had warned them to keep clear of Heracles and her words 'My little White-bottoms, you have yet to meet the great Black-bottom!' becoming proverbial, 'white-bottom' now means 'cowardly, base, or lascivious'. They would buzz around Heracles's bed in the guise of bluebottles, until one night he grabbed them, forced them to resume their proper shape, and bore them off, dangling head-downwards from a pole which he carried over his shoulder. Now, Heracles's bottom, which the lion's pelt did not cover, had been burned as black as an old leather shield by exposure to the sun, and by the fiery breaths of Cacus and of the Cretan bull; and the Cercopes burst into a fit of immoderate laughter to find themselves suspended upside-down, staring at it. Their merriment surprised Heracles, and when he learned its cause, he sat down upon a rock and laughed so heartily himself that they persuaded him to release them.

Finally, beside the Lydian river Sagiris, Heracles shot dead a gigantic serpent which was destroying men and crops; and the grateful Omphale, having at last discovered his identity and parentage, released him and sent him back to Tiryns, laden with gifts; while Zeus contrived the constellation Ophiuchus to commemorate the victory.

Omphale had bought Heracles as a lover rather than a fighter. He fathered on her three sons, namely Lamus; Agelaus, ancestor of a famous King Croesus who tried to immolate himself on a pyre when the Persians captured Sardis; and Laomedon. Some add a fourth, Tyrrhenus, who invented the trumpet and led Lydian emigrants to Etruria, where they took the name Tyrrhenians; but it is more probable that Tyrrhenus was the son of King Atys, a remote descendant of Heracles and Omphale. By one of Omphale's women, named Malis, Heracles was already the father of Cleodaeus and of Alcaeus, founder of the Lydian dynasty which King Croesus ousted from the throne of Sardis.

Reports reached Greece that Heracles had discarded his lion pelt and his aspen wreath, and instead wore jewelled necklaces, golden bracelets, a woman's turban, a purple shawl, and Maeonian girdle. There he sat — the story went — surrounded by wanton Ionian girls, teasing wool from the polished wool-basket, or spinning the thread; trembling, as he did so, when his mistress scolded him. She would strike him with her golden slipper if ever his clumsy fingers crushed the spindle, and make him recount his past achievements for her amusement; yet apparently he felt no shame. Hence painters show Heracles wearing a yellow petticoat, and letting himself be combed and manicured by Omphale's maids, while she dresses up in his lion pelt, and wields his club and bow.

What, however, had happened was no more than this. One day, when Heracles and Omphale were visiting the vineyards of Tmolus, she in a purple, gold-embroidered gown, with perfumed locks, he gallantly holding a golden parasol over her head, Pan caught sight of them from a hill. Falling in love with Omphale, he bade farewell to the mountain-goddesses, crying: 'Henceforth she alone shall be my love!' Omphale and Heracles reached their destination, a secluded grotto, where it amused them to exchange clothes. She dressed him in a net-work girdle, absurdly small for his waist, and her purple gown. Though she unlaced this to the fullest extent, he split the sleeves; and the ties of her sandals were far too short to meet across his instep.

After dinner, they went to sleep on separate couches, having

A river god (British Museum)

vowed a dawn sacrifice to Dionysus, who requires marital purity from his devotees on such occasions. At midnight, Pan crept into the grotto and, fumbling about in the darkness, found what he thought was Omphale's couch, because the sleeper was clad in silk. With trembling hands he untucked the bed-clothes from the bottom, and wormed his way in; but Heracles, waking and drawing up one foot, kicked him across the grotto. Hearing a loud crash and a howl, Omphale sprang up and called for lights, and when these came she and Heracles laughed until they cried to see Pan sprawled in a corner, nursing his bruises. After that day, Pan abhorred clothes, and summoned his officials naked to his rites; it was he who revenged himself on Heracles by spreading the rumour that his whimsical exchange of garments with Omphale was habitual and perverse.

Hesione
After serving as a slave to Queen Omphale, Heracles returned to Tiryns, his sanity now fully restored, and at once planned an expedition against Troy. His reasons were as follows. He and Telamon, either on their way back from the country of the Amazons,

Heracles wrestling with Achelous in his serpent shape. Detail of black-figured vase (British Museum)

or when they landed with the Argonauts at Sigeium, had been astonished to find Laomedon's daughter Hesione, stark naked except for her jewels, chained to a rock on the Trojan shore. It appeared that Poseidon had sent a sea-monster to punish Laomedon for having failed to pay him and Apollo their stipulated fee when they built the city walls and tended his flocks. Some say that he should have sacrificed to them all the cattle born in his kingdom that year; others, that he had promised them only a low wage as day-labourers, but even so cheated them of more than thirty Trojan drachmae. In revenge, Apollo sent a plague, and Poseidon ordered his monster to prey on the plainsfolk and ruin their fields by spewing sea water over them.

Laomedon visited the Oracle of Zeus Ammon, and was advised by him to expose Hesione on the seashore for the monster to devour. Yet he obstinately refused to do so unless the Trojan nobles would first let him sacrifice their own daughters. In despair, they consulted Apollo who, being no less angry than Poseidon, gave them little satisfaction. Most parents at once sent their children abroad for safety, but Laomedon tried to force a certain Phoenodamas, who had kept his three daughters at home, to expose one of them; upon which Phoenodamas harangued the assembly, pleading that Laomedon was alone responsible for their present distress, and should be made to suffer for it by sacrificing his daughter. In the end, it was decided to cast lots, and the lot fell upon Hesione, who was accordingly bound to the rock, where Heracles found her.

Heracles now broke her bonds, went up to the city, and offered to destroy the monster in return for the two matchless, immortal, snow-white horses, or mares, which could run over water and standing corn like the wind, and which Zeus had given Laomedon as compensation for the rape of Ganymedes. Laomedon readily agreed to the bargain.

With Athene's help, the Trojans then built Heracles a high wall which served to protect him from the monster as it poked its head out of the sea and advanced across the plain. On reaching the wall, it opened its jaws and Heracles leaped fully-armed down its throat. He spent three days in the monster's belly, and emerged victorious, although the struggle had cost him every hair on his head.

What happened next is much disputed; the most circumstantial version, however, is that Laomedon cheated Heracles by substituting mortal horses for the immortal ones; whereupon Heracles threatened to make war on Troy, and put to sea in a rage. First he visited the island of Paros, where he raised an altar to Zeus and Apollo; and then the Isthmus of Corinth, where he prophesied Laomedon's doom; finally he recruited soldiers in his own city of Tiryns.

It is disputed whether Heracles embarked for Troy with eighteen long ships of fifty oars each; or with only six small craft and scanty forces. But among his allies were Iolaus; Telamon son of Aeacus; Peleus; the Argive Oicles; and the Boeotian Deimachus.

On disembarking near Troy, Heracles left Oicles to guard the ships, while he himself led the other champions in an assault on the city. Laomedon, taken by surprise, had no time to marshal his army, but supplied the common folk with swords and torches and hurried them down to burn the fleet. Oicles resisted him to the death, fighting a noble rear-guard action, while his comrades launched the ships and escaped. Laomedon then hurried back to the city and, after a skirmish with Heracles's straggling forces, managed to re-enter and bar the gates behind him.

Having no patience for a long siege, Heracles ordered an immediate assault. The first to breach the wall and enter was Telamon, who chose the western curtain built by his father Aeacus as the weakest spot, but Heracles came hard at his heels, mad with jealousy. Telamon, suddenly aware that Heracles's drawn sword was intended for his own vitals, had the presence of mind to stoop and collect some large stones dislodged from the wall. 'What are you at?' roared Heracles. 'Building an altar to Heracles the Victor, Heracles the Averter of Ills!' answered the resourceful Telamon. 'I leave the sack of Troy to you.' Heracles thanked him briefly, and raced on. He then shot down Laomedon and all his sons, except Podarces, who alone had maintained that Heracles should be given the immortal mares; and sacked the city. After glutting his vengeance, he rewarded Telamon with the hand of Hesione, whom he gave permission to ransom any one of her fellow captives. She chose Podarces. 'Very well,' said Heracles. 'But first he must be sold as a slave.' So Podarces was put up for sale, and Hesione redeemed him with the golden veil which bound her head: hence Podarces won the name of Priam, which means 'redeemed'.

Having burned Troy and left its highways desolate, Heracles set Priam on the throne, and sailed from the Troad, taking with him Glaucia, a daughter of the river Scamander. During the seige, she had been Deimachus's mistress, and when he fell in battle, had applied to Heracles for protection. Heracles led her aboard his ship, overjoyed that the stock of so gallant a friend should survive: for Glaucia was pregnant, and she later gave birth to a son named Scamander.

Now, while Sleep lulled Zeus into drowsiness, Hera summoned Boreas to raise a storm, which drove Heracles far off his course to the island of Cos. Zeus awoke in a rage and threatened to cast Sleep down from the upper air into the gulf of Erebus; but she fled as a suppliant to Night, whom even Zeus dared not displease. In his frustration he began tossing the gods about Olympus. Some say that it was on this occasion that he chained Hera by the wrists to the rafters, tying anvils to her ankles; and hurled Hephaestus down to earth. Having thus vented his ill-temper to the full, he rescued Heracles from Cos and led

left: *Heracles with his wife Deianeira. Detail of red-figured vase (Ashmolean Museum, Oxford)*

opposite: *The Apotheosis of Heracles. Black-figured vase (Paestum Museum, Italy)*

below: *Heracles in Olympus. Black-figured vase (British Museum)*

him back to Argos.

The Conquest of Elis

Not long after his return, Heracles collected a force of Tirynthians and Arcadians and, joined by volunteers from the noblest Greek families, marched against Augeias, King of Elis, whom he owed a grudge on account of the Fifth Labour. Augeias, however, foreseeing this attack, had prepared to resist it by appointing as his generals Eurytus and Cteatus, the sons of his brother Actor and Molione, daughter of Molus; and by giving a share in the Elean government to the valiant Amarynceus, who is usually described as a son of the Thessalian immigrant Pyttius.

The sons of Actor are called Moliones, after their mother, to distinguish them from those of the other Actor, who married Aegina. They were twins, born from a silver egg, and surpassed all their contemporaries in strength; but, unlike the Dioscuri, had been joined together at the waist from birth.

Heracles did not cover himself with glory in this Elean War. He fell sick, and when the Moliones routed his army, which was encamped in the heart of Elis, the Corinthians intervened by proclaiming the Isthmian Truce. Among those wounded by the Moliones was Heracles's twin brother Iphicles; his friends carried him fainting to Pheneus in Arcadia, where he eventually died and became a hero.

When Heracles returned to Tiryns, Eurystheus accused him of designs on the high kingship in which he had himself been confirmed by Zeus, and banished him from Argolis. With his mother Alcmene, and his nephew Ioaus, Heracles then rejoined Iphicles at Pheneus, where he took Laonome, daughter of Guneus, as his mistress.

Afterwards, hearing that the Eleans were sending a procession to honour Poseidon at the Third Isthmian Festival, and that the Moliones would witness the games and take part in the sacrifices, Heracles ambushed them from a roadside thicket below Cleonae, and shot both dead; and killed their cousin, the other Eurytus, as well, a son of King Augeias.

Molione soon learned who had murdered her sons, and made the Eleans demand satisfaction from Eurystheus, on the ground that Heracles was a native of Tiryns. When Eurystheus disclaimed responsibility for the misdeeds of Heracles, whom he had banished, Molione asked the Corinthians to exclude all Argives from the Isthmian Games until satisfaction had been given for the murder. This they declined to do, whereupon Molione laid a curse on every Elean who might take part in the festival.

Heracles now borrowed the black-maned horse Arion from Oncus, mastered him, raised a new army in Argos, Thebes, and Arcadia, and sacked the city of Elis. Some say that he killed Augeias and his sons, restored Phyleus, the rightful king, and set him on the Elean throne; others, that he spared Augeias's life at least.

The Capture of Pylus

Heracles next sacked and burned the city of Pylus, because the Pylians had gone to the aid of Elis. He killed all Neleus's sons, except the youngest, Nestor, who was away at Gerania, but Neleus himself escaped with his life.

Athene, champion of justice, fought for Heracles; and Pylus was defended by Hera, Poseidon, Hades, and Ares. While Athene engaged Ares, Heracles made for Poseidon, club against trident, and forced him to give way. Next, he ran to assist Athene, spear in hand, and his third lunge pierced Ares's shield, dashing him headlong to the ground; then, with a powerful thrust at Ares's thigh, he drove deep into the divine flesh. Ares fled in anguish to Olympus, where Apollo spread soothing unguents on the wound and heeled it within the hour; so he renewed the fight, until one of Heracles's arrows pierced his shoulder, and forced him off the field for good. Meanwhile, Heracles had also wounded Hera in the right breast with a three-barbed arrow.

Neleus's eldest son, Periclymenus the Argonaut, was gifted by Poseidon with boundless strength and the power of assuming whatever shape he pleased, whether of bird, beast, or tree. On this occasion he turned himself into a lion, then into a serpent and after a while, to escape scrutiny, perched on the yoke-boss of Heracles's horses in the form of an ant, or fly, or bee. Heracles, nudged by Athene, recognized Periclymenus and reached for his club, whereupon Periclymenus became an eagle, and tried to peck out his eyes, but a sudden arrow from Heracles's bow pierced him underneath his wing. He tumbled to earth, and the arrow was driven through his neck by the fall, killing him.

Heracles gave the city of Messene to Nestor, in trust for his own descendants, remembering that Nestor had taken no part in robbing him of Geryon's cattle; and soon came to love him more even than Hylas and Iolaus. It was Nestor who first swore an oath by Heracles.

Deianeira

After spending four years in Pheneus, Heracles decided to leave the

Peloponnese. At the head of a large Arcadian force, he sailed across to Calydon in Aetolia, where he took up his residence. Having now no legitimate sons, and no wife, he courted Deianeira, the supposed daughter of Oeneus, thus keeping his promise to the ghost of her brother Meleager. But Deianeira was really the daughter of the god Dionysus, by Oeneus's wife Althaea.

Many suitors came to Oeneus's palace in Pleuron, demanding the hand of lovely Deianeira, who drove a chariot and practised the art of war; but all abandoned their claims when they found themselves in rivalry with Heracles and the River-god Achelous. It is common knowledge that immortal Achelous appears in three forms: as a bull, as a speckled serpent, and as a bull-headed man. Streams of water flow continually from his shaggy beard, and Deianeira would rather have died than marry him.

Heracles, when summoned by Oeneus to plead his suit, boasted that if he married Deianeira, she would not only have Zeus for a father-in-law, but enjoy the reflected glory of his own Twelve Labours.

Achelous (now in bull-headed form) scoffed at this, remarking that he was a well-known personage, the father of all Greek waters, not a footloose stranger like Heracles, and that the Oracle of Dodona had instruced all visitants to offer him sacrifices. Then he taunted Heracles: 'Either you are not Zeus's son, or your mother is an adulteress!

Heracles scowled. 'I am better at fighting than debating,' he said, 'and I will not hear my mother insulted!'

Achelous cast aside his green garment, and wrestled with Heracles until he was thrown on his back, whereupon he deftly turned into a speckled serpent and wriggled away.

'I strangled serpents in my cradle!' laughed Heracles, stooping to grip his throat. Next, Achelous became a bull and charged; Heracles nimbly stepped aside and, catching hold of both his horns, hurled him to the ground with such force that the right horn snapped clean off. Achelous retired, miserably ashamed, and hid his injury under a chaplet of willow-branches.

After marrying Deianeira, Heracles marched with the Calydonians against the Thesprotian city of Ephyra — later Cichyrus — where he overcame and killed King Phyleus. Among the captives was Phyleus's daughter Astyoche, by whom Heracles became the father of Tlepolemus; though some say that Tlepolemus's mother was Astydameia, daughter of Amyntor, whom Heracles abducted from

Elean Ephyra, a city famous for its poisons.

At a feast three years later, Heracles grew enraged with a young kinsman of Oeneus, named Eunomus, the son of Architeles, who was told to pour water on Heracles's hands, and clumsily splashed his legs. Heracles boxed the boys ears harder than he intended, and killed him. Though forgiven by Architeles for this accident, Heracles decided to pay the due penalty of exile, and went away with Deianeira, and their son Hyllus, to Trachis, the home of Amphitryon's nephew Ceyx.

On his way, he came with Deianeira to the river Evenus, then in full flood, where the Centaur Nessus, claiming that he was the gods' authorized ferryman and chosen because of his righteousness, offered, for a small fee, to carry Deianeira dry-shod across the water while Heracles swam. He agreed, paid Nessus the fare, threw his club and bow over the river, and plunged in. Nessus, however, instead of keeping to his bargain, galloped off in the opposite direction with Deianeira in his arms; then threw her to the ground and tried to violate her. She screamed for help, and Heracles, quickly recovering his bow, took careful aim and pierced Nessus through the breast from

Wrenching out the arrow, Nessus told Deianeira: 'If you mix the seed which I have spilt on the ground with blood from my wound, add olive oil, and secretly anoint Heracles's shirt with the mixture, you will never again have cause to complain of his unfaithfulness.' Deianeira hurriedly collected the ingredients in a jar, which she sealed and kept by her without saying a word to Heracles on the subject.

By Deianeira, Heracles had already become the father of Hyllus, Ctesippus, Glenus, Hodites; also of Macaria, his only daughter.

Heracles and Cycnus
Heracles now came to Itonus, a city of Phthiotis, where the ancient temple of Athene now stands. Here he met Cycnus, a son of Ares and Pelopia, who was constantly offering valuable prizes to guests who dared fight a chariot duel with him. The ever-victorious Cycnus would cut off their heads and use the skulls to decorate the temple of his father Ares. This, by the way, was not the Cycnus whom Ares had begotten on Pyrene and transformed into a swan when he died.

Apollo, growing vexed with Cycnus, because he waylaid and carried off herds of cattle which were being sent for sacrifice to Delphi, incited Heracles to accept Cycnus's challenge. It was agreed that Heracles should be supported by his charioteer Iolaus, and Cycnus by his father Ares. Heracles, though this was not his usual style of fighting, put on the polished bronze greaves which Hephaestus had made for him, the curiously wrought golden breast-plate given him by Athene, and a pair of iron shoulder-guards. Armed with bow and arrows, spear, helmet, and a stout shield which Zeus had ordered Hephaestus to supply, he lightly mounted his chariot.

Athene, descending from Olympus, now warned Heracles that, although empowered by Zeus to kill and despoil Cycnus, he must do no more than defend himself against Ares and, even if victorious, not deprive him of either his horses or his splendid armour. She then mounted beside Heracles and Iolaus, shaking her aegis, and Mother Earth groaned as the chariot whirled forward. Cycnus drove to meet them at full speed, and both he and Heracles were thrown to the ground by the shock of their encounter, spear against shield. Yet they sprang to their feet and, after a short combat, Heracles thrust Cycnus through the neck. He then boldly faced Ares, who hurled a spear at him; and Athene, with an angry frown, turned it aside. Ares ran at Heracles sword in hand, only to be wounded in the thigh for his pains, and Heracles would have dealt him a further blow as he lay on the ground, had not Zeus parted the combatants with a thunderbolt. Heracles and Iolaus then despoiled Cycnus's corpse, while Athene led the fainting Ares back to Olympus. Cycnus was buried by Ceyx in the valley of the Anaurus but, at Apollo's command, the swollon river washed away his headstone.

Iole
At Trachis Heracles mustered an army of Arcadians, Melians, and Epicnemidian Locrians, and marched against Oechalia to revenge himself on King Eurytus, who refused to surrender the princess Iole, fairly won in an archery contest; but he told his allies no more than that Eurytus had been unjustly exacting tribute from the Euboeans. He stormed the city, riddled Eurytus and his son with arrows and, after burying certain of his comrades who had fallen in the battle, namely Ceyx's son Hippasus, and Argeius and Melas, sons of Licymnius, pillaged Oechalia and took Iole captive. Rather than yield to Heracles, Iole had allowed him to murder her entire family before her very eyes, and then leaped from the city wall; yet she survived, because her skirts were billowed out by the wind and broke the fall. Now Heracles sent her, with other Oechalian women, to Deianeira at Trachis, while he visited the Euboean headland of Cenaeum. It should be noted here that when taking leave of Deianeira, Heracles had

divulged a prophecy: at the end of fifteen months, he was fated either to die, or to spend the remainder of his life in perfect tranquillity. The news had been conveyed to him by the twin doves of the ancient oak oracle Dodona.

The Apotheosis of Heracles

Having constructed marble altars and a sacred grove to his father Zeus on the Cenaean headland, Heracles prepared a thanksgiving sacrifice for the capture of Oechalia. He had already sent Lichas back to ask Deianeira for a fine shirt and a cloak of the sort which he regularly wore on such occasions.

Deianeira, comfortably installed at Trachis, was by now resigned to Heracles's habit of taking mistresses; and, when she recognized Iole as the latest of these, felt pity rather than resentment for the fatal beauty which had been Oechalia's ruin. Yet was it not intolerable that Heracles expected Iole and herself to live together under the same roof? Since she was no longer young, Deianeira decided to use Nessus's supposed love-charm as a means of holding her husband's affection. Having woven him a new sacrificial shirt against his safe return, she covertly unsealed the jar, soaked a piece of wool in the mixture, and rubbed the shirt with it. When Lichas arrived she locked the shirt in a chest which she gave to him, saying: 'On no account expose the shirt to light or heat until Heracles is about to wear it at the sacrifice.' Lichas had already driven off at full speed in his chariot when Deianeira, glancing at the piece of wool which she had thrown down into the sunlit courtyard, was horrified to see it burning away

Heracles pursuing Nessus. Detail of vase (British Museum)

217

like saw-dust, while red foam bubbled up from the flag-stones. Realizing that Nessus had deceived her, she sent a courier poste-haste to recall Lichas and, cursing her folly, swore that if Heracles died she would not survive him.

The courier arrived too late at the Cenaean headland. Heracles had by now put on the shirt and sacrificed twelve immaculate bulls as the first-fruits of his spoils: in all, he had brought to the altar a mixed herd of one hundred cattle. He was pouring wine from a bowl on the altars and throwing frankincense on the flames when he let out a sudden yell as if he had been bitten by a serpent. The heat had melted the Hydra's poison in Nessus's blood, which coursed all over Heracles's limbs, corroding his flesh. Soon the pain was beyond endurance and, bellowing in anguish, he overturned the altars. He tried to rip off the shirt, but it clung to him so fast that his flesh came away with it, laying bare the bones. His blood hissed and bubbled like spring water when red-hot metal is being tempered. He plunged headlong into the nearest stream, but the poison burned only the fiercer; these waters then became scalding hot and were called Thermopylae, or 'hot passage'.

Ranging over the mountain, tearing up trees as he went, Heracles came upon the terrified Lichas crouched in the hollow of a rock, his knees clasped with his hands. In vain did Lichas try to exculpate himself: Heracles seized him, whirled him thrice about his head and flung him into the Euboean Sea. There he was transformed: he became a rock of human appearance, projecting a short distance above the waves, which sailors called Lichas and on which they were afraid to tread, believing it to be sentient. The army, watching from afar, raised a great shout of lamentation, but none dared approach until, writhing in agony, Heracles summoned Hyllus, and asked to be carried away to die in solitude. Hyllus conveyed him to the foot of Mount Oeta in Trachis (a region famous for its white hellebore), the Delphic Oracle having aleady pointed this out to Licymnius and Iolaus as the destined scene of their friend's death.

Aghast at the news, Deianeira hanged herself or, some say, stabbed herself with a sword in their marriage bed. Heracles's one thought had been to punish her before he died, but when Hyllus assured him that she was innocent, as her suicide proved, he sighed forgivingly and expressed a wish that Alcmene and all his sons should assemble to hear his last words. Alcmene, however, was at Tiryns with some of his children, and most of the others had settled at Thebes. Thus he could reveal Zeus's prophecy, now fulfilled, only to Hyllus: 'No man

alive may ever kill Heracles; a dead enemy shall be his downfall.'
Hyllus then asked for instructions, and was told: 'Swear by the head
of Zeus that you will convey me to the highest peak of this mountain,
and there burn me, without lamentation, on a pyre of oak-branches
and trunks of the male wild-olive. Likewise swear to marry Iole as
soon as you come of age.' Though scandalized by these requests,
Hyllus promised to observe them.

When all had been prepared, Iolaus and his companions retired a

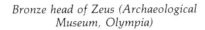

*Bronze head of Zeus (Archaeological
Museum, Olympia)*

short distance, while Heracles mounted the pyre and gave orders for its kindling. But none dared obey, until a passing Aeolian shepherd named Poeas ordered Philoctetes, his son by Demonassa, to do as Heracles asked. In gratitude, Heracles bequeathed his quiver, bow, and arrows to Philoctetes and, when the flames began to lick at the pyre, spread his lion-pelt over the platform at the summit and lay down, with his club for pillow, looking as blissful as a garlanded guest surrounded by wine-cups. Thunderbolts then fell from the sky and at once reduced the pyre to ashes.

In Olympus, Zeus congratulated himself that his favourite son had behaved so nobly. 'Heracles's immortal part', he announced, 'is safe from death, and I shall soon welcome him to this blessed region. But if anyone here grieves at his deification, so richly merited, that god or goddess must nevertheless approve it willy-nilly!' All the Olympians assented, and Hera decided to swallow the insult, which was clearly aimed at her, because she had already arranged to punish Philoctetes, for his kindly act, by the bite of a Lemnian viper.

The thunderbolts had consumed Heracles's mortal part. He no longer bore any resemblance to Alcmene but, like a snake that has cast its slough, appeared in all the majesty of his divine father. A cloud received him from his companions' sight as, amid peals of thunder, Zeus bore him up to heaven in his four-horse chariot; where Athene took him by the hand and solemnly introduced him to her fellow deities.

Now, Zeus had destined Heracles as one of the Twelve Olympians, yet was loth to expel any of the existing company of gods in order to make room for him. He therefore persuaded Hera to adopt Heracles by a ceremony of rebirth: namely, going to bed, pretending to be in labour, and then producing him from beneath her skirts — which was the adoption ritual in use among many barbarian tribes. Henceforth, Hera regarded Heracles as her son and loved him next only to Zeus. All the immortals welcomed his arrival; and Hera married him to her pretty daughter Hebe, who bore him Alexiares and Anicetus. And, indeed, Heracles had earned Hera's true gratitude in the revolt of the Giants by killing Pronomus, when he tried to violate her.

7

THE ARGONAUTS AND MEDEA

The Argonauts Assemble

AFTER THE DEATH OF KING CRETHUS the Aeolian, Pelias, son of Poseidon, already an old man, seized the Iolcan throne from his half-brother Aeson, the rightful heir. An oracle presently warning him that he would be killed by a descendant of Aeolus, Pelias put to death every prominent Aeolian he dared lay hands upon, except Aeson, whom he spared for his mother Tyro's sake, but kept a prisoner in the palace; forcing him to renounce his inheritance.

Now, Aeson had married Polymele, who bore him one son, by name Diomedes. Pelias would have destroyed the child without mercy, had not Polymele summoned her kinswomen to weep over him, as though he were still-born, and then smuggled him out of the city to Mount Pelion; where Cheiron the Centaur reared him, as he did with Asclepius, Achilles, Aeneas, and other famous heroes.

A second oracle warned Pelias to beware a one-sandalled man and when, one day on the seashore, a group of his princely allies joined him in a solemn sacrifice to Poseidon, his eye fell upon a tall, long-haired Magnesian youth, dressed in a close-fitting leather tunic and leopard-skin. He was armed with two broad-bladed spears, and wore only one sandal.

The other sandal he had lost in the muddy river Anaurus by the contrivance of a crone who, standing on the farther bank, begged passers-by to carry her across. None took pity on her, until this young stranger courteously offered her his broad back; but he found himself staggering under the weight, since she was none other than the goddess Hera in disguise. For Pelias had vexed Hera by withholding her customary sacrifices, and she was determined to punish him for this neglect.

When, therefore, Pelias asked the stranger roughly: 'Who are you, and what is your father's name?', he replied that Cheiron, his foster-

The Argonauts about to begin their voyage. Handle of a box (National Museum, Villa Giulia, Rome)

father, called him Jason, though he had formerly been known as Diomedes, son of Aeson.

Pelias glared at him balefully. 'What would you do,' he enquired suddenly, 'if an oracle announced that one of your fellow-citizens were destined to kill you?'

'I should send him to fetch the golden ram's fleece from Colchis,' Jason replied, not knowing that Hera had placed those words in his mouth. 'And, pray, whom have I the honour of addressing?'

When Pelias revealed his identity, Jason was unabashed. He boldly claimed the throne usurped by Pelias, and, since he was strongly supported by his uncle Pheres, king of Pherae, and Amathaon, king of Pylus, who had come to take part in the sacrifice, Pelias feared to deny him his birthright. 'But first,' he insisted, 'I require you to free our beloved country from a curse!'

Jason then learned that Pelias was being haunted by the ghost of Phrixus, who had fled from Orchomenus a generation before, riding on the back of a divine ram, to avoid being sacrificed. He took refuge in Colchis where, on his death, he was denied proper burial; and, according to the Delphic Oracle, the land of Iolcus, where many of Jason's Minyan relatives were settled, would never prosper unless his ghost were brought home in a ship, together with the golden ram's fleece. The fleece now hung from a tree in the grove of Colchian Ares, guarded night and day by an unsleeping dragon. Once this pious feat had been accomplished, Pelias declared, he would gladly resign the kingship, which was becoming burdensome for a man of his advanced years.

Jason could not deny Pelias this service, and therefore sent heralds to every court in Greece, calling for volunteers who would sail with him. He also prevailed upon Argus the Thespian to build him a fifty-oared ship; and this was done at Pagasae, with seasoned timber from Mount Pelion; after which Athene herself fitted an oracular beam into the *Argo*'s prow, cut from her father Zeus's oak at Dodona.

Many diffrent muster-rolls of the Argonauts — as Jason's companions are called — have been compiled at various times; but the following names are those given by the most trustworthy authorities:

Acastus, son of King Pelias
Actor, son of Deion the Phocian
Admetus, prince of Pherae
Amphiaraus, the Argive seer
Great Ancaeus of Tegea, son of Poseidon
Little Ancaeus, the Lelegian of Samos
Argus the Thespian, builder of the *Argo*
Ascalaphus the Orchomenan, son of Ares
Asterius, son of Cometes, a Pelopian
Atalanta of Calydon, the virgin huntress
Augeias, son of King Phorbas of Elis
Butes of Athens, the bee-master
Caeneus the Lapith, who had once been a woman
Calais, the winged son of Boreas

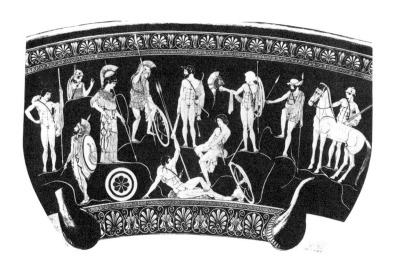

*The Argonauts with Athene. Large two-handled bowl
(Louvre)*

Canthus the Euboean
Castor, the Spartan wrestler, one of the Dioscuri
Cepheus, son of Aleus the Arcadian
Coronus the Lapith, of Gyrton in Thessaly
Echion, son of Hermes, the herald
Erginus of Miletus
Euphemus of Taenarum, the swimmer
Eurylas, son of Mecisteus, one of the Epigoni
Eurydamas the Dolopian, from Lake Xynias
Heracles of Tiryns, the strongest man who ever lived, now a god
Hylas the Dryopian, squire to Heracles
Idas, son of Aphareus of Messene
Idmon the Argive, Apollo's son
Iphicles, son of Thestius the Aetolian
Iphitus, brother of King Eurystheus of Mycenae
Jason, the captian of the expedition
Laertes, son of Acrisius the Argive
Lynceus, the look-out man, brother to Idas
Melampus of Pylus, son of Poseidon
Meleager of Calydon

Mopsus the Lapith
Nauplius the Argive, son of Poseidon, a noted navigator
Oïleus the Locrian, father of Ajax
Orpheus, the Thracian poet
Palaemon, son of Hephaestus, an Aetolian
Peleus the Myrmidon
Peneleos, son of Hippalcimus, the Boeotian
Periclymenus of Pylus, the shape-shifting son of Poseidon
Phalerus, the Athenian archer
Phanus, the Cretan son of Dionysus
Poeas, son of of Thaumacus the Magnesian
Polydeuces, the Spartan boxer, one of the Dioscuri
Polyphemus, son of Elatus, the Arcadian
Staphylus, brother of Phanus
Tiphys, the helmsman, of Boeotian Siphae
Zetes, brother of Calais

— and never before or since was so gallant a ship's company gathered together.

The Argonauts are often known as Minyans, because they brought back the ghost of Phrixus, grandson of Minyas, and the fleece of his ram; and because many of them, including Jason himself, sprang from the blood of Minyas's daughters. This Minyas, a son of Chryses, had migrated from Thessaly to Orchomenus in Boeotia, where he founded a kingdom, and was the first king ever to build a treasury.

The Lemnian Women and King Cyzicus
Heracles, after capturing the Erymanthian Boar, appeared suddenly at Pagasae, and was invited by a unanimous vote to captain the *Argo*; but generously agreed to serve under Jason who, though a novice, had planned and proclaimed the expedition. Accordingly, when the ship had been launched, and lots drawn for the benches, two oarsmen to each bench, it was Jason who sacrificed a yoke of oxen to Apollo of Embarkations. As the smoke of his sacrifice rose propitiously to heaven in dark, swirling columns, the Argonauts sat down to their farewell banquet, at which Orpheus with his lyre appeased certain drunken brawls. Sailing thence by the first light of dawn, they shaped a course for Lemnos.

About a year before this, the Lemnian men had quarrelled with their wives, complaining that they stank, and made concubines of

Thracian girls captured on raids. In revenge, the Lemnian women murdered them all without pity, old and young alike, except King Thoas, whose life his daughter Hypsipyle secretly spared, setting him adrift in an oarless boat. Now, when the *Argo* hove in sight and the Lemnian women mistook her for an enemy ship from Thrace, they donned their dead husbands' armour and ran boldly shoreward, to repel the threatened attack. The eloquent Echion, however, landing staff in hand as Jason's herald, soon set their minds at rest; and Hypsipyle called a council at which she proposed to send a gift of food and wine to the Argonauts, but not to admit them into her city of Myrine, for fear of being charged with the massacre. Polyxo, Hypsipyle's aged nurse, then rose to plead that, without men, the Lemnian race must presently become extinct. 'The wisest course', she said, 'would be to offer yourselves in love to those well-born adventurers, and thus not only place our island under strong protection, but breed a new and stalwart stock.'

This disinterested advice was loudly acclaimed, and the Argonauts were welcomed to Myrine. Hypsipyle did not, of course, tell Jason the whole truth but, stammering and blushing, explained that after much ill-treatment at the hands of their husbands, her companions had risen in arms and forced them to emigrate. The vacant throne of Lemnos, she said, was now his for the asking. Jason, although gratefully accepting her offer, declared that before settling in fertile Lemnos he must complete his quest of the Golden Fleece. Nevertheless, Hypsipyle soon persuaded the Argonauts to postpone their departure; for each adventurer was surrounded by numerous young women, all itching to bed with him. Hypsipyle claimed Jason for herself, and royally she entertained him; it was then that he begot Euneus, and his twin Nebrophonus, whom some called Deiphilus, or Thoas the Younger. Euneus eventually became king of Lemnos and supplied the Greeks with wine during the Trojan War.

Many children were begotten on this occasion by the other Argonauts too and, had it not been for Heracles, who was guarding the *Argo* and at last strode angrily into Myrine, beating upon the house doors with his club and summoning his comrades back to duty, it is unlikely that the golden fleece would ever have left Colchis. He soon forced them down to the shore; and that same night they sailed for Samothrace, where they were duly initiated into the mysteries of Persephone and her servants, the Cabeiri, who save sailors from shipwreck.

The Argonauts sailed on, leaving Imbros to starboard and, since it was well known that king Laomedon of Troy guarded the entrance to the Hellespont and let no Greek ship enter, they slipped through the Straits by night, hugging the Thracian coast, and reached the Sea of Marmara in safety. Approaching Dolionian territory, they landed at the neck of a rugged peninsula, named Arcton, which is crowned by Mount Dindymum. Here they were welcomed by King Cyzicus, the son of Aeneus, Heracles's former ally, who had just married Cleite of Phrygian Percote and warmly invited them to share his wedding banquet. While the revelry was still in progress, the *Argo*'s guards were attacked with rocks and clubs by certain six-handed Earth-born giants from the interior of the peninsula, but beat them off.

Afterwards, the Argonauts dedicated their anchor-stone to Athene and, taking aboard a heavier one, rowed away with cordial farewells, shaping a course for the Bosphorus. But a north-easterly wind suddenly whirled down upon them, and soon they were making so little way that Tiphys decided to about ship, and ran back to the lee of the peninsula. He was driven off his course; and the Argonauts, beaching their ship at random in the pitch-dark, were at once assailed by well-armed warriors. Only when they had overcome these in a fierce battle, killing some and putting the remainder to flight, did Jason discover that he had made the eastern shore of Arcton, and that noble King Cyzicus, who had mistaken the Argonauts for pirates, lay dead at his feet. Cleite, driven mad by the news, hanged herself; and the nymphs of the grove wept so piteously that their tears formed the fountain which now bears her name.

The Argonauts held funeral games in Cyzicus's honour, but remained weather-bound for many days more. At last a halcyon fluttered above Jason's head, and perched twittering on the prow of the *Argo*; whereupon Mopsus, who understood the language of birds, explained that all would be well if they placated the goddess Rhea. She had exacted Cyzicus's death in requital for that of her sacred lion's, killed by him on Mount Dindymum, and was now vexed with the Argonauts for having caused such carnage among her six-armed Earth-born brothers. They therefore raised an image to the goddess, carved by Argus from an ancient vine-stock, and danced in full armour on the mountain top. Rhea acknowledged their devotion: she made a spring gush from the neighbouring rocks. A fair breeze then arose, and they continued the voyage. The Dolionians, however, prolonged their mourning to a full month, lighting no fires, and subsisting on uncooked foods, a custom which was observed during the annual Cyzican Games.

Nymphs (Archaeological Museum, Delphi)

Hylas, Amycus and Phineus

At Heracles's challenge the Argonauts now engaged in a contest to see who could row the longest. After many laborious hours, relieved only by Orpheus's lyre, Jason, the Dioscuri, and Heracles alone held out; their comrades having each in turn confessed themselves beaten. Castor's strength began to ebb, and Polydeuces, who could not otherwise induce him to desist, shipped his own oar. Jason and Heracles, however, continued to urge the *Argo* forward, seated on opposite sides of the ship, until presently, as they reached the mouth of the river Chius in Mysia, Jason fainted. Almost at once Heracles's oar snapped. He glared about him, in anger and disgust; and his weary companions, thrusting their oars through the oar-holes again, beached the *Argo* by the riverside.

While they prepared the evening meal, Heracles went in search of a tree which would serve to make him a new oar. He uprooted an enormous fir, but when he dragged it back for trimming beside the camp fire, found that his squire Hylas had set out, an hour or two previously, to fetch water from the near-by pool of Pegae, and not yet returned; Polyphemus was away, searching for him.

Crying 'Hylas! Hylas!', Heracles plunged frantically into the woods and soon met Polyphemus, who reported: 'Alas, I heard Hylas shouting for help; and ran towards his voice. But when I reached Pegae I found no signs of a struggle either with wild beasts or with other enemies. There was only his water-pitcher lying abandoned by the pool side.' Heracles and Polyphemus continued their search all night, and forced every Mysian whom they met to join in it, but to no avail; the fact being that Dryope and her sister-nymphs of Pegae had fallen in love with Hylas, and enticed him to come and live with them in an underwater grotto.

At dawn, a favourable breeze sprang up and, since neither Heracles nor Polyphemus appeared, though everyone shouted their names until the hillsides echoed, Jason gave orders for the voyage to be resumed. This decision was loudly contested and, as the *Argo* drew farther away from the shore, several of the Argonauts accused him of having marooned Heracles to avenge his defeat at rowing. They even tried to make Tiphys turn the ship about; but Calais and Zetes interposed, which is why Heracles later killed them in the island of Tenos.

After threatening to lay Mysia waste unless the inhabitants continued their search for Hylas, dead or alive, and then leading a successful raid on Troy, Heracles resumed his Labours; but Polyphemus settled near Pegae and built the city of Crius, where he

A wall-painting of Medea. (National Museum, Naples)

opposite top: *Jason plucking the Golden Fleece from a tree. Red-figured vase (Metropolitan Museum of Art, New York)*

opposite: *The Sirens. Three-legged box for holding medicine (British Museum)*

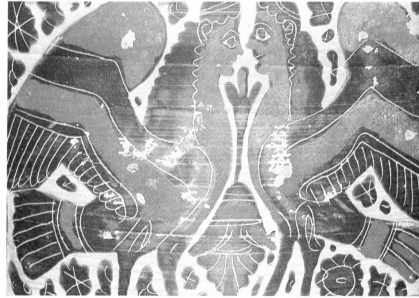

reigned until the Chalybians killed him in battle.

Next, the *Argo* touched at the island of Bebrycos, also in the Sea of Marmara, ruled by the arrogant King Amycus, a son of Poseidon. This Amycus fancied himself as a boxer, and used to challenge strangers to a match, which invariably proved their undoing; but if they declined, he flung them without ceremony over a cliff into the sea. He now approached the Argonauts, and refused them food or water unless one of their champions would meet him in the ring. Polydeuces, who had won the boxing contest at the Olympic Games, stepped forward willingly, and drew on the raw-hide gloves which Amycus offered him.

Amycus and Polydeuces went at it, hammer and tongs, in a flowery dell, not far from the beach. Amycus's gloves were studded with brazen spikes, and the muscles on his shaggy arms stood out like boulders covered with seaweed. He was by far the heavier man, and the younger by several years; but Polydeuces, fighting cautiously at first, and avoiding his bull-like rushes, soon discovered the weak points in his defence and, before long, had him spitting blood from a swollen mouth. After a prolonged bout, in which neither showed the least sign of flagging, Polydeuces broke through Amycus's guard, flattened his nose with a straight left-handed punch, and dealt further merciless punishment on either side of it, using hooks and jolts. In pain and desperation, Amycus grasped Polydeuces's left fist and tugged at it with his left hand, while he brought up a powerful right swing; but Polydeuces threw himself in the direction of the tug. The swing went wide, and he countered with a stunning right-handed hook to the ear, followed by so irresistible an upper cut that it broke the bones of Amycus's temple and killed him instantly.

When they saw their king lying dead, the Bebrycans sprang to arms, but Polydeuces's cheering companions routed them easily and sacked the royal palace. To placate Poseidon, Amycus's father, Jason then offered a holocaust of twenty red bulls, which were found among the spoils.

The Argonauts put to sea again on the next day, and came to Salmydessus in Eastern Thrace, where Phineus, the son of Agenor, reigned. He had been blinded by the gods for prophesying the future too accurately, and was also plagued by a pair of Harpies: loathsome, winged, female creatures who, at every meal, flew into the palace and snatched victuals from his table, befouling the rest, so that it stank and was inedible. When Jason asked Phineus for advice on how to win the golden fleece, he was told: 'First rid me of the Harpies!'

Phineus's servants spread the Argonauts a banquet, upon which the Harpies immediately descended, playing their usual tricks. Calais and Zetes, however, the winged sons of Boreas, arose sword in hand, and chased them into the air and far across the sea. Some say that they caught up with the Harpies at the Strophades islands, but spared their lives when they turned back and implored mercy; for Iris, Hera's messenger, intervened, promising that they would return to their cave in Cretan Dicte and never again molest Phineus.

Phineus instructed Jason how to navigate the Bosphorus, and gave him a detailed account of what weather, hospitality, and fortune to expect on his way to Colchis. He added: 'And once you have reached Colchis, trust in Aphrodite!'

Now, Phineus had married first Cleopatra, sister to Calais and Zetes and then, on her death, Idaea, a Scythian princess. Idaea was jealous of Cleopatra's two sons, and suborned false witnesses to accuse them of all manner of wickedness. Calais and Zetes, however, detecting the conspiracy, freed their nephews from prison, and Phineus restored them to favour, sending Idaea back to her father.

From the Symplegades to Colchis

Phineus had warned the Argonauts of the terrifying rocks called Symplegades which, perpetually shrouded in sea mist, guarded the entrance to the Bosphorus. When a ship attempted to pass between them, they drove together and crushed her; but, at Phineus's advice, Euphemus let loose a dove to fly ahead of the *Argo*. As soon as the rocks had nipped off her tail feathers, and recoiled again, the Argonauts rowed through with all speed, aided by Athene and by Orpheus's lyre, and lost only their stern ornament. Thereafter, in accordance with a prophecy, the rocks remained rooted, one on either side of the straits, and though the force of the current made the ship all but unmanageable, the Argonauts pulled at their oars until they bent like bows, and gained the Black Sea without disaster.

Coasting along the southern shore, they presently touched at the islet of Thynias. Thence they sailed to the city of Mariandyne and were warmly welcomed by King Lycus. News that his enemy, King Amycus, was dead had already reached Lycus by runner, and he gratefully offered the Argonauts his son Dascylus to guide them on their journey along the coast. The following day, as they were about to embark, Idmon the seer was attacked by a ferocious boar lurking in the reed-beds of the river Lycus, which gashed his thigh deeply with its great tusks. Idas sprang to Idmon's assistance and, when the boar charged again, impaled it on his spear; however, Idmon bled to death despite their care, and the Argonauts mourned him for three days. Then Tiphys sickened and died, and his comrades were plunged in grief as they raised a barrow over his ashes, beside the one that they had raised for Idmon. Great Ancaeus first, and after him Erginus, Nauplius and Euphemus, all offered to take Tiphys's place as navigator; but Ancaeus was chosen, and served them well.

From Mariandyne they continued eastward under sail for many days, until they reached Sinope in Paphlagonia, where Jason found recruits to fill three of the vacant seats on his benches: namely the brothers Deileon, Autolycus, and Phlogius, of Tricca, who had accompanied Heracles on his expedition to the Amazons but, being parted from him by accident, were now stranded in this outlandish region.

The *Argo* then sailed past the country of the Amazons; and that of the iron-working Chalybians, who neither till the soil, nor tend flocks, but live wholly on the gains of their forges; and the country of the Tibarenians, where it is the custom for husbands to groan, as if in child-bed, while their wives are in labour; and the country of the Mossynoechians, who live in wooden castles, couple promiscuously, and carry immensely long spears and white shields in the shape of ivy-leaves.

Near the islet of Ares, great flocks of birds flew over the *Argo*, dropping brazen plumes, one of which wounded Oileus in the shoulder. At this, the Argonauts, recalling Phineus's injunctions, donned their helmets and shouted at the top of their voices; half of them rowing, while the remainder protected them with shields, against which they clashed their swords. Phineus had also counselled them to land on the islet, and this they now did, driving away myriads of birds, until not one was left. That night they praised his wisdom, when a huge storm arose and four Aeolians clinging to a baulk of timber were cast ashore, close to their camp; these castaways proved to be Cytisorus, Argeus, Phrontis, and Melanion, sons of Phrixus by Chalciope, daughter to King Aeëtes of Colchis, and thus on a journey to Greece, where they were intending to claim the Orchomenan kingdom of their grandfather Athamas. Jason greeted them warmly, and all together offered sober sacrifices on a black stone in the temple of Ares. When Jason explained that his mission was to bring back the soul of Phrixus to Greece, and also recover the fleece of the golden ram on which he had ridden, Cytisorus and his brothers found themselves in a quandary: though owing devotion to their father's memory, they feared to offend their grandfather by demanding the fleece. However, what choice had they but to make common cause with these cousins who had saved their lives?

The *Argo* then coasted past the island of Philyra, and soon the Caucasus Range towered above the Argonauts, and they entered the mouth of the broad Phasis river, which waters Colchis. First pouring a libation of wine mixed with honey to the gods of the land, Jason concealed the *Argo* in a backwater, and called a council of war.

The Seizure of the Fleece
In Olympus, Hera and Athene were anxiously debating how their favourite, Jason, might win the golden fleece. At last they decided to approach Aphrodite, who undertook that her naughty little son Eros would make Medea, King Aeërtes daughter, conceive a sudden passion for him.

Meanwhile, at the council of war held in the backwater, Jason proposed going with Phrixus's sons to the near-by city of Colchian Aea, where Aeëtes ruled, and demanding the fleece as a favour; only if this were denied would they resort to guile or force. All welcomed his suggestion, and Augeias, Aeëtes's half-brother, joined the party.

As Jason and his companions approached, they were met first by Chalciope, who was surprised to see Cytisorus and her other three sons returning so soon and, when she heard their story, showered thanks on Jason for his rescue of them. Next came Aeëtes, accompanied by Eidyia and showing great displeasure — for Laomedon had undertaken to prevent all Greeks from entering the Black Sea — and asked Aegeus, his favourite grandson, to explain the intrusion. Aegeus replied that Jason, to whom he and his brothers owed their lives, had come to fetch away the golden fleece in accordance with an oracle. Seeing that Aeëtes's face wore a look of fury, he added at once: 'In return for which favour, these noble Greeks will gladly subject the Sauromatians to your Majesty's rule.' Aeëtes gave a contemptuous laugh, then ordered Jason to return whence they came, before he had their tongues cut out and their hands lopped off.

At this point, the princess Medea emerged from the palace, and when Jason answered gently and courteously, Aeëtes, somewhat ashamed of himself, undertook to yield the fleece, though on what seemed impossible terms. Jason must yoke two fire-breathing brazen-footed bulls, creations of Hephaestus; plough the Field of Ares to the extent of four ploughgates; and then sow it with the serpent's teeth given him by Athene, a few left over from Cadmus's sowing at

Thebes. Jason stood stupefied, wondering how to perform these unheard-of feats, but Eros aimed one of his arrows at Medea, and drove it into her heart, up to the feathers.

Chalciope, visiting Medea's bedroom that evening, to enlist her help on behalf of Cytisorus and his brothers, found that she had fallen head over heels in love with Jason. When Chalciope offered herself as a go-between, Medea eagerly undertook to help him yoke the fire-breathing bulls and win the fleece; making it her sole condition that she should sail back in the *Argo* as his wife.

Jason was summoned, and swore by all the gods of Olympus to keep faith with Medea for ever. She offered him a flask of lotion, blood-red juice of the two-stalked, saffron-coloured Caucasian crocus, which would protect him against the bulls' fiery breath. Jason gratefully accepted the flask and, after a libation of honey, unstoppered it and bathed his body, spear and shield in the contents. He was thus able to subdue the bulls and harness them to a plough with an adamantine yoke. All day he ploughed, and at nightfall sowed the teeth, from which armed men immediately sprouted. He provoked these to fight one against another, as Cadmus had done on a similar occasion, by throwing a stone quoit into their midst; then despatched the wounded survivors.

King Aeëtes, however, had no intention of parting with the fleece, and shamelessly repudiated his bargain. He threatened to burn the *Argo* and massacre her crew; but Medea, in whom he had unwisely confided, led Jason and a party of Argonauts to the precinct of Ares, some six miles away. There the fleece hung, guarded by a loathsome and immortal dragon of a thousand coils, larger than the *Argo* herself, and born from the blood of the monster Typhon, destroyed by Zeus. She soothed the hissing dragon with incantations and then, using freshly-cut sprigs of juniper, sprinkled soporific drops on his eyelids. Jason stealthily unfastened the fleece from the oak-tree, and together they hurried down to the beach where the *Argo* lay.

An alarm had already been raised by the priests of Ares and, in a running fight, the Colchians wounded Iphitus, Meleager, Argus, Atalanta, and Jason. Yet all of them contrived to scramble aboard the waiting *Argo*, which was rowed off in great haste, pursued by Aeëtes's galleys. Iphitus alone succumbed to his wounds; Medea soon healed the others with vulneraries of her own invention.

The Murder of Apsyrtus
Many different accounts survive of the *Argo*'s return to Thessaly,

though it is generally agreed that, following Phineus's advice, the Argonauts sailed counter-sunwise around the Black Sea. Some say that when Aeëtes overtook them, near the mouth of the Danube, Medea killed her young half-brother Apsyrtus, whom she had brought aboard, and cut him into pieces, which she consigned one by one to the swift current. This cruel strategem delayed the pursuit, because obliging Aeëtes to retrieve each piece in turn for subsequent burial at Tomi.

The most circumstantial and coherent account, however, is that Apsyrtus, sent by Aeëtes in pursuit of Jason, trapped the *Argo* at the mouth of the Danube, where the Argonauts agreed to set Medea ashore on a near-by island sacred to Artemis, leaving her in charge of a priestess for a few days; meanwhile a king of the Brygians would judge the case and decide whether she was to return home or follow Jason to Greece, and in whose possession the fleece should remain. But Medea sent a private message to Apsyrtus, pretending that she had been forcibly abducted, and begging him to rescue her. That night, when he visited the island and thereby broke the truce, Jason followed, lay in wait and struck him down from behind. He then cut off Apsyrtus's extremeties, and thrice licked up some of the fallen blood, which he spat out again each time, to prevent the ghost from pursuing him. As soon as Medea was once more aboard the *Argo*, the Argonauts attacked the leaderless Colchians, scattered their flotilla, and escaped.

After Apsyrtus's murder, the *Argo* returned by the Bosphorus, the way she had come, and passed through the Hellespont in safety, because the Trojans could no longer oppose her passage. For Heracles, on his return from Mysia, had collected six ships and surprised and destroyed the Trojan fleet. He then battered his way into Troy with his club, and demanded from King Laomedon the man-eating mares of King Diomedes, which he had left in his charge some years previously. When Laomedon denied any knowledge of these, Heracles killed him and all his sons, except the infant Podarces, or Priam, whom he appointed king in his stead.

Jason and Medea were no longer aboard the *Argo*. Her oracular beam had spoken once more, refusing to carry either of them until they had been purified of murder, and from the mouth of the Danube they had set out overland for Aeaea, the island home of Medea's aunt Circe. Medea led Jason there by the route down which the straw-wrapped gifts of the Hyperboreans are yearly brought to Delos. Circe, to whom they came as suppliants, grudgingly purified them

A terracotta Siren (Archaeological Museum, Palermo, Sicily)

opposite: *Medea pretending to rejuvenate Pelias (Museo Gregoriano Profano, Vatican)*

with the blood of a young sow.

Now, their Colchian pursuers had been warned not to come back without Medea and the fleece and, guessing that she had gone to Circe for purification, followed the *Argo* across the Aegean Sea, around the Peloponnese, and up the Illyrian coast, rightly concluding that Medea and Jason had arranged to be fetched from Aeaea.

The 'Argo' Returns to Greece

Arrived at Corcyra, which was then named Drepane, the Colchians found the *Argo* beached opposite the islet of Macris; her crew were joyfully celebrating the successful outcome of their expedition. The Colchian leader now visited King Alcinous and Queen Arete, demanding on Aeëtes's behalf the surrender of Medea and the fleece. Arete, to whom Medea had appealed for protection, kept Alcinous awake that night complaining of the ill-treatment to which fathers too often subject their errant daughters: finally prevailing upon Alcinous to tell her what judgement he would deliver next morning, namely: 'If Medea is still a virgin, she shall return to Colchis; if not, she is at liberty to stay with Jason.'

Leaving him sound asleep, Arete sent her herald to warn Jason what he must expect; and he married Medea without delay in the Cave of Macris, the daughter of Aristaeus and sometime Dionysius's nurse. The Argonauts celebrated the wedding with a sumptuous banquet and spread the golden fleece over the bridal couch. Judgement was duly delivered in the morning, Jason claimed Medea as his wife, and the Colchians could neither implement Aeëtes's orders nor, for fear of his wrath, return home. Some therefore settled in Corcyra, and others occupied those Illyrian islands, not far from Circe's Aeaea.

When, a year or two later, Aeëtes heard of these happenings, he nearly died of rage and sent a herald to Greece demanding the person of Medea and requital for the injuries done him; but was informed that no requital had yet been made for Io's abduction by men of Aeëtes's race (though the truth was that she fled because a gadfly pursued her) and none should therefore be given for the voluntary departure of Medea.

Jason now needed only to double Cape Malea, and return with the fleece to Iolcus. He cruised in safety past the Islands of the Sirens, where the ravishing strains of these bird-women were countered by the even lovelier strains of Orpheus's lyre. Butes alone sprang overboard in an attempt to swim ashore, but Aphrodite rescued him; she took him to Mount Eryx by way of Lilybaeum, and there made him her lover.

The Argonauts then sailed in fine weather along the coast of Eastern Sicily, where they watched the matchless white herds of Helius grazing on the shore, but refrained from stealing any of them. Suddenly they were struck by a frightful North Wind which, in nine days' time, drove them to the uttermost parts of Libya; there, an enormous wave swept the *Argo* over the perilous rocks which line the coast and retreated, leaving her high and dry a mile or more inland. A lifeless desert stretched as far as the eye could see, and the Argonauts had already prepared themselves for death, when the Triple-goddess Libya, clad in goat skins, appeared to Jason in a dream and gave him reassurance. At this, they took heart and, setting the *Argo* on rollers, moved her by force of their shoulders to the salt Lake Tritonis, which lay several miles off, a task that occupied twelve days. All would have died of thirst, but for a spring which Heracles, on his way to fetch the golden apples of the Hesperides, had recently caused to gush from the ground.

Canthus was now killed by Caphaurus, a Garamantian shepherd whose flocks he was driving off, but his comrades avenged him. And hardly had the two corpses been buried than Mopsus trod upon a Libyan serpent which bit him in the heel; a thick mist spread over his eyes, his hair fell out, and he died in agony. The Argonauts, after giving him a hero's burial, once more began to despair, being unable to find any outlet to the Lake.

Jason, however, before he embarked on this voyage, had consulted the Pythoness at Delphi who gave him two massive brazen tripods, with one of which Orpheus now advised him to propitiate the deities of the land. When he did so, the god Triton appeared and took up the tripod without so much of a word of thanks, but Euphemus barred his way and asked him politely: 'Pray, my lord, will you kindly direct us to the Mediterranean Sea?' For answer, Triton merely pointed towards the Tacapae river but, as an afterthought, handed him a clod of earth. Euphemus acknowledged the gift with the sacrifice of a sheep, and Triton consented to draw the *Argo* along by her keel, until once more she entered the Mediterranean Sea.

Heading northward, the Argonauts reached Crete, where they were prevented from landing by Talos the bronze sentinel, a creation of Hephaestus, who pelted the *Argo* with rocks, as was his custom. Medea called sweetly to this monster, promising to make him immortal if he drank a certain magic potion; but it was a sleeping draught and, while he slept, she removed the bronze nail which

Medea and Pelias with the cauldron. Amphora (British Museum)

stoppered the single vein running from his neck to his ankles. Out rushed the divine ichor, a colourless liquid serving him for blood, and he died.

On the following night, the *Argo* was caught in a storm from the south, but Jason invoked Apollo, who sent a flash of light, revealing to starboard the island of Anaphe, one of the Sporades, where Ancaeus managed to beach the ship. In gratitude, Jason raised an altar to Apollo.

Sailing to Aegina, they held a contest: as to who could first draw a pitcher of water and carry it back to the ship. From Aegina it was a simple voyage to Iolcus, such as scores of ships make every year, and they made it in fair weather without danger.

The Death of Pelias

One autumn evening, the Argonauts regained the well-remembered beach of Pagasae, but found no one there to greet them. Indeed, it was rumoured in Thessaly that all were dead; Pelias had therefore been emboldened to kill Jason's parents, Aeson and Polymele, and an infant son, Promachus, born to them since the departure of the *Argo*. Aeson, however, asked permission to take his own life and, his plea being granted, drank bull's blood and thus expired; whereupon Polymele killed herself with a dagger after cursing Pelias, who mercilessly dashed out Promachus's brains on the palace floor.

Jason, hearing this doleful story from a solitary boatman, forbade him to spread the news of the *Argo*'s homecoming, and summoned a council of war. All his comrades were of the opinion that Pelias deserved death, but when Jason demanded an immediate assault on Iolcus, Acastus remarked that he thought it wiser to disperse, each to his own home and there, if necessary, raise contingents for a war on Jason's behalf. Iolcus, indeed, seemed too strongly garrisoned to be stormed by a company so small as theirs.

Medea, however, spoke up and undertook to reduce the city single-handed. She instructed the Argonauts to conceal their ship, and themselves, on some wooded and secluded beach within sight of Iolcus. When they saw a torch waved from the palace roof, this would mean that Pelias was dead, the gates open, and the city theirs for the taking.

During her visit to Anaphe, Medea had found a hollow image of Artemis and brought it aboard the *Argo*. She now dressed her twelve Phaeacian bond-maidens in strange disguises and led them, each in turn carrying the image, towards Iolcus. On reaching the city gates Medea, who had given herself the appearance of a wrinkled crone, ordered the sentinels to let her pass. She cried in a shrill voice that the goddess Artemis had come from the foggy land of the Hyperboreans, in a chariot drawn by flying serpents, to bring good fortune to Iolcus. The startled sentinels dared not disobey, and Medea with her bond-maidens, raging through the streets like maenads, roused the inhabitants to a religious frenzy.

Awakened from sleep, Pelias enquired in terror what the goddess required of him. Medea answered that Artemis was about to acknowledge his piety by rejuvenating him, and thus allowing him to beget heirs in place of the unfilial Acastus, who had lately died in a shipwreck off the Libyan coast. Pelias doubted this promise, until Medea, by removing the illusion of old age that she had cast about herself, turned young again before his very eyes. 'Such is the power of Artemis!' she cried. He then watched while she cut a bleary-eyed old ram into thirteen pieces and boiled them in a cauldron. Using Colchian spells, which he mistook for Hyperborean ones, and solemnly conjuring Artemis to assist her, Medea then pretended to rejuvenate the dead ram — for a frisky lamb was hidden, with other magical gear, inside the goddess's hollow image. Pelias, now wholly deceived, consented to lie on a couch, where Medea soon charmed him to sleep. She then commanded his daughters, Alcestis, Evadne, and Amphinome, to cut him up, just as they had seen her do with the ram, and boil the pieces in the same cauldron.

Alcestis piously refused to shed her father's blood in however good a cause; but Medea, by giving further proof of her magic powers, persuaded Evadne and Amphinome to wield their knives with resolution. When the deed was done, she led them up to the roof, each carrying a torch, and explained that they must invoke the Moon while the cauldron was coming to a boil. From their ambush, the Argonauts saw the distant gleam of torches and, welcoming the signal, rushed into Iolcus, where they met with no opposition.

Jason, however, fearing Acastus's vengeance, resigned the kingdom to him, neither did he dispute the sentence of banishment passed on him by the Iolcan Council: for he hoped to sit upon a richer throne elsewhere.

As for Pelias's daughters: Alcestis married Admetus of Pherae, to whom she had long been affianced; Evadne and Amphinome were banished by Acastus to Mantinea in Arcadia where, after purification, they succeeded in making honourable marriages.

Medea at Ephyra

Jason first visited Boeotian Orchomenus, where he hung up the golden fleece in the temple of Laphystian Zeus; next, he beached the *Argo* on the Isthmus of Corinth, and there dedicated her to Poseidon.

Now, Medea was the only surviving child of Aeëtes, the rightful king of Corinth, who when he emigrated to Colchis had left behind as his regent a certain Bunus. The throne having fallen vacant, by the death without issue of the usurper Corinthus, son of Marathon (who styled himself 'Son of Zeus'), Medea claimed it, and the Corinthians accepted Jason as their king. But, after reigning for ten prosperous and happy years, he came to suspect that Medea had secured his succession by poisoning Corinthus; and proposed to divorce her in favour of Glauce the Theban, daughter of King Creon.

Medea, while not denying her crime, held Jason to the oath which he had sworn at Aea in the name of all the gods, and when he protested that a forced oath was invalid, pointed out that he also owed the throne of Corinth to her. He answered: 'True, but the Corinthians have learned to have more respect for me than for you.' Since he continued obdurate Medea, feigning submission, sent Glauce a wedding gift by the hands of the royal princes — for she had borne Jason seven sons and seven daughters — namely, a golden crown and a long white robe. No sooner had Glauce put them on, than unquenchable flames shot up, and consumed not only her — although she plunged headlong into the palace fountain — but King Creon, a crowd of other distinguished Theban guests, and everyone else assembled in the palace, except Jason; who escaped by leaping from an upper window.

At this point Zeus, greatly admiring Medea's spirit, fell in love with her, but she repulsed all his advances. Hera was grateful: 'I will make your children immortal,' said she, 'if you lay them on the sacrificial altar in my temple.' Medea did so; and then fled in a chariot drawn by winged serpents, a loan from her grandfather Helius, after bequeathing the kingdom to Sisyphus.

Medea in Exile

Medea fled first to Heracles at Thebes, where he had promised to shelter her should Jason ever prove unfaithful, and cured him of the madness that had made him kill his children; nevertheless, the Thebans would not permit her to take up residence among them because Creon, whom she had murdered, was their King. So she went to Athens, and King Aegeus was glad to marry her. Next, banished

Medea and her children. Terracotta
(Archaeological Museum, Avignon)

from Athens for her attempted poisoning of Theseus, she sailed to Italy and taught the Marrubians the art of snake-charming. After a brief visit to Thessaly, where she unsuccessfully competed with Thetis in a beauty contest judged by Idomeneus the Cretan, she married an Asian king.

Hearing, finally, that Aeëtes's Colchian throne had been usurped by her uncle Perses, Medea went to Colchis with Medeius, who killed Perses, set Aeëtes on his throne again, and enlarged the kingdom of Colchis to include Media. Some pretend that she was by that time reconciled to Jason, but the truth is that Jason, having forfeited the favour of the gods, whose names he had taken in vain when he broke faith with Medea, wandered homeless from city to city, hated of men. In old age he came once more to Corinth, and sat down in the shadow of the *Argo* remembering his past glories, and grieving for the disasters that had overwhelmed him. He was about to hang himself from the prow, when it suddenly toppled forward and killed him. Poseidon then placed the image of the *Argo*'s stern, which was innocent of homicide, among the stars.

Medea never died, but became an immortal and reigned in the Elysian Fields where some say that she, rather than Helen, married Achilles.

As for Athamas, whose failure to sacrifice Phrixus had been the cause of the Argonauts' expedition, he was on the point of being himself sacrificed at Orchomenus, as the sin-offering demanded by the Oracle of Laphystian Zeus, when his grandson Cytisorus returned from Aeaea and rescued him.

INDEX

Typesetting by TAP Ltd
London
Separations by MULLIS-MORGAN Ltd
London
Printed and Bound by BREPOLS
Turnhout